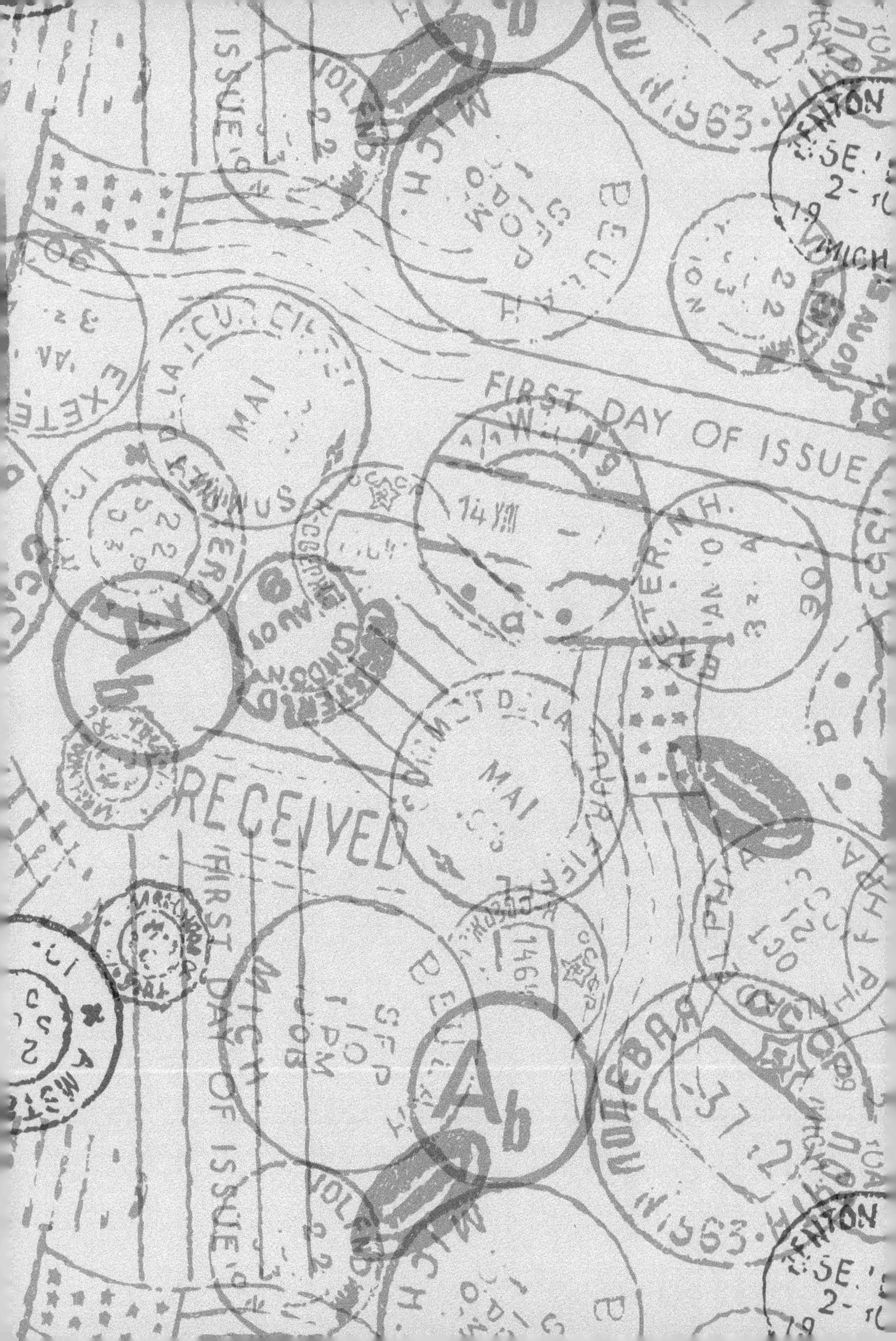
FIRST DAY OF ISSUE
RECEIVED
MAI
MICH
1963

DO
SOMETHING
WITH THIS
BOOK

THINK

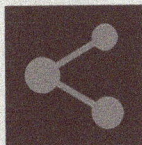
SHARE

NOTE

PRESENT

APPLY

SUBSCRIBE

TAKE ON TRIP

BOOKMARK

REFLECT

DISCUSS

HAVE A CUP

FOR OTHERS

OTHER BOOKS BY LEANDRO HERRERO:

The Flipping Point
Deprogramming Management

The Trouble with Management (out of print)

The Leader with Seven Faces
Finding your own ways of practicing leadership in today's organization

New Leaders Wanted: Now Hiring!
12 kinds of people you must find, seduce, hire and create a job for

Viral Change™
The Alternative To Slow, Painful and Unsuccessful Management of Change in Organizations

Disruptive Ideas. 10+10+10=1000
The maths of Viral Change™ that transform organizations

Ideas Rompedoras
Las reglas del Cambio Viral para transformer organizaciones

Homo Imitans
The art of social infection: Viral Change™ in action

However
Work Could Be Remarkable

SOON TO BE AVAILABLE:

The Little Book of Big Change
Universal rules for change makers

Unplugged
Organizations under new management

Homo Imitans
(second edition)

Exotics on the payroll
The anthropology of life in organizations

Victims or agents?
The modern choices of employee engagement

All books are available on Amazon, Barnes and Noble, Blackwell's, Waterstones, Books Etc. and many other bookshops.

For book enquiries and bulk orders please contact:
meetingminds@thechalfontproject.com

Text copyright © 2021 Leandro Herrero

Designed by Rachel Barker

Images used under license from Shutterstock.com

Leandro Herrero has asserted his moral right to be identified as the author of this work in accordance with the Copyright, Design and Patents Act 1988.

Disclaimer

First published in 2021 by: **Meetingminds**

Meetingminds is a division of The Chalfont Project.

MEETINGMINDS
PUBLISHING

The Chalfont Project Ltd, Charter Building, Charter Place, Uxbridge, United Kingdom UB8 1JG

Email: **meetingminds@thechalfontproject.com**

ISBN 978-1-905776-20-7

A CIP catalogue record for this title is available from the British Library.

CAMINO

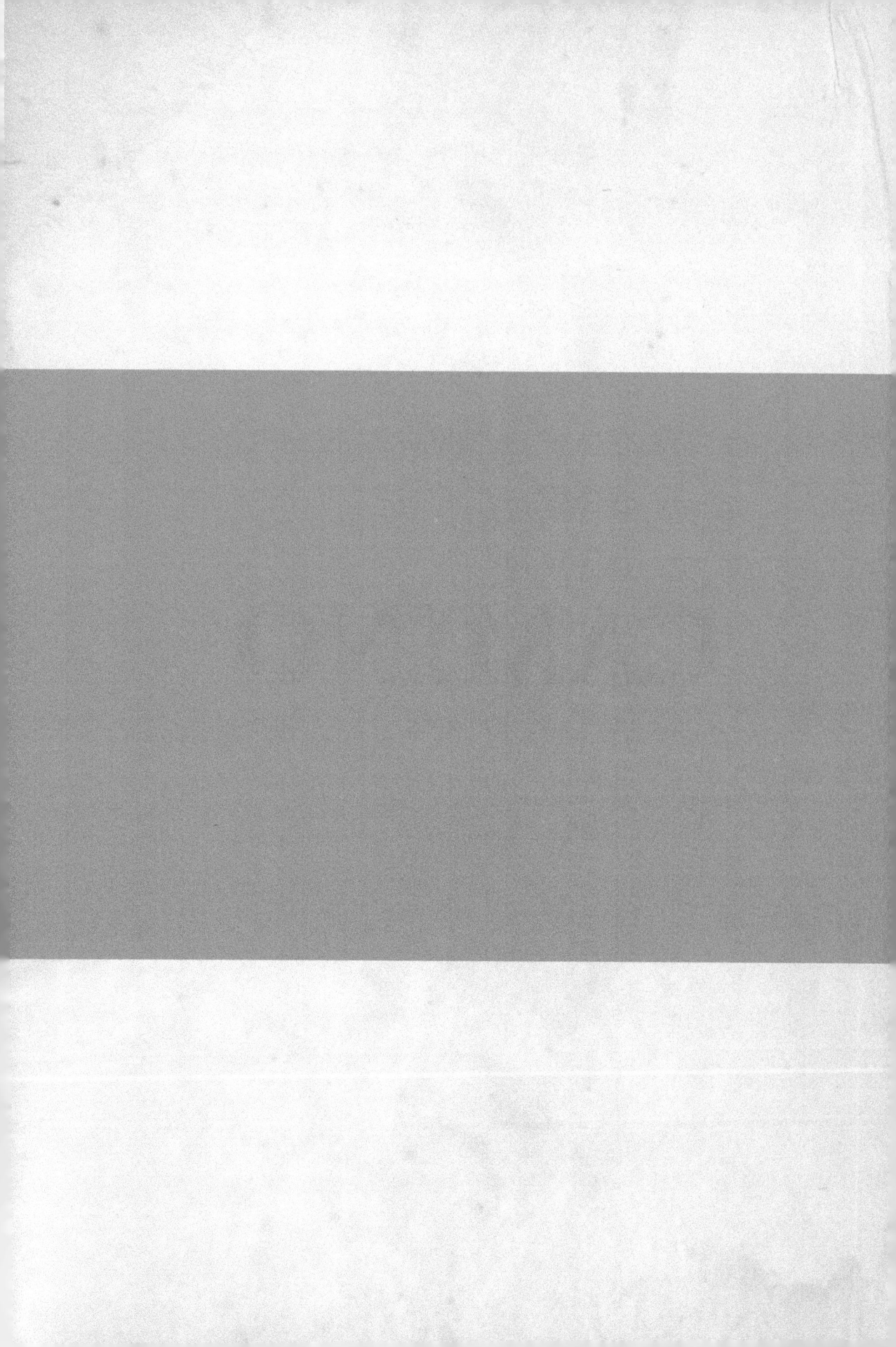

CAMINO

LEADERSHIP NOTES ON THE ROAD

LEANDRO HERRERO

MEETINGMINDS
PUBLISHING

To everybody in my team at The Chalfont Project,
Camino fellows and builders of remarkable organizations

JOURNEY

CADAQUÉS, EL MARITIM

SALAMANCA, PLAZA MAYOR

SANTIAGO DE COMPOSTELA, PRAZA DO OBRADOIRO

LA HABANA, PARQUE CENTRAL

BASE CAMP

Philosopher Martin Heidegger requested before his death that the collection of his writings be called 'paths, not works'. He had used the word 'paths' several times. It provides, according to some interpreters of his 'works', an image of 'leading' but not necessarily to anywhere in particular; like many paths do in the woods.

The great Spanish poet Antonio Machado said it well in one of his most acclaimed poems. It would read in English something like this: 'Walker, there is no path, you make the path by walking'.

The allegory of the path, whether Machado's path making or Heidegger's 'paths, not works', is a good metaphor for leadership. I really believe that cartography and leadership are twin sisters.

Pilgrimage is also another good metaphor for the leadership journey, a journey that can be done in solitude but also accompanied by followers. The pilgrimage has both the personal and the collective, all in one. The journey contains all sorts of challenges and discoveries for the pilgrim, as it does for the leader. The difference in the pilgrimage is that it has a fixed destination. But arriving is never landing by helicopter. You have to walk, to go, to move, bit by bit, and then sense, learn, live.

Every year, about 300,000 people walk the Camino de Santiago (The Way of St James) a network of routes starting in France or Portugal, or Spain itself, and that ends in Santiago de Compostela, in Galicia, Spain. Probably a minority will walk the 'required' last 100 km on pure religious grounds. But most will talk later about the transformative effects of the Camino, the route, the pilgrimage.

Constantine P. Cavafy is one of my favourite poets, and *Ithaca* my favourite one. He describes the perils of the journey to the mythical Ithaca. A destination. 'Keep Ithaca always in your mind. Arriving there is what you're destined for'. But he says that most of those perils may be in your head. And then he recommends to take your time, not to rush, go slowly, stop in all the ports, learn from the locals, and buy their perfumes. And he warns, maybe when you finally get to Ithaca, you'll be disappointed. It has nothing to offer compared with all you've learnt and lived and changed. 'Wise as you will have become, so full of experience, you will have understood by then what these Ithacas mean'.

Good leaders are good path makers. Sometimes the journey is not clear. The destination may still be ambiguous. Again, it's all about cartography. For me, a leader is the cartographer in chief who, whilst walking with others, also becomes an architect and a builder. If this is about journeys, and maps, and building, and Cavafy's 'enter (ing) harbours you're seeing for the first time and stopping at Phoenician trading stations, to buy fine things', then there is almost no end to it.

On my imaginary journey inside my head, I took notes and articulated ideas. Most became a Daily Thought, a blog I have been running for years. This is a collection of those notes. Don't look for Harvard here, there are only harbours and other places that have generously adopted the content between them.

In this Camino of mine, I have also learnt to spot the real things, the fundamentals, the rocks. These are my Rules. A small collection of warnings, strong views and discoveries that I do not intend to be transferable. After all, the journey is not transferable, nobody can walk the Camino for you. Liberated by the idea that I don't need to impart universal wisdom to end in a sterile case study and that I can share these rules like one shares a meal without having to explain the chemistry of the ingredients, here they are, still full of dust from my journey. The one I have only just begun.

1. Earn credibility all the time. Stocks deplete easily.

2. Act as if you do not have anything to lose.

3. Be unreasonable in your demands, the reasonable ones are taken.

4. Detect bullshit and become proficient at detecting it. Then, protect yourself and others.

5. Exercise provocation with panache and respect. Aim at being appreciated, not hated, for it.

6. Don't be a provocateur, rebel, maverick, contrarian or challenger for the sake of it. Have a good 'because' ready.

7. Infect others, don't do it alone.

8. Be restless, be uncomfortable (and foolish and hungry and the rest...). They're the only things that confirm that you are alive.

9. Watch your ego. Most of the time it is not your friend. Rule of thumb, most of the time it's not about you.

10. Never settle for one possibility only.

11. Don't waste your time managing the 'inevitable'. There is a lot of 'possible' waiting for a leader. Look for what would not happen without you.

12. Seek unpredictable answers. The predictable ones are already seeking you.

13. Don't be against anything. Don't create enemies. The exceptions are mediocrity and dishonesty.

14. Write down your little bit of daily legacy in a secret little book.

15. There is only one test: what will you tell the children? (that you do, you did, you didn't do).

16. More important than what you say is what people hear when you are saying it.

17. Practice 'I don't know', possibly followed by 'and I don't think you know either, so let's figure it out'.

18. Make things happen first, then clean up the process for the next time. In that order.

19. The unexamined leadership, like the unexamined life, is not worth living.

20. Play as many roles as you want, but never a victim or an enemy. Both being 'victim' or 'enemy', requires your full consent.

Off to the next harbour.

Kinvara, The Harbour

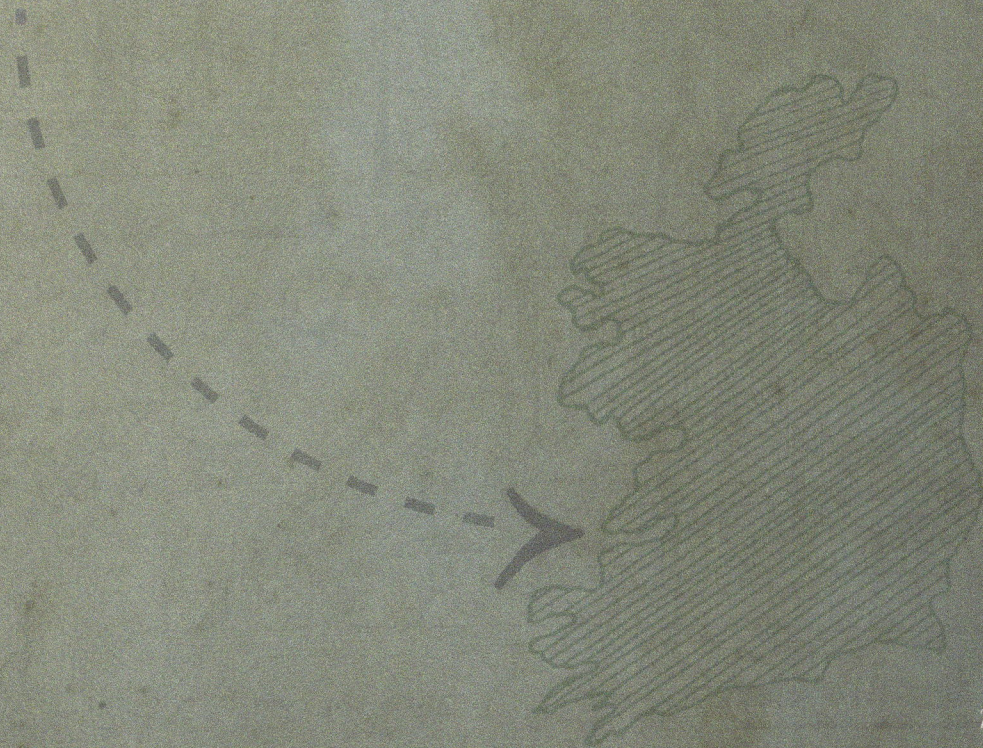

'What if the problem is me ?'
An uncomfortable, key question for leaders

Reflective leadership has gone into progressively short supply. In an era where prescriptive answers seem to dominate reflective ones, it has become more difficult to stop and think, to question, to wonder. After all, we have ready made 7 Habits for This and 8 Attributes for That, which seem to provide universal answers. Introspection has never been favoured by traditional management, or at least, not by 'mass management'. Granted, some elites that have been given access to some forms of executive development may have had the opportunity. Even in that territory, however, self-reflection is rarely, if ever, at the top of the agenda.

An old psychological concept from the 60s may help to understand why leaders differ in their ability to self-reflect on their leadership and the impact of their actions. It's called 'external vs internal locus of control'. People with a predominant 'external locus of control' tend to attribute events to external forces. In the opposite extreme, people with a predominant 'internal locus of control' will see themselves more in charge or as protagonists of the events in their lives. It follows that the external people will end up blaming other people more, whilst internal people will look more at themselves first.

This crude distinction is particularly important in areas such as Safety. In our Viral Safety™ programmes we use this unsophisticated parameter a lot. Safety professionals, or simply employees, with high 'external locus of control' will tend to see safety problems as something

produced mainly by others and will focus more on somebody else's behaviours, versus considering that the safety is of their own making.

Leadership can be seen through similar lenses. Some leaders seem to never contemplate the possibility that they are the problem, it's always somebody else's fault. If there is any reflection, it's certainly outwards. You need a good dose of 'internal locus of control' to realise that maybe the problem is you.

In my consulting practice I find this leadership problem one of the hardest to solve. 'Internal vs external locus of control' is very entrenched in personality. It's hard, but not impossible through good coaching, for example, to turn a high external individual around.

My behavioural hat however, has a clear, if not answered, guidance for this: create a habit of asking the question 'what if (this problem, what is happening, what I see) has to do with me? What if the issue is me?'

THE HABIT OF REPEATED QUESTIONING IS A GOOD WAY TO OPEN THE DOOR TO BETTER REFLECTION, AND, WHO KNOWS, THE DISCOVERY OF A NEW WORLD INSIDE OF YOU!

Emotional Ignorance needs a book

EMOTIONAL INTELLIGENCE WAS A PARAGRAPH-LENGTH CONCEPT EXPRESSED IN A LIBRARY OF PUBLICATIONS. AT THE TIME IT WAS A SHOCK TO THE SYSTEM. DO YOU REALLY MEAN EMOTIONS COUNT IN HARD MANAGEMENT AND LEADERSHIP? WOW!

The Emotional Intelligence industry (that created subsequent sequels in the form of social intelligence, even spiritual intelligence) has continued to warn about the need for 'broader intelligences', in plural. And there is a place for this! But what really needs a book is Emotional Ignorance. Or two books, or... errr. Day after day we see people in high places oblivious to what is happening on the human side of the enterprise: too complex, too soft (soft and hard are still used as terms), too distracting. They are the ones who think they have a high emotional score but behave like blind men in the land of people dynamics.

It's this Ignorance that worries me: robotic management, robotic processes, robotic systems managed by people who want ... innovation, entrepreneurship and risk taking.

20 Reasons
why I trust you

1. I trust you because I can say 'I haven't got a clue' and you don't think I am an idiot
2. I can be vulnerable and won't be penalised
3. I can be emotional and you won't think I am weak
4. I made a mistake and you said you did as well
5. I opened my heart and I did not regret it
6. I told you something in confidence and you kept it private
7. I shared my doubts and I did not go down the ranking
8. I showed you my tiredness and you didn't think I wasn't capable
9. I am not as strong as you think, but you could see strengths in me that I didn't
10. You said that you'll help me and you did
11. You said I could call you and you meant it
12. I felt overwhelmed and you did not broadcast it
13. When I screwed up, you could have avoided me, but you gave me your public hand
14. You knew how much I depended on that piece of work and you delivered it to me earlier
15. I got mad and you didn't
16. You always keep your promises
17. You represent me and I can sleep
18. You protected me and did not send the bill
19. You always tell me the truth even when I don't want to hear it
20. You never grow at the expense of my shrinking

Bring ‹character› back

We call it character assassination for a reason. It's the ultimate attack. The attack on the uniqueness of an individual, to the moral scaffolding of the person, to the sum of his qualities, a sum which has a unique blend of components that makes that character so distinctive. Stripped from anything else, character remains. The Greek and Latin etymology of the word links character to a set of qualities, which mark or design (like the characters of a text), 'an imprint on the soul'.

When politicians run out of policy arguments against opponents, they may resort to character. In fact, this is always a flag, a sign of desperation and weakness, not a strength, on the part of the assassin.

Character is often translated into a set of words including trust, courage, honesty, respect, moral integrity etc. A solid set of values seem to be at the core of the DNA of character.

We need to bring character back to the table of Leadership. Why back? I seem to imply it has gone. Not quite, but it's gone for long sabbaticals. The organizational airtime for character has been taken over by other more prosaic and often neon-like visible flashes of 'what the leader does', and even more, by 'the 10 things successful leaders do' and the 'so many habits'. This is not bad in itself. Mirrors and examples and models are welcome, provided they are taken with a pinch of salt. However, these are shortcuts that avoid a deeper discussion.

But, it's easier to talk about how good leaders empower, delegate, communicate well and set expectations, than to get down to the cave and look for the soul. In the choice between soul and the '10 traits of

successful leaders', the latter sells much more. Also, we are told, C level business people don't do soul.

I believe that the ultimate discussion about leadership is about character. Not even about personality. After all, personality has to do with the persona, the exterior, the mask, still not deep enough. Abraham Lincoln said that 'Character is like a tree and reputation like its shadow. The shadow is what we think of it; the tree is the real thing'. Instead of reputation we could also say the visible persona, the external behavioural 'presentations in everyday life', as Erving Goffman would have said.

The main challenge I see is that, as I said before, character has been evicted from the organizational/business/people conversation and now we tend to find it dwelling in the Self Help, New Age or Spiritual shelves. Even Western educational systems seem to be shy of the word these days.

I could picture an entire Leadership Development Programme devoted to Character, including its corrosion, to use Richard Sennett's 1998 title of his book.

THOSE OF US WHO OCCUPY THIS TERRITORY (YOU, ME, MANAGERS, PRACTITIONERS, CONSULTANTS) SHOULD BE BOLD ENOUGH TO UNAPOLOGETICALLY RESCUE CHARACTER FROM ITS TRAVELS TO OTHER LANDS, SO THAT IT OCCUPIES AGAIN THE CENTRE OF THE DIALOGUE, A CENTRE THAT IT SHOULDN'T HAVE LEFT.

Pilot or pastor ?
From the No Nonsense Francis School of Leadership

POPE FRANCIS HAS DONE IT AGAIN. I MEAN, HIS PROBABLY WEEKLY, PLAIN ENGLISH (WELL, ITALIAN OR SPANISH), BIT OF NUDGING TO HIS TROOPS. AND, AS IT IS NOW NORMAL, A NEW PIECE OF WISDOM AND UNSOPHISTICATED, UNCOMPLICATED GUIDANCE, IS OUT FOR COLLECTION.

This plain, off-the-cuff talking drives his holy apparatus nuts and is often seen (mostly heard) with horror by the ones who expect the Catholic Pope to speak nothing other than extremely complicated and theologically unintelligible language. But many people, even those not close to the Catholic Church, also systematically receive it as fresh air.

Francis' authenticity is such raw material that many people think of it as calculated spin of a 'super-skilled politician'. We have come to believe that authenticity is suspicious. Who could blame the thinkers? After all, we are short of that authenticity, so seeing a real Endangered Species live next to us, shocks us.

Francis was this time talking to the Italian Bishops about the importance of the laity. Read normal people not in the church hierarchy. He told them that they did not need a bishop-pilot ('to assume their responsibilities at all levels, political, social, economic or legislative') but a bishop-pastor. The implication was: you are piloting too much. So, pilot or pastor?

Everybody knows what a pilot is. The ones who do the job, take you to places, whilst you sit behind in comfortable seats (of some sort), often going off to sleep. Pilot-leadership style is similar. 'They' at the top will do, decide, will tell us what to do. The CEO is the pilot, the COO the co-pilot, the CFO the second co-pilot and so on.

Pastor and pastoral care not only has a religious connotation in itself, but a broader meaning of 'emotional and spiritual support'. In the UK, in particular, the term 'pastoral care' is used in education in a non-religious way, to refer to 'the practice of looking after the personal and social well-being of children or students under the care of a teacher or rabbi'. It can encompass a wide variety of issues including health, social and moral education, behaviour management and emotional support.

Pastor-leadership is therefore more about creating the conditions, the environment, the space. It's about care (same root as cure, and in other languages as dear or loved).

MANY WELL-MEANING LEADERSHIP TEAMS EMBRACE PROGRESSIVELY INCREASING LEVELS OF PILOTING WITHOUT EVEN BEING CONSCIOUS OF IT. THE PILOT MODEL IS VERY VISIBLE IN ORGANIZATIONAL CULTURES WHERE TOP LEADERSHIP OR TOP MANAGEMENT TEAMS HAVE A DISPROPORTIONATE AMOUNT OF TOPICS TO 'APPROVE AND DECIDE' ON THEIR AGENDA. THESE GROUPS AND TEAMS ARE SO BUSY PILOTING FROM THE FIFTH OR TENTH FLOOR HQ COCKPIT THEY HAVE NO TIME TO COME DOWN TO THE PASTURES AND DO SOME PASTORAL STUFF.

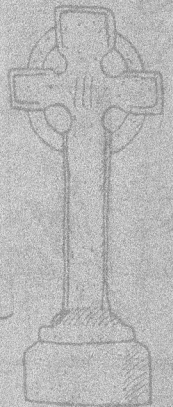

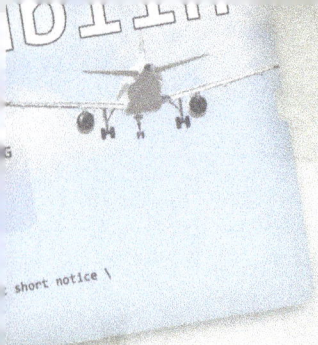

His greatest success was not to fail

Many people, many of them in high managerial positions, succeed by avoiding failure. They become unmemorable by design. A new head teacher was appointed in an important school. The press went back to past pupils and asked what they remembered of him: 'he fell downstairs once'. A new pharma R&D leader is nicknamed 'The Chronic Survivor' because everybody else in his top team has left or been fired but he managed to survive unscathed from all the storms. People can't remember any mistake he has ever made. People can't remember anything, period, other than the fact that he survives.

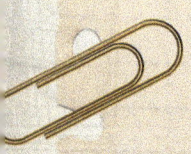

THESE TWO VIGNETTES ARE REAL AND PART OF MY PAST EXPERIENCE. MANY LEADERS MAY REMAIN UNNOTICED AND IN THE UNMEMORABLE CATEGORY. THEY ARE SQUATTERS IN THE ORGANIZATIONAL CHART. 'WHAT DO YOU WANT TO BE REMEMBERED FOR?' IS A CRUCIAL QUESTION WE DON'T ASK OFTEN ENOUGH.

Do visionary leaders nominate non-visionary successors ?

HARDLY A QUESTION I CAN ANSWER WITH STATISTICS, BUT I WOULD TEND TO AGREE. AN ARTICLE WRITTEN BY STEVE BLANK ON QUARTZ.COM POINTS IN THAT DIRECTION ALTHOUGH ONLY CITING TWO ICONIC COMPANIES.

This is how it goes:

Apple. Visionary Jobs innovates and innovates. Followed by Cook, non-visionary, not really new products, certainly not à la Jobs.

Microsoft. Visionary and innovator Gates is followed by non-visionary not innovating, revenue super boosting Ballmer. Here's the good news: followed by Nadella, visionary again and new innovations coming out.

Hardly a scientific experiment, but it made me think. I've seen these alternations in small scale again and again, more of the Apple type than the Microsoft, that in fact has gone back to the core and soul of the company as Nadella puts it in his book *Hit Refresh*.

I think the article is harsh with Cook and Ballmer, The Great Successors, but there is something there.

For whatever it's worth I think that visionary leaders should be followed by visionary leaders. It is not true, for example, that there isn't another Jobs. There is, they're just called something else.

What the organization needs is a simple and healthy internal balance between vision and execution, the latter not at the expense of compromising the former.

Are we following here too much a form of the Great Man Theory of History? Perhaps. But the observations by Steve Blank made me think.

Rambling, yet it makes me think.

In doubt,
make it personal

INVITED TO PRESENT AT TEDX EAST LONDON, I HAD LOTS
OF CONVERSATIONS WITH ITS WONDERFUL CURATOR MARYAM
PASHA. THE THEME OF THE TEDX WAS 'SOCIETY BEYOND
BORDERS'. I HAD A FLOW OF IDEAS ABOUT HOW THE DIGITAL
WORLD HAS FORCED A REDEFINITION OF BORDERS AND THE
CONSEQUENT PARADOXES: THE END OF SPACE AND TIME THAT
DOES NOT INCREASE OUR PROXIMITY; HYPER-CONNECTIVITY
THAT DOES NOT MAKE US HYPER-COLLABORATIVE, ETC.

I had a clear idea of the first part of the flow of the talk. What was less clear to me was 'Part 2' or the 'So what?'. Like those TV contests, some movies and some video games, I had two possible endings for the script. I could go for the logical 'commercial' side easily. After all, my consulting work has to do with large scale behavioural change and we use the power of peer-to-peer influence as a currency. We know about networks and human connectivity. This is natural territory for me. Or I could perhaps go for a more personal side: the liabilities of a lack of borders for the Self and the Soul in the new digital world. In praising 'no borders' ('Anything without Borders' has a head start), we have forgotten the dangers of full disclosure of the Self that many people seem so comfortable with.

Option A's end was clear, but Option B's ending was fuzzy, more of a nagging problem in my head: adolescents living in that world of full disclosure, the relinquishing of privacy, the cult of transparency, identity in cyberspace, etc. My old psychiatric hat was nagging me too much to let me avoid these themes.

I did offer Maryam both Option A and Option B, quite convinced that A (the logical, commercial, well-crafted version) would win. I was wrong. In her gentle and firm curatorship, I was directed towards the corridor of my unfinished thoughts. 'Make it personal', she said. The same week I had a chat with a business partner and I shared with him my dilemma. He asked me straight: 'Where is your heart?' I confessed, B. 'Well, no brainer then, that would be You talking!'.

YES, PERSONAL WINS. PERSONAL WON ON THE DAY.
IT WAS GOOD ADVICE FOR WHEN IN DOUBT.
I SHOULD HAVE KNOWN ... BUT I NEEDED A GOOD CURATOR
AND A GOOD BUSINESS PARTNER TO TAKE ME
TO THE MORE DIFFICULT AND LESS
OBVIOUS OPTION.

The death of the charismatic leadership has been grossly exaggerated

As Mark Twain said of himself, 'The death of the charismatic leader has been grossly exaggerated'. The problem is that 'charisma' has changed its face. Many years ago, charismatic leadership sounded loud. A charismatic leader was supposed to mesmerise, exhibit exuberant passion (stereotype of the American leader?), be extraordinarily persuasive (would sell ice to Eskimos) and be able to command an almost unconditional following. Of course, I am in caricature mode here. It took a lot of time to realise that many exceptional leaders, according to this profile, were not charismatic at all.

Perhaps charismatic leadership today has a different profile. His or her inspiration comes from being emotionally and socially brilliant. The new charismatic leader sees and feels the social environment around them, they 'get' the people and the dynamics of the organization. He or she is a master of giving the stage to others, something that I have described as Backstage Leadership™. Above all, the new charismatic leaders have less of a 'push' style (messaging) and are more able to 'pull' behaviours around him. They would be firm and visible but also far more humble.

I have a little rule of thumb about trust and charismatic leadership. The old type sometimes used to trigger feelings such as: 'he is brilliant, great charisma, I am not sure I trust him, though'. The new type produces first an 'I trust this guy', and then other traits follow. Don't look for any science behind my rule.

Perhaps new forms of charisma have been evolving all the time, but the death of charisma itself has been grossly exaggerated.

It reminds me of an old thing when I started medical school. Students used to repeat (and shout) the mantra; 'we don't want magisterial lectures' – the ones given by chair professors in front of hundreds of people for sixty minutes or so, non-stop, in huge amphitheatres, as was the norm. I always thought that the main reason for disliking them, was because we did not have good 'magisters'. Had we had good ones, I personally would not have minded at all.

I WONDER WHETHER THE FALL FROM GRACE OF
THE CHARISMATIC LEADER (AS HAS BEEN THE CASE
IN RECENT YEARS) HAS TO DO WITH THE SCARCITY OF THEM.
JUST A THOUGHT.

The era of Narcissus

IN GREEK MYTHOLOGY, NARCISSUS FELL IN LOVE WITH HIMSELF WHEN LOOKING AT HIS OWN IMAGE REFLECTED IN THE WATER. IT WAS, OF COURSE, ALL NEMESIS' FAULT, WHO HAD NOTICED NARCISSUS' FONDNESS FOR HIMSELF AND TOOK HIM TO A POOL OF WATER WHERE NARCISSUS DISCOVERED HOW BEAUTIFUL HE REALLY WAS. HE DIED, ADMIRING HIMSELF, STUCK LOOKING AT THAT POOL.

That was when the Selfie was born, but, of course, neither Narcissus nor Nemesis had a chance to patent this new concept. Narcissus did not have a smartphone to take a picture of himself, just the water as a high resolution camera.

Never in history has humankind had the opportunity to be more self-centred. The instant broadcasting of 'Me', plus the colossal interconnectedness between individuals, coupled with 'the end of distance', 'the end of time', and the ubiquitous social media, makes Narcissus' possibilities unlimited. The new digital world is a Narcissus pool of water of pan-galactic dimensions.

What is the point of posting that you've just arrived at Frankfurt airport and it's raining? Or posting a picture of your bowl of cereal on the breakfast table? Perhaps pictures of yourself looking at yourself via your iPhone? Downloading an entire dictionary of quotations, one quote an hour on Twitter? Checking in with yourself? The point? To reaffirm your own existence, I suppose.

(Nothing as irritating as David Cameron, when UK Prime Minister, congratulating the Duke and Duchess of Cambridge on the birth of their newborn baby, via a post on ... LinkedIn!).

'Come on!', my Jiminy Cricket/ Pepe Grillo says, tapping on my shoulder. And, as with the conscience of the Disney character, Pinocchio, I must pay attention to him. 'Ease up!', he says, 'it's all good. It's all sharing. You use social media too Leandro (yes I do, modestly, but not on the cereals side) and you write and broadcast Daily Thoughts (yes, until I stop making sense)'. OK, I'll ease up now.

I still worry about the self-centrism that we are generating. I must confess I worry less about adults taking pictures of themselves 'because they can' than kids learning that the centre of the Universe is that image that they can see in their smartphone screen.

As I flip screens on my MacBook Air on a quiet Saturday morning, I see the world around me. One Facebook screen shows three selfies of 'friends' last night after a few drinks. Next screen is the BBC's news on Ebola and some Dantesque pictures in Africa. A twitter feed has just popped up with somebody I don't know telling me that 'He has absolutely zero motivation this morning'. Another screen on *The Guardian* online shows me an article entitled 'Big pharma has an interest in rich people being sick'. An alien, just landed, would say: 'What kind of mad world is this?'

OK, this is my world this morning. Mad.

PERHAPS TAKING PICTURES OF ONESELF IS NOT SO BAD AFTER ALL. BUT, OF ME? DON'T EVEN THINK ABOUT IT.

Leadership 's hearing problems

'AND THOSE WHO WERE SEEN DANCING WERE THOUGHT TO BE INSANE BY THOSE WHO COULD NOT HEAR THE MUSIC'.

Friedrich Nietzsche's quote is a great reminder. The advanced mind, the individual a bit ahead of the game, the team challenging the default position, the company pushing for the unconventional, they are all singing something that perhaps others cannot hear. Or cannot hear yet.

In the famous 1997 Apple ad *Think Different*, a list of people are quoted: 'the misfits, the rebels, the troublemakers (...) the ones who see things differently'. I agree that we need these minds, but we also need a company environment that can host these rebels. Above all, we need leaders that can hear.

I have written a few times about my misgivings about 'the rebels for the sake of it', or the promotion of the 'rebel' category as a major player in 'change management'. This is all very well, but I am more interested in the creation of environments where the ones who can dance can actually dance, and where leaders are not deaf and can actually hear different music.

Every time you or your team are about to declare some idea or initiative as 'insane', double check your hearing. Perhaps you can't hear that music. The problem may be you, not those dancing.

'AND THOSE WHO WERE SEEN DANCING WERE THOUGHT TO BE INSANE BY THOSE WHO COULD NOT HEAR THE MUSIC'. A GREAT QUOTE BY NIETZSCHE, WHICH NIETZSCHE ACTUALLY NEVER SAID. IT HAS BEEN QUOTED A MILLION TIMES. WE HAVE HEARD HIM SAYING IT. BUT HE NEVER DID. YOU SEE, STILL HEARING PROBLEMS.

5 things very successful leaders have in common

1. They don't read blogs entitled '5 things very successful leaders have in common'.

2. They don't care about lists of platitudes such as: be yourself, know where you are going, give feedback, be proactive, listen to people and don't leave things for tomorrow.

3. They don't think they have anything in common with other successful leaders other than success.

4. Actually, very successful leaders have in common a pair of legs, a pair of eyes, one heart, they were all babies before, and they will all die.

5. Courage, determination, resilience, honesty and fantastic communication skills. These 5 attributes of very successful leaders are equally found in very unsuccessful leaders.

I BEG YOU:
Stop thinking like a printout. Stop spamming with a list of platitudes. Say something that is better than silence. Stop writing as if you have found the Meaning of the Universe. Starting the phrase with "research shows that' does not necessarily give credibility to your argument.

By all means, share ideas, personal and subjective. That is not the problem. On the contrary, that may be the solution to Robotic Psychological Pollution. I love biased and subjective ideas associated to a name. Then I know I am talking to a human being. I may agree or not, but I will know where people stand.

Disclosure. There are no 5 things that very successful leaders have in common. Or 10 things. Or Harvard research with the solution. These attributional lists have the solidity of a cream cake. Father Christmas is your dad. Management thinking is exhausted. We can't milk more Google lists anymore.

RICHARD III UPDATE: 'A HUMAN AND CRITICAL THINKING CONVERSATION, MY KINGDOM FOR A HUMAN AND CRITICAL THINKING CONVERSATION'. IT'S THE BATTLE FOR IDEAS, NOT LISTS.

To be a better leader, take a holiday from yourself

THE SPACE OF YOUR SELF IS OCCUPIED. BY YOU. THIS IS GOOD NEWS AND BAD NEWS. ON ONE HAND, YOU ARE ALWAYS WITH YOUR SELF. ON THE OTHER HAND, YOU MAY BE TOO MUCH WITH YOUR SELF. THE SELF CAN BE YOUR WORST ENEMY ('WE ARE OUR OWN WORST ENEMIES') BUT COULD ALSO BE YOUR BEST FRIEND. BEST FRIENDS OCCASIONALLY IRRITATE YOU, PRECISELY BECAUSE OF THEIR CLOSENESS, THEIR PROXIMITY. PERHAPS YOU HAVE WISHED, A FEW TIMES, TO TAKE A LITTLE BREAK FROM A 'BEST FRIEND'.

Leaders need to be good friends with themselves. They need to have the insight and the maturity to see their Self in action: taking too much space? Too little space?

There are times when you should take a holiday from 'yourself', as the late John O'Donohue would say. It does not have to be a long, exotic holiday, but more of a time out or a break.

THERE ARE FIVE SETS OF SYMPTOMS WHICH MAY SUGGEST THAT YOU SHOULD CONSIDER THAT HOLIDAY (SOON):

1.   You find you're talking too much about yourself

2.   For a little while you have been too harsh, perhaps too unkind, to yourself, blaming yourself for an unusual number of things

3.   You are missing some life-lines (not dead-lines) such as kids birthdays, anniversaries, reunions. People seem to have the habit of having birthdays and anniversaries the days you are travelling or absent

4.   You find yourself interfering too much in other people's lives, professional or personal

5.   You have not had a chance recently to ask yourself that question about 'what your legacy as a leader is?', 'what kind of house are you building?', 'what are you leaving behind?'

There may be more symptoms, but these are pretty important. Trust me, I am a doctor.

Sure, to identify the symptoms some insight capacity is required. Which I am assuming a leader has. If not, the case is terminal, anyway.

YOU MAY NOT HAVE THESE FLAGGED IN A TRADITIONAL 'LEADERSHIP MANUAL'. THIS IS PART OF THE 'NOT-OFF-THE-SHELF-LEADERSHIP-STUFF' SERIES.

Choosing between honest arrogance and hypocritical humility

'EARLY IN LIFE I HAD TO CHOOSE BETWEEN HONEST ARROGANCE AND HYPOCRITICAL HUMILITY. I CHOSE THE FORMER AND HAVE SEEN NO REASON TO CHANGE'.

This is a quote by Frank Lloyd Wright (1867-1959), pioneering architect, critical and conceptual thinker of spaces and places, father of a movement and a style, a great mind and an often controversial figure.

This is a great quote. A great frame for leaders. There are always choices, big choices and small choices, mundane choices and existential choices.

I respect them all.

But I recognise my choice in the honest arrogant side: as a consulting company we operate with fixed 'honestly arrogant' principles. For example, we don't sell our time. Yep! It is simply something we don't sell. We sell advice, outcomes, help, value, hands on implementation, motivation, engagement, ideas, critical thinking, dreams, realities. We are organizational architects. We sell organizational houses, not the time that it takes to build them.

Our 'honest arrogance' drives Procurement Departments nuts, delights great customers and puzzles others. How easy it is to default to hypocritical humility.

Oh, I forgot, we also sell restlessness, sometimes comfort.

I will draw a parallel with leadership, the really interesting topic, not me. Leadership needs authenticity, clarity of the value it brings, unapologetic stances, its own 'honest arrogance'. Respect for others, driving others to better pathways, mobilizing energies and, in general, 'taking others with you', start from a position of authenticity. This is often seen as arrogant or superior. How sad that 'hypocritical humility' is far more politically correct and far more accepted.

I've seen (I meet every day) weak leaders, middle of the road CEOs, unauthentic leaders, dishonest arrogant ones, and anything in between. But I also see great leaders and great minds. From the latter, all of them have in common the right imbalance between that honest arrogance and hypocritical humility. As for the best I know (whether clients, friends, not clients, not friends) it is crystal clear what they stand for. Whether I like it or not.

Even my favourite ones, the ones who don't profess to have all the answers, the ones who don't have a fixed destination, the ones who are more Travellers and Cartographers than anything else, do all these things from a position of strength. Their humility is a strength, not hypocritical. Their honesty may come across as arrogance. But most of them are the most anti-arrogant people I have ever met. In a world of often weak principles, strong ones may come across as self-important, too proud or superior.

Most historical religious, political or civic leaders, did not say, 'have black, or perhaps pink, it does not really matter, red is good as well, but if you like green, so be it; it's all the same, it's all relative, don't worry about it; it all depends on circumstances'. Nope. It does not.

MY COLLEAGUE AND BUSINESS PARTNER CAROLINE TIERNEY, BRINGS THE LLOYD WRIGHT QUOTE TO THE TABLE MANY TIMES: 'ARE WE BUILDING A LLOYD WRIGHT HOUSE OR A DRIVE-THROUGH MCDONALDS?' THE HORROR OF THE WRONG CHOICE KEEPS US ON TRACK.

Leadership is a social concept, not an individual trait

But we are fascinated by the individual stock

Leadership is a term that describes a relationship. No relationship, no leadership. Leadership can only be defined in terms of followers. No followers, no leadership. Cut across this apparent platitude for a minute and suspend judgement.

The early centuries' desert hermits were not great leaders at the time. Then, some of their writings were diffused over centuries. Some are considered thought leaders today, even if they never had troops around. Can a hermit be a leader? If he has followers, yes he can. What would describe them as leaders is not a sort of intrinsic set of characteristics (wisdom, humility, vision) but the existence of a relationship which entails people following them.

Harrison White, (*Identity and Control*, 1992, 2008) one of the greatest living sociologists, has been very clear about what he considers the error of attributing traits to 'leadership', despite the thousands of books that do so. These are not universal here. It's not something that you have. It's what you practice and the how.

For every set of attributes associated to a good leader (or a good company, or successful organization for that matter) one has to see if some or all of those attributes are also found in not particularly good leaders (or unsuccessful organizations).

We know more about the liabilities of not having something than the benefits of having it. Translation: we know that a leader that is not honest, that has little integrity, that treats people like commodities and has an ego bigger than the Sun, is bad news. He will have that negative influence, will run the organization in a particular way, will be a disaster.

Now, let's have the opposite. A leader that is very honest, has tremendous integrity, treats people with high respect, is humble and a servant, is surely a gem to have. Do the combination of all these make him a good leader? No, sorry. It makes him a great human being. Those 'good attributes' are not exclusive of that category/concept called 'leadership'. But it's great to have this around.

A great deal of so-called research, which in pop-business-culture is often translated into those 10 habits, 10 characteristics, 10 things, 10 attributes, is flawed. That does not make it 'not interesting' and, for sure, it does not seem a handicap to write a book about it.

LEADERSHIP IS NOT SOMETHING THAT ONE HAS OR NOT, IT IS SOMETHING THAT ONE PRACTICES IN A SOCIAL CONTEXT AND THAT TRANSLATES INTO PATTERNS OF BEHAVIOURS AND RELATIONSHIPS. OUR 'INDIVIDUAL INTEREST' IS OUT OF FOCUS.

Your most important list of personal assets. Take time. Now ?

THERE ARE MANY WAYS TO LIST OUR OWN ASSETS. AND THAT IS SOMETHING THAT IS VERY HEALTHY TO DO. PRACTICE IT FROM TIME TO TIME, NOT JUST WHEN TALKING TO RECRUITERS.

1. **WHAT WE'VE DONE.** This is the first thing that comes to mind. Many CV/resumes are travel books, with a bit of TripAdvisor. This list will give you the 'been there, done that'. It may look impressive or may not. But it's not the most important list, even if you have the heroic assignments in the Amazon (the forest and the online).

2. **WHAT WE KNOW.** Ah! This is the bit that usually deals with qualifications and 'experience'. Experts, experts! Can you really list what you know and don't know? OK, but this is not the most important list anyway.

3. **WHAT WE CARE ABOUT.** That's another list. Try it. Seriously. (Now?!) Hard sometimes. It's the list of values. But don't call it values, it's a bit devalued. Call it *'The Things I Seriously Care About List'*. This is a very, very important list, but not the most important list.

4. **WHAT WE DO AND LIKE, THAT NOT EVERYBODY KNOWS, PROBABLY NOT IN THE COMPANY ANYWAY.** Training kids, singing

in a choir, driving old ladies to the doctor, making mojitos. Very important list, but not the most import list.

5. **THE THAT'S ME LIST IN FRONT OF A MIRROR.** What is unique about you, from all the lists above, that defines you, when you look at yourself in the mirror and say, Ah! I know that guy. This is the you as 'the only world expert of your own experience' (William Stafford). This is the unique blend of good and bad, and less good, and those unique pieces of the other lists. This is the most important list.

Can you make that list? Just as well, because whilst somebody else can list the things that you have done, the marvellous things you are an expert of, your values and your secret likes, nobody else other than you can write list number 5.

It's also a choice to define yourself by (1) what you do, (2) what you know, (3) what you like and are good at, (4) what you care about, or (5) what is it only you and nobody else knows about.

PS. Note that the default position in introducing people is to talk about what we do. Nice to meet you Peter, nice to meet you John, so, what do you do? Well, I run the IT back office for Super Duper. And you?

Now, imagine this: Nice to meet you Peter, nice to meet you John, so, what do you care about? Well, these are the things: kids, fishing, and global warming, no particular order. Awkward? But why? It's a perfectly legitimate question.

I am digressing. Make that list 5.

The many 'me' inside Me need some discovery: have a go
They all seem to come for dinner

Continuing the conversation on leadership. Yes, we could go on forever. Let me make an assumption: that miraculously you'll have some quieter time soon to slow down a tiny bit. Summer: that magic word that means lots and lots of days for many of my clients and just a little break if you are in the US. Apologies to those who don't have summer when we do have one. I know that you down South take revenge and have a warm Christmas.

If you have some extra time for reflection, of some sort, well, (your) leadership is not a bad topic to focus on. Read, think, take notes?

If you start deep inside you here is an idea: list your contradictions. Yep. How you like A but also B, which is so opposite. How you criticise X and love Y, but you are X as well, and you don't criticise yourself. Greet the many *yous* that live together.

Frankly, in my case, sometimes it looks like a 70's commune of uninvited people taking over the living room and camping in the garden. There are so many *mes*.

I really believe that perhaps step one for any reflective leadership is to acknowledge the contradictions inside, welcome the paradoxes and do some discovery work.

And then, remain calm.

ELIAS CANETTI (1905–1994) WINNER OF THE NOBEL PRIZE IN LITERATURE SAID: 'I WOULD LIKE TO REMAIN SIMPLE, SO AS NOT TO CONFUSE THE MANY IDENTITIES I AM COMPOSED OF'.

PRECISELY. I SAY CALM INSTEAD OF SIMPLE. MAYBE BOTH ARE THE SAME.

Heaven is empty
of self-centred people

These were recent words of Pope Francis to the Italian bishops, apparently too preoccupied with their own careers and favours in the Vatican.

These are also words of wisdom for leadership. Leadership and self-centred attitudes do not go well together. Self-centred leaders are bad leaders, dangerous leaders. Leadership requires a servant attitude and this is incompatible with a self-centred focus. In fact, a refocusing of 'the centre' may even be a requisite for success.

There was a moment in the 2008 Obama campaign when the grassroots movement began to be organized. Almost in passing, David Plouffe, the then manager of the campaign, wrote in his later book, *The Audacity to Win: The Inside Story* and *Lessons of Barack Obama's Historic Victory*, that the message to the grassroots was: 'It's not about him, it's about you!'. Obama was very good at refocusing attention from himself to the issues and to the activists.

Self-centred leadership is an oxymoron, a dangerous one. The good news is that these pseudo-leaders are very visible at a distance. My advice: avoid them like the plague, because whatever they pretend to lead, the focus is most likely on them and not on the real issues of concern.

There are good leaders, excellent leaders, and Gold leaders

This is what Gold looks like

GOLD LEADERSHIP IS THE ONE ABOVE SILVER AND BRONZE, THAT'S IT. SORRY IF YOU WERE EXPECTING A VERY SOPHISTICATED DEFINITION.

If I describe the Gold, you can figure out what Silver and Bronze would be. Certainly, a very rich set as well, all excellent. Just not Gold.

THIS IS GOLD:

1. Ahead of the game, a few or more steps than anybody else. A bad leader thinks that this Gold leader is on a different planet. But the Gold leader is not; he/she simply sees this planet from a different angle. An angle that not many people see. This is visioning at its best, not dreaming. He/she is also not entirely apologetic about this.

2. Imagination at work, which needs some (often irritating sounding) detachment from daily life; even if that daily life sucks the Gold leader into factual problem solving. Even a crisis that is in the process of being addressed, by no means solved, elicits in the Gold leader the thinking of how to avoid a new one, or different one, which annoys people trying to solve the crisis of the day.

3. The Gold leader refuses to obey the 'one thing at a time' rule. For the Gold leader, sequential stuff is overrated.

4. The Gold leader refuses to see 'focus' as something you see through a tiny hole. Focus is often confused with determination. The Gold leader is focused but has more than one target to focus on. He or she particularly likes

people who can have a broad vision and a good helicopter view, and then can focus. Which confuses some.

5. The Gold leader thinks legacy, even when nobody expects that he or she thinks legacy, not yet. It's mainly not personal or ego legacy but thinking about the building that is being built. Sometimes nobody seems to see the walls. Gold leaders do.

6. Creates space and time by stealing them, by refusing to be drawn to busyness. This is both for himself/herself and for others. It has nothing to do with 'free time' and 'thinking time'. It has to do with the War on Stupid Busyness.

7. The Gold leader is brilliant at enhancing the possibilities and life of people. He/she puts people in the right places, which also stretches them. There is nothing altruistic or naive in this. He or she has perhaps an innate hope in human beings but may not be too vocal about it.

8. The Gold leader refuses to play the role of having all the answers or knowing the exact point of destination, but at the same time brings others to figure out the journey (and may close the door and throw the key out of the window until everybody is on the same path).

9. The Gold leader not only accepts but promotes areas of ineffectiveness in the life of the organization, where things are not super perfect and super clear and perhaps there are elements of waste. The Gold leader knows that this is the only way to get better and better, and succeed. But he or she can sometimes be seen as too tolerant with some ambiguity.

10. The Gold leader is both very strategic and very tactical, so it does not fit into the assumed bipolar view of the world. In fact, the Gold leader surprises others with the apparent confusion. Often some tactical moves for others are very strategic for the Gold leaders and vice-versa. That distinction does not sit comfortably in the Gold leader's mind.

IF YOU SEE ONE OF THESE, WORK FOR OR WITH ONE OF THESE, CONGRATULATIONS. IF YOU ARE ONE OF THESE, THINK PLATINUM.

Leadership dialects : you are supposed to join a party, but don't get an invitation

The language of leadership is often plain and monotone. Used to explain slides, with a screen behind them, leadership language can be dull. I often sit in large corporate meetings and think that the TV weather forecast guy does a better job.

There are many types of 'leadership dialects' but these 3 are quite relevant. This is why:

FACTUAL, DESCRIPTIVE: 'this is the strategic plan, these are the goals, and the challenges; this is what we need to achieve; this is the ambition'. This style is rather common. It's based upon the assumption of the universal goodness of communication. It is informational. If coming from the very top, it may or may not contain a revelation, something new. I am always surprised by how much no-newness is included in some top corporate speeches. Of course, as usual, the value is in the ritual of the top leader addressing the troops. It is 'hearing it from him', more than hearing something new.

ASPIRATIONAL: 'we thought it would take us 3 years, here we are today. It's possible, yes, we can do this; we are our own limits'. This dialect is pulling quite a lot of emotions. It helps with the visualisation of a destiny, small d or capital D. It's not incompatible with the 'factual dialect' but goes well beyond. Obama is here in his acceptance and inauguration speeches.

INVITATIONAL: 'come with me, I need you, let's do it together; I can't do it on my own'. It builds upon factual and aspirational, but it creates a new 'pull effect'. I am actually inviting you not just to understand the facts, not only to imagine a future, but to come with me and start walking. In my experience in the corporate arena seeing and hearing leaders talk, these are my informal statistics of what I find: it is about 80% factual, 15% aspirational and 5% invitational. Many leaders simply forget the invitation.

Formal communication training often stops at the obvious: (1) style: be authentic, be yourself, be clear; and (2) content: have key messages, be on target, be specific.

The key question, however, on top of the above, is to know what behaviours you want to trigger. The factual dialect produces, perhaps, clarification, rational and emotional understanding. The aspirational dialect produces motivation. The invitational dialect is trying to trigger action.

THE INVITATIONAL DIALECT IS THE MOST FORGOTTEN, YET POTENTIALLY THE MOST POWERFUL. DON'T LEAVE THE ROOM WITHOUT AN INVITATION TO PEOPLE. SMALL ROOM, BIG ROOM, SMALL DESTINY, BIG DESTINY, INVITE, ALWAYS INVITE.

The leader as a blank screen, on which others project

IN HIS 2003 BOOK *THE AUDACITY OF HOPE*, BARACK OBAMA WROTE:

'I SERVE AS A BLANK SCREEN ON WHICH PEOPLE OF VASTLY DIFFERENT POLITICAL STRIPES PROJECT THEIR OWN VIEWS. AS SUCH, I AM BOUND TO DISAPPOINT SOME, IF NOT ALL OF THEM'.

In his last months in the White House, the Accountants of Hope landed to count the Audacity of Hope and were ready to list the done and still-to-do, will never be done. And there were disappointments, as he predicted.

I am not an American. I am a political voyeur, world citizen with a Spanish passport, an organization architect as a profession, passionate about people mobilization in organizations. I am biased. (You too). I do believe that in the not too distant future, not that entity that we call 'History' that we all refer to, meaning several generations back, Obama will be seen as one of the greatest presidents that country has had. And, in saying so, I am of course on a collision course with those who thought that 'Making America Great Again', as Mr Trump's slogan said, would happen by building big walls, widespread insults, carpet bombing and a populist circus.

I am digressing. This Daily Thought was not meant to be a political chat. I think that the little line in Obama's book, 'a blank screen on which people project their own views', is a great metaphor for leadership. We project on leaders our hopes and expectations, also our rejections and judgements. We see on that blank screen what we want to see, not what is there; hear what we want to hear, maybe not what he says; and make judgements on 'the screen' itself with no other foundations than what we want to project, the achievements that we want to see or the disappointments that we have perhaps previously decided we will see.

A reflective leader then should look at himself or herself and watch that projection, see the movie, hear the music.

AS A LEADER, WHAT I SAY MAY NOT BE WHAT PEOPLE HEAR, WHAT I DO MAY NOT BE WHAT PEOPLE SEE AND WHAT I BUILD MAYBE A HOUSE THAT PEOPLE DON'T WANT. MAYBE, THE TRICK IS, INVENT A SORT OF OUT-OF-BODY EXPERIENCE, AND WATCH. THAT MAYBE THE BEST AND HANDIEST LEADERSHIP DEVELOPMENT NEEDED.

'Human' and 'leadership' can go together by inviting our demons for dinner

IF LEADERSHIP IS A PRAXIS, SOMETHING THAT 'I' DO (NAME AND SURNAME HERE, PLEASE), THEN, KNOWING A LITTLE BIT ABOUT THE 'I' SHOULD HELP. THAT IS WHY REFLECTION AND SELF-AWARENESS ARE SO IMPORTANT.

Some HR practices have reduced 'awareness' to 360 degree feedback. As useful and as mis-used as this is, this is not a substitute for self-reflection.

When deepening into that 'I', seriously, a stock of little Pandora's boxes may be opened. It could be scary, also fun, liberating, depressing and God knows what.

One of those little Pandora's boxes is labelled 'contradictions'. This is where all of them are stored. We are bound to find them in pairs, the good and the bad, the ones we like and the ones we don't, the opposites, our Jekyll & Hyde, our Yin and Yang, what we see and the ones other people see in us etc.

Rejecting half of them (the bad ones) is rejecting half of the 'I'.

I think it was Friedrich Nietzsche (I am pretty sure but I can't remember where I got it from, and also I am paraphrasing ad libitum, sorry Fred) who said that the best liberating moment was when he invited all his negative traits, dark sides and flaws to be his friends. Making friends with those, allowed him, will allow us, to invite them to the conversation. Rejecting, abandoning, pretending that they don't exist, will never lead to any progress.

If we have to 'rethink our humanity', as many voices are now saying, for different reasons, including the digitalisation of our life, how about starting by inviting our demons for dinner?

Perhaps, to acknowledge our contradictions (in thinking, in attitudes, in values, in behaviours) it is a good foundation for the practice of leadership. And, by inviting them all to the table, I am pretty sure our humanity coefficient would increase. A good injection of mental health. A good starting point for a healthier 'practice of leadership'.

Bring the whole 'I' for dinner.

Why people 'with leadership traits' don't become leaders

THE LATE JACK WELCH, EX CEO OF GE AND SUZY WELCH, JOURNALIST, AUTHOR, AND JACK'S WIFE WROTE ON LINKEDIN, IN ONE OF THEIR MULTIPLE WELL-PROMOTED ARTICLES, ABOUT THE FIVE ESSENTIAL TRAITS OF LEADERSHIP. HERE IT GOES:

'From our experience, the first essential trait of leadership is positive energy — the capacity to go-go-go with healthy vigour and an upbeat attitude through good times and bad.

The second is the ability to energize others, releasing their positive energy, to take any hill.

The third trait is edge — the ability to make tough calls, to say yes or no, not maybe.

The fourth trait is the talent to execute — very simply, get things done.

Fifth and finally, leaders have passion. They care deeply. They sweat; they believe'.

So, there you are: positive energy, ability to energise others, edge, talent to execute and passion. The five traits of leadership. Positive energy and ability to energise others are 'hard wired' or 'personality'. Passion is also inborn. The other two are more teachable and trainable.

218,759 views, 12,682 likes and 707 comments for the original LinkedIn post. 'Great post', 'totally agree' and 'Please also add...' are quite general comments.

Difficult to disagree. Imagine that we were to say that leaders have low energy, do not energise people, have no edge, don't know how to execute and have no passion. No article.

The trouble with these assertions that only people with the Welch surname and associated to GE can get away with, is that they are meaningless. Nobody can disagree. They could only become more solid (from their present state of gas, not even liquid) if you can tell what makes people within these traits become leaders, (and how, would also be helpful) and, more importantly, why probably many, many others with the same traits will never become a leader.

Yes, my hypothesis is that for each person with positive energy, ability to energise others, edge, talent to execute and passion, who is or has become a leader, there are many times where more people with the same traits don't become a leader.

Now let's throw in another five: clear communication of a destiny, ability to bring others along, stand on a model of 'servant, that is serving others, humility, and ability to learn and change gears fast when needed. Another five?

By the way, there is no definition of frame of 'leadership' in that article, so I imagine the Welches have many cases and situations in mind, but my guess is that they are talking business organizations.

For the record, on the package of positive energy, ability to energise others, edge, talent to execute and passion, the following people I know fit the bill: the hairdresser at the end of the street (I don't know whether she leads people but she has lots and lots of customers; does that count?), a local priest I know, one of my kids' teachers (but he is a real pain though, and creates more antibodies than recognition), Mary in the Post Room of my client's HQ, oh, yes, Mary, and the manager of my local supermarket.

'Self, us and now': the very old, uncomfortable trio for a modern look at leadership

HILLEL THE ELDER, OR 'RABBI' HILLEL, THE JEWISH LEADER WHO DIED IN 10 CE, IS REMEMBERED OUTSIDE THE JEWISH TRADITION BY HIS SAYING 'IF I AM NOT FOR MYSELF WHO IS FOR ME? AND BEING FOR MY OWN SELF, WHAT AM 'I'? AND IF NOT NOW, WHEN?'.

There are some variations of the saying depending on translation liberties, but the three pillars 'myself', 'only about myself' and 'now' have remained intact. It is often simplified as "If not us, who?" If not now, when?", and, as a commentator put it, 'it involves discussion from Hillel to George W. Romney to Robert F. Kennedy to Ronald Reagan to Barack Obama to Saturday Night Live'. In other words... the triad has resisted time magnificently and it constitutes perhaps the simplest model of leadership thinking.

It starts with reflection about oneself. The first time you read it, it even sounds a bit selfish and self-centric. But it isn't. It's looking inside oneself. The second part is very direct and bold. It does not ask for who you are but 'what', as in what kind of beast? The third part, is a part in a hurry: so, if not now, when on earth?

Marshall Ganz, father of modern social activism and leadership for collective action (Kennedy School of Government) uses a matching trio when it comes to the use of storytelling as part of that leadership development. He talks about 'the story of self' (personal introspection, testimonial, sharing with others); 'the story of us' (the collective, the group, the activists) and 'the story of now' (the sense of urgency, the now). These are Hillel's translations.

This terribly simple trio has helped me enormously in the framing of my leadership work. It also reminds me of the need for us in managerial and leadership positions of some sort, to tap into historical sources of wisdom, as opposed to, say, the Twitter feed!

Of course, all this can be trivialised, packaged and Mcdonaldised, and yes, since 'all that is solid can melt in the air', (Rabbi Marx?) all that is wisdom can become a car sticker.

BUT FOR ME, THE 'IF NOT US, WHO; IF NOT NOW, WHEN?' IS A CONSTANT CALL TO ACTION, SMALL OR BIG. A SHOT OF MOTIVATION DIFFICULT TO RESIST. 'SELF, US AND NOW', COULD BE THE BEST LEADERSHIP SLOGAN IF YOU NEED ONE. I HAVE ADOPTED IT.

EUROPA
ÉIRE 30

There is something only you can do : be yourself
Everything else can be outsourced

THERE IS SOMETHING ONLY YOU CAN LIVE: YOUR LIFE.
SOCRATES SAID THAT 'THE UNEXAMINED LIFE IS NOT WORTH
LIVING'. BEING ONESELF, LIVING YOUR LIFE AND EXAMINING IT,
ALL THESE THINGS NEED REFLECTION TIME. CALL IT
HOW YOU WANT, BUT IT'S 'STOP AND THINK'.

Reflection is for me the key ingredient of leadership. A super doer, super achiever, super energetic leader with little reflection attached is not a good leader. An energy-sucking machine is not the same as a strong leadership.

So, what's reflection time? You can have it in many forms and shapes. The universal way is a myth. Some people need to disappear to a remote and exotic land to do that. Great! Well, great for them if it works. Other people, more prosaic ways of life, need 'time outs'. But not all time out is reflective. It may be restful, or energising, but not necessarily reflective. Long journeys or short ones, you need to find your way.

There is a tradition in many spiritual writings (and, as such, attributed to many authors) that says that the true spiritual journey is one inch long. That is, look inside your head. My geometrical version of this is that instead of a 360 degree feedback system, so overused and abused in management; people need to learn the 45 degree feedback first: look yourself in the eye in the mirror. Small angle, short journey, you see? All manageable!

To be reflective is to ask questions. It sounds simple but, since we have been educated to produce answers (look at the state of current education systems) more than in the art of questioning, it may be harder than we think. It's inevitable that some psychological conditions such as lack of distractions are required. Again, spiritual traditions of many sorts practice the 3S: silence, stillness and solitude. These are the hardest things you can ask many leaders to do. Trust me, I try. I run a leadership retreat based on them. In the absence of perfect conditions, I ask leaders to practice very small tricks as 'initiation' (!): drive with the radio off is a very popular one.

There is no obvious substitute for reflection in leadership. Perhaps the first steps are about reflecting on all these topics! The best books on leadership are books of questions. The best leadership development programmes are programmes full of questions. One of the greatest investments we can make in personal and professional development is the art of questioning.

REFLECTION AND QUESTIONING ARE BROTHERS. AGAIN, NON-OUTSOURCEABLE. NOBODY CAN REFLECT OR QUESTION FOR YOU.

My contradictions are my friends, and they come with me as leader

WE PRAISE PEOPLE BECAUSE OF THEIR 'CLARITY OF MIND'. WE SAY, 'SHE IS A GOOD MANAGER, SHE KNOWS WHAT SHE WANTS, AND WE KNOW WHAT SHE WANTS'. WE APPRECIATE, WELCOME AND, PERHAPS, EVEN EDIFY CERTAINTY. 'THAT MANAGER'S CERTAINTY GIVES US COMFORT'. WE SAY: 'IF EVERYBODY WAS AS CLEAR AS SHE IS, WE WOULD BE IN A BETTER PLACE'. CLARITY AND CERTAINTY ARE SUDDENLY MARRIED.

The trouble with certainty is that, whilst it spreads and injects comfort, it may be simply misleading. In a complex world, full of uncertainty, some of the people who are apparently blessed with 'clarity' and 'certainty' may be just wrong! Or maybe not.

In any case, it is more 'dangerous' and more politically (managerially) incorrect to declare your doubts or undecided views. Having doubts sounds like a lack of clarity about things. So, it takes even more leadership maturity to hold contradictory views, acknowledge them, and avoid a 'premature closure' declaring a position absolutely and unequivocally correct. Doubts? Contradictory views? Mmm!

I have always loved F Scott Fitzgerald's quote: 'The test of a first-rate intelligence is the ability to hold two opposing ideas in mind at the same time and still retain the ability to function'.

Many people are too intolerant to contradictions, mostly those of other people. As leaders, we are 'expected' not to have them. We are expected to project 'clarity, confidence and certainty', a 'package' traditionally associated to good stewardship.

To acknowledge our own contradictions and even, dare I say, share them, makes us vulnerable. We have also been told that vulnerability is not good. Certainly not for a good leader! But a child is vulnerable, a person in a new relationship is vulnerable, a leader pulled in many directions makes him vulnerable.

To be human is to accept being vulnerable. A non-vulnerable leader is a robot. Trust, by the way, is linked to vulnerability. 'I trust you' means I can be vulnerable and you will not abuse me.

Bringing your own contradictions to the table, your own clouded or untidy areas of thought, your own uncertainties, is a first pass to showing the human side of leadership (is there any other?). Your people will have a human role model of leadership, one that anybody (other than robots) can relate to.

BRINGING YOUR OWN CONTRADICTIONS TO THE TABLE IS BRINGING YOUR BEST FRIENDS TO DINNER, ONE TO WHICH YOU HAVE ALSO INVITED THE PEOPLE REPORTING TO YOU.

My shopping list for new leaders :

1. DEPOLARISATION

F. Scott Fitzgerald is one of many who have described this, but his articulation is the one widely quoted: 'The test of a first rate intelligence is the ability to hold two opposed ideas in mind at the same time and still retain the ability to function'.

It turns out that there are some cognitive studies that tend to validate this ability, whether related to 'intelligence' or not, as something of great importance in 'cognitive power' terms.

For me, the opposite is something we are all seeing everywhere: polarisation. The extremes or the tendency to the extremes. In political ideas, in society, and also in positions of views and behaviours in organizations. This or that. You can't have both, we are told. We have built an entire management system that is bipolar: cost or differentiation, quality or speed, leader or manager. It does not hold water today.

Depolarising people's views is a key transformative skill of leadership. Having a critical view of those poles and being able to bring others to assess them on their own merits, is a gem of a skill. 'The ability to hold two opposed ideas in mind at the same time and still retain the ability to function' may or may not be first rate intelligence, but it sure is first rate leadership, circa 2020 AT (Anno Trumpini).

The key, however, is not to default to the 'halfway fallacy' either. The idea that, systematically, one has to agree that somehow the truth is somewhere in the middle. Most of the time it isn't. Which is not a popular assertion.

Note that the sentence reads 'ability to hold two opposed ideas in mind at the same time and still retain the ability to function', not 'the ability to hold two opposed ideas in mind and find a lower common denominator'.

Depolarising is de-dramatising. It's cleaning up an emotionally charged idea confronting another emotionally charged idea about to reach a bland, plain vanilla common ground. Once uncritically landed in that common ground, you are stuck with its anxiolytic effect. 'All is fine now, in fact we are saying the same with different words'. Most of the time this is not true. We are not saying the same at all, but our minds are crying for mercy.

Depolarising is humanising. It's cleaning up the 'ad hominem' dust (character assassination) to bring the conversation to facts, truths and own merits.

Depolarising is re-polarising. It's acknowledging the poles but finding a non-plain-vanilla-common-lower-denominator ground, perhaps higher purpose for both poles.

And yes, still retain 'ability to function', or perhaps going beyond that to a new, unknown common territory in which the poles don't see that confrontational after all.

2. REFRAMING

I have referred before to George Lakoff's work and his little book *Don't think of an elephant*, which makes the point of how easy is to think of an elephant. If you want to learn reframing, read Lakoff.

On my shopping list of a-little-unconventional skills in the enormous supermarkets attributed to leadership, reframing scores very high.

We need leaders who have less answers and more ability to ask questions. But asking questions is an art, and the whole 'reframing plus critical thinking' lenses are more needed than ever.

1. The question on the table is A, what if the question were B?

2. We are about to make decision X. What are the preconceived ideas that we bring to the decision?

3. We all agree on Z. Are we agreeing too much?

4. We talk about the cost of doing N. What is the cost of not doing it?

5. We have a plan to succeed. Can we create a plan to completely screw up and compare?

6. Let's brainstorm for very bad ideas.

7. How much time do we dedicate to problem solving? What is it that we are building?

8. We have a list of competitors to compare ourselves with. Can we compare ourselves with anybody not on the list?

9. Can we compare all our 'why we are doing this?' Let's compare our own reasons. Let's get all the invisible whys visible.

10. What is the question behind the question? Why is X asking this? What if she is asking a different question but it has just come up disguised as this one?

These are 10 examples that require only practice to make them live. Not a special brain but going to the critical thinking gym frequently. Accountants relax: the cost of this is zero, the benefits infinite.

If leaders take upon themselves the role of master reframing practitioners, others will see it, and hear it, and feel it, and will copy, and will follow.

Taking the reality around us at face value only facilitates automatic pilot answers. We will never learn and will apply standard answers to predictable questions.

The Leader reframer may make some people restless and uncomfortable. And this is precisely a good outcome of leadership for our days.

3. BRIDGE BUILDERS

The word Pontifex (Pontiff in English) is the term associated with the Pope (Twitter account...err.. @pontifex, what else?).

I love this term for what it means. Historically, this has been equal to High Priest in Roman culture, a position occupied by patricians, never a plebian, until 254 BCE according to my search. But the etymology, the origins of the word, is fascinating. It's a combination of 'pons' (bridge) and 'fex' (maker or producer). So, literally, what it means is 'one who builds bridges'.

On my shopping list for new leaders, I want this in: bridge builder, broker between A and B, connecting ideas and people. OK, let's stretch it: making impossible associations, declaring and seeking connection, not isolation, mastering brokership, unifier.

Most good pontifex-leaders I know seem to work in the background. They are not the usual suspects with the PowerPoint pack. In some cases that I know well, they are 'the second', not the first. The ones who facilitate the human encounters behind the Visible First.

Social Network Analysis (SNA), as we practice it, finds these individuals sometimes hidden more or less somewhere in the organizational chart jungle. Semi-invisible trees that the forest hides.

Whatever their position in the social network (which any organization is), what I have called in my book, *Homo Imitans* (our social GPS), bridge builders (pontifex) are a gem. A few of them solve an enormous amount of organizational dysfunctions.

Being at the very top, or close by, in the organization will make that brokership more visible and it's bound to be imitated as a role model of good leadership.

Yes, there are, of course, the bridge-builders and the bridge-burners, I know. But building is for me the quintessence of leadership. When many moons ago we in The Chalfont Project chose to call ourselves 'Organization Architects', I had more than one eyebrow raised around me, friends and colleagues. It was for a reason. Very simply, my obsession with 'building', as opposed to solving, fixing, changing, transforming or any other term in the Organizational Development Thesaurus.

I am not a natural networker, as in cocktail networking. And this characteristic in my list is not about this. I am not talking about the multiple and skilful networker, navigator in the jungle of weak and strong ties of ten new networkracies. These are, by definition, the new employees, the sailors in the new idea of 'work'. Leadership goes beyond that. Perhaps from the visible tribal cocktail campfires, to the less visible connecting the unconnected key people.

Perhaps I could say that Bridge Building is 'making it happen' by closing the encounter of otherwise distant people. And distant may be the next office, or somebody in New Zealand, or two people/clusters/units/ organizations that did not know they could connect, or did not feel the need, or combinations.

Bring the bridge engineers in anyway.

4. INVITATIONAL PEOPLE

I have held the view for many years that management is 'by invitation'.

For example, I am against Leadership Teams composed exclusively of the direct reports of the leader. A Leadership Team should be composed of people invited to be part of the Leadership team, not by the opportunistic presence in a particular geographical GPS position in the organizational chart. The Leadership Team could include, indeed, all direct reports and/or some, and/or invited advisers, or members of other teams, and dare I say external people, similar to the function of Non-Executive Directors on Anglo-Saxon Boards.

Being a member of a Leadership Team should not be an automatic entitlement given to a particular box in the organizational chart. Yes, that automatic pilot composition is handy in terms of sharing information, for example, but that's all. Having all the generals in the room helps. I get it.

OK, this is a conversation for another day. However, it's linked with the fourth theme on my shopping list: invitation.

Early in 2006 in my book, *The Leader with Seven Faces*, I talked about the invitational language (or lack of it) in leadership. 'Come with me, let's do it, I need you, join me, let's cook it together, invite Jim', etc. Most of our leadership language is factual weather forecast type.

Religious traditions, certainly the Christian one, have invitational language embedded. Come with me.

On my shopping list for new leaders, I put high in the list leaders-who-invite, as opposed to leaders who explain, or dictate, or read the weather forecast of the Strategic Plan. Come with me. Join me.

I remember the famous pitch from Steve Jobs to the then CEO of Coca Cola, John Sculley: 'Do you want to spend the rest of your life selling brown water, or do you want to change the world?' Sculley joined Apple as CEO. And then he did not change the world, but changed Jobs, firing him. Many moons ago I spoke to John Sculley about that paradox in a technology Congress party in the US. He did not find my observation amusing. At all. But he signed my copy of his book *Odyssey*.

Invite. Come with me. I need you. Would you like to change the world? I know some may find this a bit of a cliché. I am finding these days that more of the old clichés are more solid than the plain vanilla current leadership discourse.

(If you are in a leadership position in a corporation and find 'change the world' irritating, cliché and childish, you should 'reconsider your position', as used by political language).

We invite less than we should. We either take the guests at the party for granted, or they are already there occupying their chairs, or we tell them what to do, or read them the weather forecast. We have lots of uninvited people in management and leadership teams. We need to reclaim 'invitation'.

RSVP.

5. MOBILIZERS

Managing? Leading? Probably one of the worst dichotomies ever invented. Another day.

Engaging? Motivating? Committing?

Consider Mobilizing! It means...what it means. Get people in motion, act, stop the paralysis, the reservations, the permissions. It contains engaging, motivating and the rest.

Mobilizing also means organizing. Using language from social movements, 'organizing for collective action'.

In our Viral Change™ programmes, there is a particular role called 'Mobilizers' who are colleagues coordinating pockets of grassroots activities.

Mobilizing also means a road, a map, a direction, a pace, a sense of destiny. It also resonates with collective energy and common purpose. It refers to a sense of duty of addressing injustice, or simply shaping something better for the future. Hopefully leaving behind some legacy.

It's at the core of large scale behavioural and cultural change. That means culture. That means culture as a social movement. That's what my team does for a living.

On my shopping list for new leaders, my last in the list is Mobilizing. Mobilizer, leaders who invite, bridge builders, reframers and depolarisers, (as per my previous four) forgive my language, are a good bunch. I love their company.

RTN

536936910

4.20

OXFORD,
BLACKWELL'S

Five spaces that the organizational leader needs to design and nurture

What about the leader as a designer of spaces, a social architect that creates places (physical) and spaces? Not hard to imagine, but I think it is an underestimated concept, perhaps lost in the rhetoric, in the analogy.

Leaders need to create space for employee voices. For that read opportunities, platforms (digital and analogue), vehicles, processes and systems if needed, and, above all, the encouragement of behaviours: speak up, make yourself heard, provide an input, contribute, not just 'doing your job'. This is the first space.

The second space is the informal organization, the one that does not 'contain' teams, committees, task forces, fixed conference calls and any other formal structure. Here, read the corridors, the buffer time, the cafeteria, the informal brainstorm. The informal organization is the oxygen of the company. Shrink that supply at your peril. This second space is also a mixture of physical and psychological spaces. Table tennis in a corner is not enough, if there is not a culture of informal conversations or if the culture sees them – those spaces, those semi-artificial break outs - as a waste.

The third space is personal. The space to think and reflect, to look at things with a critical view, to digest and compare, to form an opinion, to open yourself to the possible aha! To say, "I have a Wednesday afternoon free for this", does not work.

It must be embedded in the culture. A culture of 24/7 busyness does not provide that space.

The fourth space is also personal. It is the space of professional and personal development. It includes, of course, formal courses and training but goes well beyond these to mentoring, to time to shadow somebody, to do something that is not in the job description, or well beyond these, stretching people's skills and imagination. This space requires the leader to not only accept, but create some slack in the system, some redundancy, some buffer that is not considered a waste. 'Personal' and 'professional' are blurred here. The thing not to do is to be obsessed with the ROI, with how doing this could have an immediate return. As soon as you start counting these beans, the desired effect goes out of the window.

The fifth space is collective. It's the space for experimentation with ideas, the generation of as many bad ones as possible, the mental prototyping of possibilities, the playing with 'unfinished thoughts' and half-baked opportunities. Many leaders hate this. These are the ones putting off employees by saying, 'come back when you have a perfect business case'. Since there is no such thing, people never go back.

Yes, leaders need to see themselves as architects, as space designers, creators, and implementors.

This is an area where, what the leader says counts less than what the leader does in this social engineering. It is therefore very silent, but the spaces will be very visible and the legacy will be enormous.

'The things you do not have to say make you rich'

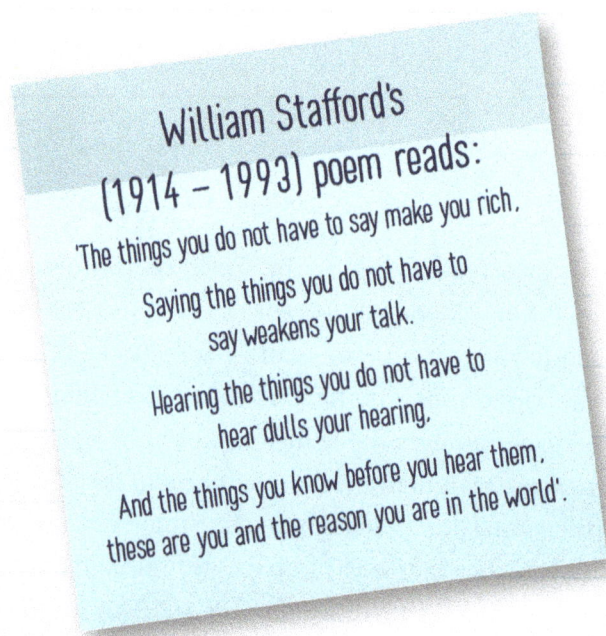

William Stafford's
(1914 – 1993) poem reads:
'The things you do not have to say make you rich,

Saying the things you do not have to
say weakens your talk.

Hearing the things you do not have to
hear dulls your hearing,

And the things you know before you hear them,
these are you and the reason you are in the world'.

Attention leaders. Judging by the above, we are pretty poor. We talk too much, we command too much, we say too much, we repeat.

I am not against the famous 'walk the talk'. It's just that I think the order is wrong. Walk first and then do the talking about the walk: why the walk, the benefits of the walk, why others should join the walk… Talk the walk!

If people see you walking, maybe then you will have less to say. And, if as a leader, you accumulate more and more things that you don't have to say, you are rich, and you are doing great as leader. This is lesson One of Disruptive Economics for Leadership.

'The things you don't have to say make you a rich leader'.

'You don't have to attend every argument to which you are invited'

This quote is from an unknown author. He or she must have known a thing or two about the futility of engaging in every single discussion that comes your way. The quote is also a proxy for 'pick your battles'. There are battles worth fighting and battles that are not. It may also serve as a reflection on what leaders choose to do.

In organizational life, people are often pulled in too many directions, where 'signal' and 'noise' get confused all the time. Big things get mixed up with small things. The important gets confused with the urgent. The strategic and the tactical become mixed up. All things become equally important, equally relevant, equally necessitating a response, to have a say, to send an 'I agree' message.

I am not fond of the word 'prioritisation'. Not that I don't believe in the need to prioritise, but I have little faith in our standard ways of doing this. For leaders, a better angle is 'What will make the difference?' Or better, 'What can I personally do that will make the difference, and perhaps only I can do?'.

We need to switch from spending our time on 'managing the inevitable', to leading what will not happen unless we lead it.

In this quest, you don't, as leader, have to attend every argument to which you are invited, you don't have to get involved in everything and certainly, you don't have to spend your time fighting every battle. The magic word is choice. Choices are always in front of you.

A 6th Century Leadership Manual starts with the word 'Listen!'

It's impossible to listen in a noisy room. If you want to listen to your breathing, you need silence. You can't listen in busyness mode; we hear lots of things, we listen to few.

Listening to music through your earphones when walking around is more hearing the music than listening to it.

We hear other people, we hear the CEO, we hear the news, we hear our team members, we hear complaints, we hear people suffering. It does not follow that we listen to any of them.

Listening is becoming a rare quality. It requires active willingness to do it.

There are four magic questions for leaders about listening:

(1) What am I saying?

(2) Am I being heard?

(3) Is anybody listening?

(4) How do I know any of the above?

In, *The Leader with Seven Faces*, one of my books and the basis for my Leadership Programmes, language is face number one. The above questions are key leadership hearing aids.

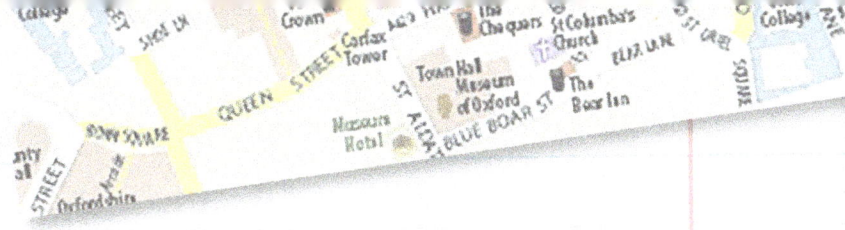

Listening is sometimes an anxious request. Listen to me! Would you listen! One of the oldest Standard Operating Procedures (SOP) and Leadership Manuals in the world is *The Rule of Saint Benedict*, written in the 6th Century for monks in monasteries, although there were other similar Rules even before. For centuries, it has inspired religious and non-religious life. It caters for all needs in the community and provides guidance and solutions to potential problems. Still today this Rule, with its modern adaptation, is in place in all Benedictine communities around the world. Benedict of Nursia, patron saint of Europe, wrote his Rule in ordinary Latin. It has a Prologue and seventy-three chapters, not bad for an SOP! The Rule starts with one single latin word, on its own: 'Ausculta', that is, Listen! Perhaps he anticipated modern organizational life.

For leadership, look around, not in research papers

Leadership has traditional sources of learning, reflection, role modelling and a 'body of knowledge'. There are four that dominate. This is my humble classification: The Military, Corporations, Civic and Religious models, and Sports.

Where do organizations borrow from for leadership models? The military source is mostly about language (as opposed to individuals). The language of war is well embedded in organizational and business thinking: killing the competition, price wars, winning and losing markets etc. Occasionally there is reference to true military strategy and leadership, but not too frequently. Civic and religious leadership is also referred to, but here instead, only with the accent on individuals. 'I have a dream' and Luther King must be the most admired example. Business organizations love sports analogies which, in my opinion, are overrated and oversized.

There is a point here, however. There are multiple sources from which to learn, mirror, copy, study, draw conclusions about Leadership. Multiple models and examples. It was in this context that some time ago, I was taken aback when invited to participate in a round table on the topic at a prestigious global business school. The Head of Research presented their five-year research data on the future of leadership. It consisted of in-depth interviews with most of the Chairmen and CEOs of top FTSE 500 companies and from this he claimed that they now knew what the future of leadership looked like. That was it!

I put it to them that they had completely missed the point and the views of the Chairman of Coca Cola, for example, (with all due respect to the Chairman of Coca Cola) were hardly relevant to day to day leadership in organizations.

There is a myriad – I pointed out – of small or not so small enterprises that are full of people 'leading' from day to day, navigating through life, with different degrees of resilience and most of them without a golden parachute should they screw up. 'Where was that data?' I inquired.

I didn't like the way he looked at me and I realised I was turning into a Martian to them. I am sure that 'the research team' enjoyed a pleasant travel budget and found the research rewarding, but to call this the latest on the leadership of the future was slightly insulting to say the least.

Every day we miss the reality that is there in front of our eyes, in favour of the big names and big label position papers and reports. For leadership, it's easy: look around. Don't look up at The Big Names. Or don't look at them only. Try schools, neighbourhoods, community leaders, small companies, medium and big, churches, public servants, good CEOs even if not those on the front page of the newspapers. We are rich in examples of good leadership. As rich as we are poor in so-called 'research'.

Sorry, it's not about what the CEOs of the FTSE 500 think. Leadership, good or bad, is all around us, because it's a praxis.

If we are serious about research in leadership, we need to come down to earth and do a whole lot better than interviewing the usual suspects. Update: I keep waiting for an invitation to another of their roundtables – but they haven't called me.

The three 'magic' words: transparency, clarity and fairness

These three organizational 'magic' words manage to get mixed up a lot. It's hard to believe because they are so different. But people love the mixing because the use of language in organizational life has a sort of 'complete freedom', which results in lots of 'prêt-à-porter' word concepts. So, 'magic' here has to be interpreted as producing an abracadabra effect: use them and many doors will be open (even if their meaning is mixed up).

More than once I have seen these three 'magic' words in a single value system as if their combination validates the good intentions of the company and provides a stamp of integrity and honesty (incidentally, two more 'magic' words).

Organizations seem to thrive in conceptual muddle. My friend and brilliant inter-cultural consultant, David Trickey, calls this 'a conspiracy of self-inflicted ambiguity'.

My definitions, to dispel the magic a bit:

Transparency: everybody can see it, there are no secrets

Clarity: everybody understands

Fairness: nobody is discriminated against

That's it!

Something may be transparent to the staff, but unclear, even opaque. Something may be clear for management, but not transparent to others. Something may be fair to people, but it's not clear or transparent.

Problems arise when there is a free, interchangeable use of the three. People tend to assume that something is unfair when it's not transparent. But transparency does not make it automatically fair. There is nothing unfair about not making something transparent to everybody. It may or may not be unfair. Some managers preach transparency, but they mean clarity. Other managers preach fairness, on the basis of clarity and transparency to all. But the issue may be very unfair, yet, clear.

I suggest you carry on playing with the permutations but avoid at any cost the indiscriminate use. Beware of the prolongation of 'self-inflicted ambiguity'.

I hope I am clear, have been transparent
in my intentions and you find these points fair.
If not, I will have to start again.

Trust is like pregnancy. You can't have a bit of it.

Statements such as 'I don't trust him too much', in reality, means I don't trust him at all. The 'too much' is a softener that we impose upon ourselves to make it a little bit questionable, just in case there is still some hope of full trust.

Trust is a funny non-linear thing, excuse my language. It takes time to build, sometimes with considerable effort, reaches maturity, stabilizes, but can suddenly go out the window very quickly following even a small breach. Non-linear. Most non-linear effects are associated with the expression 'it's not fair!'. That is, not fair that you have delivered A, B and C in a superb way, but you failed to deliver D and your trust drops at the speed of light. Life is not fair (life is not linear).

Trust is built in different ways but, at the core, it's always a game of vulnerability. Can I make myself vulnerable to Peter and know that Peter will not abuse this? Can I be wrong and not be told off or penalised? Can I make mistakes and not be sacked? Can I disclose what I don't know, how doubtful I may be, my questions marks, my homework not done, my declaration of unpreparedness, and still be confident that Peter, John or Mary will not jump on me, disclose my weakness to others or put me in their black books or simply lose faith in me?

When thinking about trust, I am very binary. Yes or No. I know that anything in between is more an expression of hope (in either direction) than a reality.

3 versions of speed

ANDREW GROVE, EX INTEL
'This business about speed has its limits. Brains don't speed up. The exchange of ideas does not really speed up, only the overhead that slowed down the exchange. When it comes down to the bulk of knowledge work, the 21st century works the same as the 20th century. You can reach people around the clock, but they won't think any better or any faster just because you've reached them faster. The give and take remains a limiting factor'.

JOHN CHAMBERS, CISCO
'Companies that are successful will have cultures that thrive on change, even though change makes most people very uncomfortable. In the end, you might just have speed, talent, and branding. Those things may be the only differentiators'.

JOE HYAMS, ZEN IN THE MARTIAL ARTS
'A young boy travelled across Japan to study with a famous martial artist. The master asked him what he wanted. The young boy told him he wanted to be the finest martial artist in the land and asked how long he had to study. 'Ten years at least', the master answered. 'But what if I studied twice as hard as all your other students', the young boy responded. 'Twenty years', the master replied. 'Twenty years! What if I practice day and night with all my effort?'. 'Thirty years', was the master's reply. The boy was thoroughly confused. 'How is it that each time I say I will work harder, you tell me that it will take longer?', the boy asked. 'The answer is clear. When one eye is fixed upon your destination, there is only one eye left with which to find the Way'.

3 versions, 3 approaches, worth reflecting.
Let's take stock individually, make our own conclusions.

10 Rules of Self-Survival: The Border Diet

My TEDx East London Talk I delivered a few years ago ended with a proposal. The Border Diet: A diet to protect yourself against persistent Full Disclosure that the digital world forces upon you. The late John O'Donohue, in another context, spoke of 'inner eviction and outer exile' of our Selves. I think this is an epidemic in need of serious warning. Sherry Turkle of MIT, wrote about this in her 2011 book and with the wonderful title: *Alone Together*. My point of the talk was: don't get sucked into Total Transparency, Total Disclosure, I-Have-No-Secrets philosophy. It has consequences.

SO THIS IS MY BORDER DIET:

1. Have a list of secrets, make an inventory, keep them. Review them monthly. Having no secrets is a symptom of Self depletion. There are sacred secrets of your soul and in your soul. They are your real friends, because they are the closest to you.

2. Take social media sabbaticals. Make yourself not just 'unavailable' (this is the analogue term) but 'undiscoverable' (digital). Or choose selectively to whom you make your Self discoverable. And how much and for how long.

3. Drop Pilates, take Pascal classes. Pascal said that 'All of humanity's problems stem from man's inability to sit quietly in a room alone'. That has not changed since the 17th Century, if anything it is incredibly more difficult today. The

21st Century human can't 'sit': we have become restless, attention deficit disorder beings.

4. Make an inventory of assets you can give to others: start with time, ideas, attention and care. Keep stocks high. Make sure you don't give too much at a time.

5. Practice daily silence. Start simple: radio off, earphones off. Despite common belief, it is possible. Silence will help you listen to your Self, and who knows, beyond. Not for nothing has silence been called God's language.

6. Practice stillness. Stop moving, jogging, going to the gym. Well, not all the time. Don't do anything, I repeat, anything, for a good 30 minutes a day. Try. It won't kill you. Notice I have not said meditation. Meditation is doing something.

7. You would not choose to be in a room full of smoke or a contaminated nuclear area. Mental pollution is much worse than these. It's the greatest digital health hazard. Avoid systematic mental exposure to trivia as much as you would avoid breathing smoke.

8. Don't be open, transparent and an exhibitionist. You are fooled by your ego. Hard as it is to accept for many people, nobody really cares about you checking in at the airport of X, having cereal Y for breakfast today or just changing your cover photo in Z. You are mainly reporting to yourself, what your Self already knows.

9. Reconcile with your borders, protect your distances, go back to your inner house. Then you can give from within. But you need to protect your Self from all open windows and all open doors. The Self may catch a cold.

10. Then, go back to number one.

It's official: the single, magic bullet that characterises good leadership is to back off

It should not surprise us that people are constantly looking for the magic bullet of leadership. What makes a good leader? We are not short of answers. Reams of paper and servers full of gigabytes will give you any answer you wish. There is, for example, the typical list of values: integrity, courage, honesty, sensitivity, emotional and social intelligence etc. Trouble is, these lists of universal values are not very specific. They would apply equally well to being a good father, indeed to being a good human being.

I am sympathetic to the approach that asks a more refined question: 'What would it take to be a leader here, in company A, B, C?' Still you wish you could find the universal magic bullet, even with lots of translations and context.

But thanks to Google, we are a step closer to the bullet, or at least to understanding the potential magic. The data is interesting. It answers the question for Google and leaves us with a big hypothesis: could we extrapolate this to our own non-Google-esque environments?

The reason why Google 'has the answer', is because a long time ago, Google decided to apply to their Human Resources the same rigour applied to their engineering. That is, using something Google has in good supply: data. Google is not shy to say that it is carrying out its own People Analytics all the time.

Consistently, through their internal analytics, Google finds that the single characteristic of the successful leader is '**predictability**'. Not very exciting, in fact, somewhat of an anti-climax at first reading. It means that people in Google feel that their (good) leaders are those who will not interfere or change their mind all the time. They will be consistent. That leads them to talk about the other side of the magic bullet: autonomy. People feel with them that, within some parameters, they are free to act, make the most of themselves and be themselves. The predictable, consistent leader removes the main obstacle: himself or herself. From here, it follows that, another way they describe this singular characteristic of leadership is 'autonomy support'. Summary: the best Google leaders are consistent, therefore predictable. That gives autonomy to me, to make the best of me. They support my autonomy. Nice Human Algorithm.

The data is solid. No other parameters, from IQ to university grades or mental capacity correlate with 'good leadership'. I don't know how Google-esque we all are these days but the 'Google evidence' is a clear reinforcement of the concept I have used formally since 2006, '**Backstage Leadership™**': the art of leaders giving the stage to others who can act. In the case of **Viral Change™**, the 'others' are those elected volunteers, highly connected and influential individuals within the organization. Outside the Viral Change™ framework, they are subordinates, team members or other colleagues.

This idea is also consistent with an old obsession of mine: space. That is, that leadership should be concerned with the creation and protection of space both for themselves and for others (***The Leader with Seven Faces***, 2006). That this all closes the loop nicely on my own thinking is irrelevant here. What it does say, however, is that, at the very least, this is a hypothesis worth testing in your organization.

If, as I see it, a mature version of leadership is actually to back off, as opposed to stepping in, then this has significant implications for leadership development. The single objection I get about my Backstage Leadership™ is people saying, 'If I do that, it will be a disaster, my people won't deliver'. If this is the case, you have a problem. It's called you!

Either you are in full command and control mode, so the problem is you, or you don't have the right people. If the latter, the problem is still you, unless you have inherited a colony of aliens.

Leadership's
Splendid Expeditions

'The history of mankind might be described by a cynic as a series of splendid expeditions towards the wrong goal or towards no goal at all, led by men who have all the gifts of leadership except a sense of direction, and every endowment for achieving their ends except a knowledge of ends worth achieving'.

These words by Sir Richard Livingstone (1880 – 1960) still resonate today. His focus was education, which is where he spent his life (Oxford and Queen's in Belfast), but this paragraph should be kept as one of these perennial quotes and pieces on leadership.

The 'splendid expeditions towards the wrong goal or towards no goal at all', reminds us that not everything that looks like an expedition may be worth it. We may make leadership complex and even well-orchestrated, but this also needs 'a sense of direction'. It seems so trivial to simply state this. I particularly like 'sense of direction' as opposed to a fixed destination. The second part of the statement talks about 'ends worth achieving'. Again, leadership may look like an expedition towards ends, but the little qualification', 'worth achieving' hits the nail on the head.

I have treasured this piece for many years and still it comes back to my mind again and again. I use it with my clients within leadership work, individual or collective, as a piece for reflection, even digestion of all of its parts.

The long quote continues with a second part on education:

'We must not forget in our education this element, a sense of direction. We do forget it, if we are content that our schools should merely impart knowledge, develop and discipline the intelligence, train character in the narrow sense. They must also be places where the mind is enriched by the right visions and where the ends of life are learned'.

Education systems in the Western world are struggling. 'Places where the mind is enriched' is still a goal that is not well achieved. Perhaps leadership starts in school. Perhaps this is why true leadership is still not well entrenched in many people in organizations. However, it's true to say as well, that many people are genuine in its quest, sometimes intuitive, sometimes guided. In the true sense of Livingstone's view of the world, I regard leadership development as 'education'. In the etymological sense of the word: to get, from inside, that which is already there in the person.

I guess many of us, you and me, are on some kind of splendid, leadership expedition. Worth checking for the right maps.

'I told them once; they didn't understand. I told them twice; they didn't understand. I told them three times and I understood'.

I don't know where this quote comes from, but I have always seen it as a source of reflection on leadership. It describes the leadership journey in which true understanding is emergent, even for the leader who thought he understood himself very well in the first place.

It tells us that leadership is social, a praxis, something that one learns, something one becomes. Becoming a leader is a better term than being a leader. We are always becoming and, in that journey, sometimes we have to tell 'them' three times so that we understand, finally.

I worry about the kind of leadership that has all the answers, that has 'arrived at the destination' as if there was an organizational Sat Nav, a Leadership Tom Tom, or Garmin, or Google map, that takes you exactly to a GPS destination point.

Leadership is not real leadership without an invitation. The invitation is for others to navigate and find better ways, better success, better lands. But it requires this human, humble element of 'understanding together'.

Perhaps by the third time!

'Grasp the facts, misses the meaning': The Leadership Dyslexia upon us

Did we ever, ever have more facts around us?
Certainly not. We talk about Big Data. It is of course
Colossal Data, monstrous, whatever we want to call it.

In this overwhelming availability of facts, there is a type of manager, leader and executive that grasps the facts, but misses the meaning. It's a type of leadership dyslexia of some sort. From all the attributes of leadership, the ones people write down, the ones that I myself have criticised as 'the impossible list', if I were to choose one single word, just one, it would be meaning. Meaning for himself or herself first, and then for all, for the followers, for the organization.

In day to day management, we spend a lot of time accumulating facts. Inevitable. Desirable, if you think of the alternative. But we have come to fooling ourselves that the presence of rich facts equals meaning. Sense, making sense, providing meaning, this is the gem. The rest is commentary.

This leadership dyslexia with an abundance of facts and missing the meaning, may even go unnoticed, unseen. The Digital Tsunami will not be tolerant; will not wait for meaning until a second wave. It does not stop. It assumes you filter noise and signal. And this is a hell of an assumption.

At the very least, we need to redirect our Leadership Programmes to provide the abilities, perhaps the toolkits, for an anti-dyslexic operation. The size of the dysfunction is enormous.

Off-the-shelf, 'this is how you lead in circumstances X',
will not do the trick. So, what do we do?

It takes only one question to know about your model of leadership (and there is always an alternative question, just in case)

Don't define leadership for me. Tell me what legacy you want to leave behind and I'll know.

What am I leaving behind as leader? What am I building? What will be left when I am not here? What will my legacy look like? These questions and similar ones (all a variant) are important questions that leaders should ask themselves. There are all types of leaders, from the ones who have an answer to these questions to the others, at the other end of the spectrum, who not only don't have an answer, but have never asked themselves the questions.

There are not good or bad answers. If you want to leave behind a company that has made the Top List of Something, great. Perhaps a new product or a service. Perhaps a transformation in your industry.

If you want to define your legacy by a number (market share, top line, profitability, earnings per share, number 1 in 'X') fine as well. I once met a new CEO who spent the entire introductory dinner with his new Leadership Team explaining how he went from a 3.5% market share, somewhere on the planet, to a 9.5% market share when he left. You could have said that the audience was not overwhelmed with joy. He defined his leadership style in one dinner. But, hey, he is still at the helm in his company and making tons of money!

The legacy question must be asked, that is the point. Some leaders feel a bit uncomfortable; others are puzzled and concede that they have never thought about it in a specific way. I always ask 'the question' to anybody in a leadership position. The question is always personal, so I expect a personal answer.

I am interested in the discipline of the questioning, perhaps privately first, then more collectively at leadership team level. 'The legacy' is one of the Seven Faces in my model of leadership. It's always a tricky one. Well, not too much if taken superficially, but a complex one if one is serious about it.

I sometimes get stuck in the conversation with leaders about this topic. This is often the point when the client starts speaking Corporate Tribe Dialect and involving shareholder value. At this point, a reframing of the question is due in order to get to the bottom of a good answer.

My favourite alternative question is: 'What will you tell your children that you've done?'.

'If you want to revenge someone, prepare two graves'. On leadership and digging.

This is one of the many pearls of wisdom from Confucius. Your revenge may kill the adversary but a bit of you will be dying as well.

Let's get a less dramatic interpretation. When we inflict pain on fellow human beings, some of us will require some painkillers at some time as well.

Leaders are required to lead with a good dose of emotional and social intelligence, not precisely new concepts, but perhaps never fully captured. Leaders lead and in doing so, they are impacting on the life of others. I am stating the obvious. Many leaders seem oblivious to the consequences of their leadership. Some macho styles may sound like this: 'I need to make the tough decisions so, I am sorry, it's not me, it's the tough decision and anything else will be weak leadership and seen as weakness'.

But nobody says the leader should not make 'the tough decisions'. This is perfectly compatible with being very sensitive to the consequences, particularly the negative ones for the life of the followers.

In my consulting work, for many years I have seen and still see today, the whole spectrum of sensitiveness. I have seen and see, leaders laying off people and doing so in an extraordinarily sensitive and human way. I've seen and see, the opposite. I've seen gratuitous power exercises. I have seen leaders with the social skills of a dead fish. I've seen great leaders with a sense and knowledge of their environments that not a dozen Employee Engagement surveys could provide.

So, here is another leadership question: how deep is my grave?
How is the digging going?

If you are not a good, sensitive, emotional and socially intelligent leader, carry on, but be careful when moving around with that hole in the ground that seems to get bigger every day.

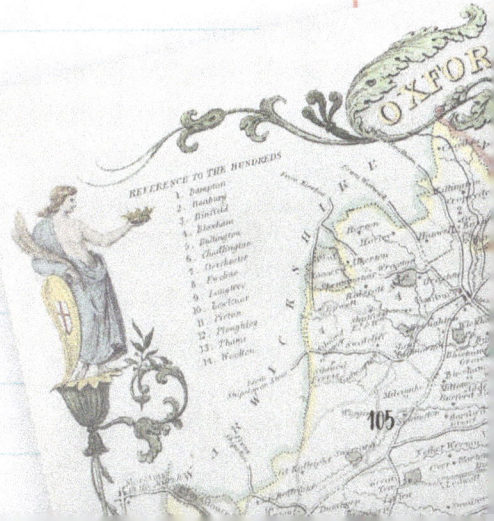

The moral choices of leadership, courtesy of Pedro, my taxi driver in Panama

I broke my antisocial tradition during taxi rides and started a conversation with my Panama driver. I asked him who was the best President they had ever had.

I was intrigued enough to ask. I was going to be there for a few hours, working with a client and I had very little time for sightseeing, so the hotel introduced me to Pedro. I was, officially, 'an English doctor who speaks rather good Spanish'. Flattered by the 'rather good' ranking of my native language and amused by me suddenly acquiring a new nationality, I went for a three hour overpriced private tour.

I am usually quiet, hiding at the back of cars. I'm the opposite of some friends of mine who always talk to taxi drivers, as if they knew them from primary school and were suddenly reunited.

I did not get an initial answer about a President, but Pedro gave me the mental frame instead, perhaps so I could make my own judgment. 'Mister' – Pedro started any sentence with Mister – 'there are two types', he said, 'the ones who do a lot for the country, but they steal a lot, and the ones who don't steal, but they don't do anything'.

The binary world of Pedro was there in front of me, naked, crude, and solid. It was expressed with the conviction of a first-hand receiver, a native; somebody who seemed to know what he was talking about.

There is something universal in the inevitability of the world of Pedro. We are prone to accept binary worlds. They are solid frames. 'One of us' or 'not one of us'. Remember the launch of the so-called War on Terror? 'With us or against us'. Pedro's moral choices of political leadership are also present in our narrative of leadership of organizations, not so crude, but often equally bipolar. Strong, decisive leaders, will also be authoritarian and leave little room for empowerment. Kind, sensitive and human leaders will also be weak. We may not notice it, but we are always unconsciously pairing bits of reality all the time, as Pedro does with his Presidents. And the pairing goes beyond leadership: quality work will be slow, fast and hurried, will compromise quality, etc.

Unbundling moral choices may be a necessary step to take a fresh look at the reality in front. But I did not get any unbundling from Pedro, nor when I pursued the conversation, absorbed as I was for a while in the little digestion of his binary world.

Having broken my silence vow when at the back of cars, Pedro felt free to follow his own questioning about things, for him much more interesting than the morality of leaders, so I had to oblige with answers: no, I had not watched Manchester United matches live; no, we don't have the Euro in the UK; yes, it's possible to go to Paris by train; no, it's not raining all the time; no, Berlusconi was not the President of Europe; yes, we still have queens and kings in Europe, fancy that!

Lead in Poetry, manage in Prose

I am of course paraphrasing Mario Cuomo's 'You campaign in poetry; you govern in prose'.

Cuomo (1932-2015) was an American lawyer, a Democrat, a devout Catholic, a Governor of New York (1983-1995) and very fond of phrases. He did 'Poetry' a lot. He once said: 'I talk and talk and talk, and I haven't taught people in 50 years what my father taught by example in one week'. Mario Coumo did talk. Perhaps the Italian genes.

For all his visible and memorable 'Poetry', the Poetry of 'Yes-We-Can' and 'Hope', Obama, another lawyer, had to be coached and coerced into Poetry by his formidable team of political campaigners. Believe it or not, Obama was more comfortable with Prose. It's the lawyer within. He much preferred to give long and articulated explanations of the reason for a particular policy, than summaries and power-lines; driving his Communicators and Advisers nuts.

He was asked to be concise many times during the 2012 campaign, in particular, and he failed miserably at the beginning, for example, in his first TV debate with Romney. He had to be reminded again and again (and to the point of people around being close to resigning in desperation) that, as leader, he needed to continue with the Poetry.

After the elections, he used to complain to David Axelrod, his key campaign architect, saying: 'I am not campaigning anymore!', meaning, 'I can leave the Poetry and get into Prose', such as his long Harvard lawyer explanations on social justice for example. He was told, as firmly as a friendship of many years could handle, that he was very wrong. 'You are campaigning all the time', Axelrod shouted at him. *(David Axelrod, 'Believer', Penguin Press 2015).*

It would be a mistake to equate Poetry with spin. 'Poetry' here means inspiration, purpose, drive, making sense, driving commitment, inviting to a place, a dream, a goal, elevating the logic to a higher purpose. Leadership Poetry can be (must be) sincere and honest, but, has to elevate the narrative to a place of destiny; I don't mind small d or big D.

The same honesty and sincerity applies to Prose. Prose means the day to day managing, governing, making things happen, driving to results. After all, 'manage' has its roots in the Latin 'manus' (hands). Hands on things happening, that is.

The problem arises when a natural Prose-person holds a top leadership position, and when a top leader Poet is sent to manage the troops. I know, I know, this is too black and white, too binary, particularly for those who always say 'you-have-to-have both' (a *Deus Ex Machina* we all have handy when we want to kill a good debate). But it makes the point for me.

As leader, never stop the Poetry. Small p, big P, it does not matter. Even if you are also comfortable with the War and Peace side of writing.

Prose make things happen. Poetry explains why.

'The tyranny of the moment'. Liberating Leaders Wanted.

Thomas Hylland Eriksen is a Norwegian Anthropology professor who has achieved more than any of his fellow anthropologists: you only need to read his books once.

His books are gems. My favourite is ***Small Places — Large Issues***, followed by ***The Tyranny of the Moment***.

And we have a lot of this tyranny in management. The book feels dated more than a decade after being written, but its principles are sound and even more prominent today. For example, the argument in favour of 'private periods' of thinking without interruption. Have you heard about that one?

In the 24/7 regime we live in, the instant is a premium. Forget instant coffee, it is instant knowledge and an instant answer. It is instant broadcasting and posting, and liking it, and requesting an (instant) answer. Prisoners of the moment, our concept of space and time is changing fast.

The world is split between the ones who say that we are going in the wrong direction, the ones who say this is great, and the other third who say, what the hell are you talking about? The latter is Age Related Incomprehension to ridiculous dilemmas.

There is a tyranny of the moment in our management lives. You'll find it in the Outlook calendar booked weeks in advance, the secretary responding with the usual, I don't know if this will be possible until (read here months in advance and the Overall Kingdom of Busyness for the Sake of It).

Again, another little leadership reflection. Much of this may be self-inflicted. This is bad enough. But as leaders, we are inflicting that tyranny on those working for us. Surely, we must stop and think.

(Wait a minute, did you mean now? In this very moment? What a Tyrant!)

Perhaps there is a form of Liberating Leadership waiting for a book.

'The top leaders are not specific, they don't tell us what they expect'. This is very good news.

Talking about leadership teams at the top, I often hear 'they launch these words but they don't give specifics', or 'we don't really know what their expectations are', or 'they don't tell us exactly what they think or what to do'.

There are many reasons why a leadership team at the top is not explicit about directions or give answers, or tell you exactly what to do. But one good bet is that they do not have a clue themselves.

Don't be disappointed, they are human. OK, highly paid humans, but human.

Most times when I see my client worrying about what the leadership team really thinks, 'because they don't tell us', I tell them that this is very good news. Other than the humanity thing, they may be asking you to figure out what the answer is. Without telling you, because this is a tiny little bit of exposure.

In my leadership development programmes, I spend a bit of time with clients convincing them that the world of receiving specific instructions to execute is far less lovable, that they are lucky, that they could shape the answer ('occupy that street', I say) and that they should be grateful.

Ok, the improvement in the dynamics comes from being more honest. I agree with this. This honesty may look like this: 'We have to go North. Not South, not East, although we were thinking about West. We don't have a good map. We don't know about stops and sleep overs. You go and figure it out'.

That is in fact pretty good leadership stuff.

'Meeting their (leadership team) expectations' is a reasonable expectation, but it assumes that the leadership team has in fact clear expectations, which is a hell of an assumption. They themselves are navigating through uncertainty. They have been elevated to the 10th floor, that is true, but their brains are not made of special material.

It's a game and not a malicious one, actually quite a human one. Detach yourself and read between the lines.

Maybe all could be summarised in a single word: help! Could it be that?

All thoughts come out of silence. Leadership development may turn out to be free after all.

Perhaps one of the most difficult things a leader has to do, is to be mindful of his/her own thinking. Not just the content and the style, and what is transformed into language, spoken or written, but also the filters, the biases, the traps, the shortcuts. Our heuristic brain allows us to shortcut, to use intuition, bets, rule of thumb, guesses. It's a wonderful ability that we have, which frees us from the algorithmic, step by step, check it all, be completely safe and sure. But even people who claim to be good at intuition are subject to those possible traps and biases. It would be wonderful to have the ability to rate our own thinking in terms of solidity and robustness. (I sometimes imagine a sort of Tripadvisor for corporate thinking where we can give stars, not to the outcome, but the clarity of thinking).

We have little luxury in organizational life to reflect, on almost anything. Thanks to those 'lessons learnt' we have a chance, but many 'lessons learnt' are in fact 'lessons learnt sessions', with the emphasis on having the session. Certainly, useful and important, usually collective, we need them big time. But, in my view, nothing compares to individual reflection, the ability to look at oneself, hear oneself, smell oneself, smile at oneself and see our own tricks and our own thoughts playing together in the background.

The thinking brigade inside our brains shapes our emotions and our behaviours. The late Irish poet and philosopher John O'Donohue spoke of 'thoughts as lenses' and 'thoughts in search of action'. I think that we also often have 'thoughts

in search of questions' since we have learnt to produce a reservoir of answers that seem to be permanently on standby.

For all those leadership development programmes on offer, all those learning and development packages, all those often readymade answers with an executive and management development brand on the label, nothing can substitute the personal reflection time, with or without help. And as soon as you touch 'personal reflection', you touch the most elusive, difficult, challenging, even disruptive 'human activity': silence.

I don't think I have to remind ourselves that our world goes against it. If we don't fill in our silence quick, we will be restless, many perhaps feel guilty and may want to rush to 'do something'. In the West, we have put silence on the same shelf as void and we think that, in any case, it is something only a few people really live in. Mainly monks, and those New Age meditative people back from a trip to Nepal.

I think that if silence could be packaged, we could sell it at a premium price.

All thoughts come out of silence. The quality of the silence impacts on the quality of the thoughts. The monk, Thomas Keating, has predictably put it in a religious frame: 'Silence is the language God speaks, and everything else is a bad translation'.

I think we should aim at good translations. The first and second, and lots of other lessons in silence, are actually free: practice it. Then, after a reasonable preamble in silence, try to hear, feel and smell what you have just said to your team in that very long and noisy Leadership Team meeting. That reflection may surprise you. Then go back to silence. Anything inside the sandwich made of silence, tastes very differently.

Leaders who have little control of things, but who think they have a lot of it, are the ones who fear losing control the most

Fear of losing control is a funny thing. It does not seem to correlate with how much control you have in the first place.

I find that leaders who in fact have very little control, but who think this is not the case, fear losing control and talk a lot about it. Typically my teams encounter this in the context of a Viral Change™ programme, in which the engine of change is at the grassroots and leadership is distributed in the form of highly connected 'activists' who are shaping the organization in an orchestrated, bottom up, peer-to-peer way. The contrast with a traditional 'change programme' which has top down communication, with lots of cascading workshops through the hierarchical lines, is striking.

Very often leaders feel that, in the old-fashioned top down way, they are in control, and that in Viral Change™ they lose/may lose/will lose control. This is actually not a hard one for us to redirect because it's exactly the opposite. The only control you have in top down systems is the number of workshops, the number of people attending and the content. Once this is done, you close your eyes and pray. You have very little control over what happens next, even from the time of people returning to the car park.

In the Viral Change™ antipode territory, the pool of highly connected people engaged and leading, working with us, (activists, champions, connectors) are so close to the ground on a day to day basis that you know what is going on, by the

minute if you wanted. Paradoxically, Viral Change™ provides higher levels of control than the traditional top down change systems.

But this is not the topic. The topic is how many leaders kid themselves, thinking that they have great control in the first place, something that they fear they may lose, which is unsettling to them. But to lose something you have to have it first, and, believe me, this is not always the case.

Control is often, in fact, 'an illusion of control' only fuelled by the times you see an input and output working. You asked people to attend a seminar, they did. You prepare a communication package and digitalised it in powerpoints and it has been cascaded down to all. Is this control? Only of the information tsunami. Try the same with changing behaviours.

My rule of thumb is to always ask my clients to reflect on 'how much (control) they have' before addressing the 'how much they will lose'. Never allow the conversation about losing, without knowing how much is in the bank.

A wonderful way to stop worrying about losing
control is to realise that you don't have much in the
first place. Then to figure out the level of control 'required'.
This is a conversation for another day.

'A desk is a dangerous place from which to view the world'

The late John le Carré, British ex secret intelligence serviceman, espionage writer, knew about danger, and apparently about the danger of desks.

You can lead the company from a desk on the 15th floor in an insulated office in the corner. Or practice something like 'Management by wandering around', a term usually attributed to Tom Peters, although it may be much older than his 1982 *In Search of Excellence book*.

But this 'get out of your office' (and avoid the risks of the desk as a platform to view the world) is not the same as Management Tourism (trademark pending), the practice of visiting affiliates, sites, plants and, of course, 'customers', but not getting dirty on those floors. Seeing but not listening. Hearing but not understanding. Leaving those places with a superficial insight and simply ticking boxes in a plan. For that, perhaps the desk is better.

In the past, I have known of a US senior executive visiting her very distributed sites in dozens of States and spending little time in each, almost invisible, rushing back to the airport for an HQ meeting the following day. I have seen this repeated a hundred times. Is it ego? Indispensable? Zero social skills? Love of air miles?

I see people 'descending from HQ' all the time and creating disruption by generating extra work through one-to-ones and presentations, and nobody saying, excuse me, and the point of all this is?

An executive desk is a dangerous place from which to view the world, but intellectual Management Tourism is even more dangerous. Move around, wander around, get out of your office, but wear the shoes of the people you visit, properly, deeply, like a curious amateur anthropologist. Practice the H2H (human to human), absorb, reflect, enrich, have a few ahas! Or, stay at your desk.

Le Carré thought it was dangerous, but, unless you do the above, people you visit in those affiliates, plants and sites, will think that the real danger is to have you visiting.

Certainty is addictive. Leaders, handle with care.

I've come across by chance a short video interview with Tony Robbins, life coach, health guru, motivational speaker, author, self-made multi millionaire and celebrity pal. In his typical firm and reassuring way, he said something that I had in store in my own cooking for my Daily Thoughts. Speaking about the US presidential candidates, he gave his views on them in short summaries. The interview was about leadership, so the choice of topic was very pertinent. [I wrote this at the time, keeping my notes here] Speaking of Donald Trump, Robbins said that he provided certainty and that in an uncertain world, people liked that, regardless. He was not saying whether that was right or wrong, just making the point that certainty was his currency. In fact, a few sentences later, he criticised what I suppose you could call Trump's false certainty. The interpretation is mostly mine.

At the core of this simple observation one thing is very true, and this is why I'm bringing it here for reflection. Certainty sells, but also, certainty is a powerful home for safety. As parents, we often project a certain world. The kids need that to feel safe, be safe. Somebody has the answers. At least for a few early years, until they figure out that there are at least fifty shades of grey in that black and white paternal certainty. But this early, safe, certainty is vital for the development of the children. At some point, of course, Father Christmas looks remarkably similar to granddad and doubts about reality start to flourish.

You could say that certainty is a key ingredient of leadership. Robbins says so, although apparently not the Trump's one. So, is it any certainty? The true one? Or, it doesn't really matter?

It's always said that, in times of crisis, people look for leaders with strong views, determination and drive, a sense of direction and willpower. (Like the ones who invade countries?). Nobody wants hesitating, weak, simple indecisive leaders in the middle of a catastrophe. Ok, so here is another word for all those expectations: certainty.

But when certainty dominates in a way that there is no room for alternative views, we have a problem. Certainty as 'there is one single view, and it's not yours', does not seem to me as a clever leadership quality. In fact, in the long term (or short? or medium?) the power is in 'I don't know, let's figure this out together, to get close to more certainty'. Or something like that.

So perhaps we have to be aware of the addictive powers of certainty. The 'I don't know, let's figure this out together, to get close to more certainty School of Leadership' is no doubt much harder. It can't be exercised without the emotional and social intelligence needed to master the apparent vulnerability and its potential un-safe-territory effects.

For me, Certainty, capital C, whether the one of the leader with a clear destination (his/hers) or the atheist who knows, or the people with all the answers, is of the scary type.

The fact that we are not well-equipped with toolkits for an uncertain world, does not imply that we have to ban uncertainty to make our toolkits work.

Back to Tony (I am sure he would not mind if I call him Tony), the irony is that he is the world master in selling certainty via his psychological, physical and social persona. And he does that very, very well.

Human behaviour laws are unfair. Positive or negative consequences are disproportionate to the causes. Get used to it as leader.

An old patient was concerned about her hair. A nurse came in at 7am to put colour in her hair. 'Nurses are saints', she said. All nurses? That's unfair. (A real example from one of our Viral Change™ programmes).

We have a reasonable level of trust between us. We help each other. But I have just let you down. Just once. Trust goes out of the window. This is unfair. How can trust be so vulnerable. (Because it is).

The doctor was hesitant, perhaps confused, maybe she had a bad day, but she missed a vital sign. Doctors don't really know what is going on. There is a big problem in this hospital. You can see how everybody is so stressed. That is unfair.

Twelve nurses in the hospital ward were kind, attentive and considerate. One was terrible, uncaring, dismissive, awful. The nursing staff in this ward have an attitude problem. (All? But you've just said…) That is unfair.

Again and again human behaviours and human emotions are not linear. We love unconditionally with very little objectivity. We hate deeply for perhaps a small feature.

These are non-linear maths. We are stuck with them. This maths may be needed to (be seen as running) run a brilliant organization out of a small set of positive behaviours or a dysfunctional organization out of a few bad apples. With these stats, 'a few bad apples' has no meaning. 'Few' is all you need to create havoc. In traditional, linear (organizational) maths, a few bad apples is just 'a small proportion' not to worry too much about.

In our day to day non-linear world, those few bad apples need to be identified and addressed. There may be more than one way, but leaving it to the comfort of 'it is a small number' is a bad idea.

The most powerful leadership instructions are the ones that are unsaid

And that can be good or bad.
Usually bad.

Islamic terrorists, who follow strict orders from ISIS, have a plan, a structure, a set of orders. They are part of an articulated strategy. They are 'proper soldiers'. To some extent this type of terrorism still follows some traditional warfare rules and could be tackled as such.

But another type is the one in which there is no direct military link, no written order, perhaps not even support. An individual, or several, act following an ideology, following a generic call, throwing to the pot their own interpretations, grievances, psychopathic personalities and a self-granted membership of the Cause. Nobody at HQ sent them the memo. The orders were unsaid.

The case of the Nice atrocities on 14th July 2016 seem to be one of these, regardless of the obvious post-hoc, Return on Investment (and I bet ISIS' core structure has a strategic manual somewhere showing the statistics around the ROI of lone wolves) zero cost message:

'The person who carried out the operation in Nice, France, to run down people was one of the soldiers of the Islamic State. He carried out the operation in response to calls to target nationals of states that are part of the coalition fighting the Islamic State'.

'Of course', ISIS would say. What else? It's the cheapest headcount of all. You don't even need to fund extreme fundamentalist schools and mosques. Drunk psychopaths with gambling addictions will do nicely.

Acting on behalf of a cause without talking to the heads of the cause, is not that dissimilar to guessing what the CEO wants and deploying some actions. Horror, how can I compare? I just did. Most top down, particularly cultural, dictations, instructions, and directions are not written. They are a derivative of original frames that top leadership establish. In many cases, they end up being interpretations of interpretations, or just copycat behaviours. In my original 2006 and second edition 2008 *Viral Change*™ book, I gave the example of a new CEO who changed dramatically in days, the style of meetings (no one-to-ones for him anymore, no crazy travel for him) and 'influenced' the organization to a rapid decrease of both, management meetings and travel. Interviewed by me months later about his cunning plan, he said to me, "what plan?".

That one may have ended up as a good thing, but it may not always be the case.

Leaders, not just the ones at the top, lead in Homo Sapien mode but underestimate the power of Homo Imitans. They don't need to just 'say', but question what has been heard and how the unsaid will be used.

The unsaid is dangerously powerful. After all, Henry II of England didn't say 'Go and kill this unbearable Thomas Becket Archbishop of Canterbury', but 'What miserable drones and traitors have I nourished and brought up in my household, who let their lord be treated with such shameful contempt by a low-born cleric?'. Copy that.

Leadership and the art of managing disappointments

A less spoken feature of great leadership is the art of managing the disappointments created by that same leadership. I call it the art of explaining 'no, we can't'. Or we couldn't. 'Yes, we can' is motivational and inspirational. 'No, we can't', is its inconvenient ugly sister.

There will be disappointed people. I can assure you: the ambitions that could not be fulfilled completely; the compromises that others may find unpalatable.

Some people will feel you did not go far enough. Other people may feel you went too far. Dealing with satisfied followers is the easy part. Explaining to the dissatisfied is harder, but a noble feature of strong leadership.

There may be trade-offs to explain. Chances are some may have been invisible. There may be emergent barriers. Perhaps we were more resource constrained than we thought. Perhaps there was a high expectation of achieving X and we did not. But X is still the aim. Maybe some goals need postponing.

Explaining the disappointments is not the end of the story, but will embrace an extra percentage of people who will see honesty, courage, and guts; perhaps boldness. The winner of acknowledging and explaining disappointments is trust.

For each piece of 'yes, we can', find and explain the 'we cannot, however'. This yin yang of expectations is powerful and often overlooked.

Throw embarrassment out of the window.
Practice the humble act of saying 'no', explaining why,
and describing what we can, however do and will do.
You coming with me?

Reflection is subversive.
Uprise! Slow down!

Space to reflect? Where is that? Are you saying
we are not reflective? Don't we have intelligence?
Are you suggesting we don't think properly?
Hey! Hold on! Stop the shouting.

Believe me, some people get offended. They may not express it as vocally as this.

Reflection needs space. And time. Which is the same thing but twice.

I really love the analogy (discovered in Julian Baggini's book, *How the world thinks*) of being on a train at high speed and only being able to see a blurred landscape through the window. Only slowing down will let you see the trees and the countryside with all the details.

Many organizations run at high speed. People are unable to reflect on those trees because they can't see them. The subversive thing to say, and do, is slow down, pause, breathe.

We have had a 'slow food movement'. We need a 'slow down the train' one.

I know, I know, those unmanageable and irresponsible people ('they') will never get anything done. What about all those 327 KPIs in the strategic plan? What is going to happen to them? Surely nothing with a low speed train.

I hear that music.

Some managers/leaders are so worried about this! Yet, of course some organizations need to inject speed, not the opposite. Back to my train, some organizations are such a slow train that they always see the same tree. Some are so insanely speedy that they can't see any trees.

Leaders are in charge of speed limits. Up or down.

Cruise control is a leader's key competence.

The collaboration of rivals is always the strongest. Try it!

The author Doris Kearns Goodwin wrote a most interesting book about the Lincoln presidency: *Team of Rivals*. It says it all.

John Kerry teamed up with John McCain for years to fix problems. Before that, Kerry the anti-war and pacifist, and McCain, war veteran, prisoner of war, did not speak to each other for 10 years.

Spain's 1978 constitution, post Franco, was literally written and signed at once by great minds from the ex-Franco system, the Christian Democrats, the Socialist Party, Communist party and Nationalist parties. They were genuinely at war with each other well before, for years.

South Africa came out of apartheid with the two opposite poles teaming up. Mandela offered government places to people who had 'managed' his prison.

The Good Friday agreement in Ireland managed to get together irreconcilable positions, historical, political and religious.

If all this can happen in the big, real world, it can happen to you and me in our real small worlds. You and I work in or with corporations. We have rivals with a small 'r'. OK, sometimes the font is big. It looks like a big 'R'. But usually we are not asked to write constitutions with people who wanted to kill us.

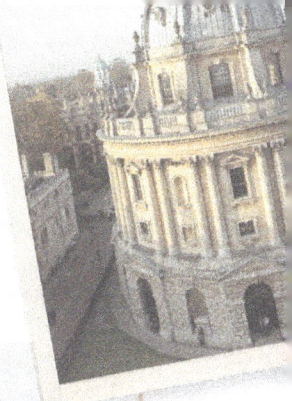

This is a five-point winning strategy:

- List your rivals

- Invite them to team up

- Watch their faces of surprise

- Insist

- Surprise everybody

- You are on the path to success big time.

Try it. It has probably never been done around you.

(I thought you wanted innovation).

'Leave it with me' is a magic behaviour. Spontaneous 'jumping in' and helping, if widespread, is like winning the lottery.

Something short of a miracle occurs in some lucky organizations where leaders spontaneously 'jump in' and take over a piece of orphan responsibility or lend a helping hand to other colleagues without having been asked.

Perhaps the most beautiful music in the lucky organization is the expression 'leave it with me'.

The key, and the trick, is the term spontaneous. It does not have to be. It is not dictated by the boss or top leaders. The expression 'taking accountability' in English means precisely that: to take. It does not have to be given.

Accountability is a term that does not translate well outside English. In many other languages it translates as responsibility.

I've written many times that the key to the logic of differentiation, if you want one, is in the etymology. Accountability belongs to counting, call to account. Responsibility belongs to responding. My heuristic rule is to suggest to clients that responsibility (responding) is something that can be shared, whilst accountability is not.

But one or the other, when spontaneity kicks in, when it is not in your job description to 'jump in and help', to volunteer a 'leave it with me', then the magic starts. It is the magic of collective leadership.

There are not many ways to inject this in the system, but, fortunately, the few there are can be very effective.

One, hire people with that attitude, those who can navigate that element of ambiguity, those who can cross borders and are not hooked into a rigid job description as expectation.

Two, once you see this thing happen, make it very visible. 'Jumping in' and 'leave it with me' are behaviours, therefore they are contagious, it's Homo Imitans. It will spread, it will be copied.

It can't be dictated, but it can be orchestrated ('planted') and multiplied.

With my behavioural hat on, this is a simple behaviour that has a very high impact. If you have it in your company DNA, you are lucky. But don't take it for granted. Nurture it, reinforce it, make it visible, give it airtime.

If you don't have it, start somewhere with some role models, particularly with highly connected and visible people. Then reinforce, celebrate, talk about it. It is not the anecdotal case that is important. It is how we can make it normal, embed it into the culture.

Your mental frame, as defined by words, will dictate your actions. Even your values. Words are dictators.

The purpose of the organization is... The objectives of the strategy are... The reason why we have restructured is...

From then on, any word used will dictate more than a few actions. What comes after is the frame, which is the same as saying the box, the borders, the spirit behind. So, for example, here are some frames: fixing, building, creating, protecting, solving, defending, and winning. Each word decides a set of values, a course of action.

Solving a poor customer relationship system is not the same as building a culture of customer-centrism.

Defending the brand is not the same as creating a community of brand fans.

Winning a position in the market is not the same as creating a market.

The frame dictates.

I can hear people saying that it is the other way around, that first is the intention, then strategy and then the words. But I see day after day the use of words that nobody knows exactly why they are used and that seem to be (vaguely?) related to the purpose. In many cases I know, the words have taken over. Perhaps irreversibly. In that case, words dictate, they are not dictated.

Words are cheap, their consequences are not.

Restructuring to align processes and systems better, to concentrate leadership and/or serve a customer sector in a better, more logical and more effective way, maybe done for all those purposes, but simply heard as cost cutting and people leaving. The latter may be so, but in reality, a new structure (I am not making a judgement as to whether good or bad, sensible or not) is born. Taking this under the building mode, for example, may just create a completely different future. Building, as a forgotten frame, is a lost opportunity to align people on a new and exciting journey.

It is far from semantic games. Words dictate us, not the other way around. Words produce emotions, from excitement to boredom, from emotional engagement to cynicism, from possibilities gained to paradise lost.

Framing is a key skill for leaders. Poor leaders will take this as a word game that an advertising or consulting agency will craft for them. Good leaders will start with asking others around to choose a frame, to explore the consequences, decide and stick to it.

In the beginning it was the mental frame.

Bold leadership pays off. It can also be killed by those who are highly paid to be professionally afraid.

Years ago, I persuaded a pharmaceutical client to make three bold moves in one:

(1) To create a New Product Incubator Unit (NPI) in charge of fast assessment/fast fail of very early stage development of medicines, including those offered for in-licensing by outsiders. The client was slow in this crucial filtering phase of the value chain and applied to this well-known bottleneck in medicines development the same laws and management criteria used in the rest of the company. We created an Incubator from what it was, a Slow Incinerator.

(2) To give the NPI complete autonomy with different governance from the mainstream company, for example, allowing a different reporting system and different levels of risk management (read: high). In many companies, uniformity and homogeneity of processes, systems and reporting, sold as the quintessence of, otherwise flawed, good management efficiency, is the only way to go. To carve out spaces (we call it 'cohabitation of spaces' in our Organizational Design method) with different laws and rules of the game, sometimes seems to management like a non-affordable nightmare. But the only reasons for the non-affordability, though, are simply of the managerial convenience type. It is indeed more difficult and painful to manage an organization which de facto works as a host of different designs, units, and rules of the game, a diversity of spaces, not one mansion with all the windows and toilets looking the same.

(3) To put somebody in charge with a technology/engineering background, not medical or pharmaceutical. This bright gentleman, out of ignorance, started asking all sorts of uncomfortable questions about speed, decision making, risk levels, resources and deliverables. The client anticipated a big backlash from 'the professionals' but, in fact, we had next to none, 'professionals' largely welcoming the alien and his awkward questions that nobody else had asked before.

This all-in-one bold move worked extraordinarily well on all counts. It got rid of all the backlog of assessment of molecules. It attracted bright people who wanted to join in. In fact, its permanent headcount was low, but we had a long queue of good brains wanting to join as secondments from other parts of the company. The NPI was 'the place to be'. It was a fast moving, high risk, work intensive, stimulating, high output, thought provoking environment. And did deliver big time.

When later on the company was acquired by a Big-All-Things-Corporation, it took the new owners just a few days to dismantle this alien, avant-garde, magnetic structure. None of the new acquiring executives descending from heaven with a McKinsey cookbook understood this apparent madness and the most successful experimentation in the long history of the company, going back to the 50s, died unceremoniously.

I made a big mistake at the beginning. I took for
granted that success would always be protected, proven
innovation would always win, and even Big Consulting Thinking
would always acknowledge bold moves.
I am slightly less stupid now.

For any 'what you say' there are always many 'how you say it'. Impact is in the how.

Take a look at these 5 reframes. You should see the differences not just the simple literary ones but the very different outcomes that each of them trigger.

1. Only 30% of people have responded./Already 30% of people have responded.

Only 30% of people have responded. [Struggle, disappointment, way to go, help!] vs. Already 30% of people have responded. [Doing well! Join in, improve! Don't miss the boat]. The 30% is the same in both.

2. Do you have any questions?/What questions do you have?

Do you have any questions? [Maybe! Don't know. Maybe not, look around]. What questions do you have? [There are questions, taken for granted].

3. You can have A or B./Which one do you want, A or B?

You can have A or B. [OK thanks, I'll think about it]. Which one do you want, A or B? [I must choose].

4. Do you want to participate?/Tell me if you don't want to participate.

Do you want to participate? [Opt in please, make an effort]. Tell me if you don't want to participate. [Otherwise you are in]. Opt out structures are very powerful.

5. This is a failure – No, it is not a failure!/This is a failure –
   I have a very different view.

This is a failure – No, it is not a failure! [The word failure is repeated,
it smells like failure]. This is a failure – I have a very different view.
[I don't agree and I am not trapped here].

The formula is simple:

Content x Intention x Frame = Outcome.

Change the frame, change the outcome.

The formula is never Content = Outcome. Never.

Leaders should be trained in minimal reframing techniques. I run Reframing
workshops occasionally, when I have time outside projects, or within the project
itself. They are most rewarding.

Try to play with
these five above.
It won't hurt you.

10 reasons why leaders need to focus on the (unmanaging of the) informal organization

Our traditional management education has almost 100% focused on the formal organization, the structural fabric of teams, divisions, groups, committees and reporting lines.

The informal organization, often also called the 'invisible organization', has always been a ghost: you know it's there but can't see it, can't manage it, can't measure it, so I don't do anything about it. A few years ago, many leaders considered the informal side a waste, a detractor from the core and the formal, that is, doing your job. It seems only yesterday when a friend of mine, a very successful business owner, spent a lot of time writing (handwriting for his secretary to type) memos to staff about not using email for personal reasons or the internet for that matter. Forget that online shopping and Ticketmaster deal. Not in his company.

Today, the role of the informal organization is more recognised. But still it is important to remind ourselves of what the informal social networks inside the organization, the web of connections, the largely (but not totally) invisible side does, and why it is inexcusable for leaders today to ignore it, or even treat it as an anecdote.

1. Connectedness (= network) Obviously!

The issue here is fluidity. Informal social networks inside the organization could become non-fluid if you attempt to formalise them, 'convert them into a team' or corporatise them. They then become clubs (women in leadership, expats) which have their own utility, but they are not strictly speaking an informal network. The real connectedness dwells in the informal organization, well above the 'forced connectedness' of teams and task forces.

2. Information traffic and communication.

The travel, the social life of information, uses two highways: the top down hierarchical system of communication (the pipes) and the informal network (chatter, rumours and all versions of Chinese whispering). You can't exercise a role, for example, like Internal Communications without mastering the social life of the rumour. So, you need to know how the invisible organization works.

3. Clustering.

In the internal social network, people who know/do/did X, also know/do/did Y. There is an entire social cartography that can be considered. The informal organization loves clustering. Find an element, chances are you'll find the others. It's 'people like me do this'.

4. Listening. Receiving feedback.

The informal organization/internal social networks are very good at listening and closing the loop with people. If you see the organization as a listening organism, then you need to focus on the informal organization, not the structural and formal of teams and committees. What the formal organization hears is then listened to in the informal one.

5. 24/7 Q&A.

The informal organization is a 24/7 Q&A system you can tap into. The 24/7 Q&A knows no boundaries. The fluidity and use of the informal organization and its clusters of (informal) social networks allows for the bypass of a formal 'expert system'. It is literally a 'can anybody tell me about X?', assuming that everybody is a possible 'expert'. You don't need to catalogue them anymore.

6. Ideas generation/crowdsourcing.

Tapping into intellectual capital, idea generation and fast idea qualification requires the entire network. Internal crowdsourcing is only possible if the fluidity of the social network is respected.

7. Ties.

The social network is the generator of ties, strong or weak. The weaker the ties, the greater the potential for innovation. Strong ties are more predictable (you already guessed what your team members John and Peter and Mary are going to say) and are not particularly good for innovation. The informal network hosts the weak ties, which are often the most powerful ones.

8. Social capital.

The network is a constant creator of relationships, a self-configuring one. It is therefore the strongest social capital builder; social capital defined as the sum of qualitative and quantitative relationships.

9. Host of conversations.

The true conversations take place outside the straitjacket of the team meeting.

10. Stories.

The informal organization is a big campfire for stories to be told. Their nodes in the informal organization (you and me) are raconteurs. The employees in the formal structures are more on the information traffic side.

Leaders should be curators of the informal organization, masters of the invisible world and keepers of the fluidity, avoiding any attempt, from anybody, to corporatise or formalise it. It is the art of unmanaging to reach full potential.

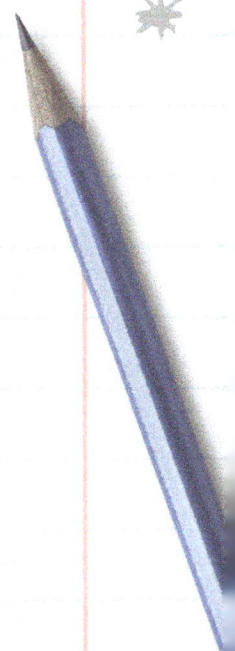

CADAQUÉS, EL MARITIM

IF I WERE THE CEO'S SPEECHWRITER FOR A DAY, THIS IS THE SPEECH I WOULD PASS ON

Don't look at us as the leadership at the top. We are the wrong mirror. Of course, we are committed to being the best possible role models for the organization. It is our duty and privilege. But we may get it wrong from time to time. Our potentially bad example, I very much hope transitory, should make you aim even harder at excellence.

The real leaders in the organization are people like you, managing groups, divisions and teams. Leadership is completely distributed amongst us – actually, we are rich in it. How you, sitting in different layers of management in the organization, do things, how you move forward, is what matters. You are the real day to day role models. Other colleagues will look at you first, before even thinking of looking up to the leadership team. You see? Leadership modelling is mostly about you and between you. This is where you have to look, every day. It is your own environment that will serve as a mirror first. Look sideways, not up. Shape the environment around you. You have the power I don't have.

Don't get me wrong. We all, in the leadership team at the top of the organization, are committed to our values, to constantly shaping a culture based upon them. If any of us don't live by those values, if we create barriers instead of breaking them down, we will have a big problem. I promise you, we will get better and better.

Not there yet. But small, or not small, failure or disappointment in us at the top level, should not be an excuse for anybody to relax the values, to steer the organization in the wrong direction.

If you see any of us in the leadership team, including myself, deviating from the right course, tell us. I know, it's not easy. Most people won't be comfortable with that. And that includes the messengers and the receivers. We are all human and sometimes don't like to be told that something we are doing is not right, particularly if we are in a top position in the hierarchy. But, this is the deal. I promise you that I, personally, as CEO, will always welcome any comment, any input or piece of feedback. I promise you, I will hear it clearly. I can't promise that I will always be able to react immediately, but I can assure you, your effort won't be wasted.

Let me repeat. Don't waste your energies analysing what happens at the top of the organization. Shape the culture according to our values, with your own teams and above all teaming up, joining forces with your own peers. You don't need permission for this. Other managers and leaders like you, have similar issues and challenges. Some will be better than others at finding solutions: people issues, organizational issues, barriers, resources, any challenge. Your peers, not the top leadership team, will be more able to help. This is your first port to collectively move forward. You and your peers have more power than you think to shape things around you, certainly, more than us in the leadership team.

I, with the top leaders with me, am moving forward with all my capacity, to make this company the best there is. This is my personal invitation. Come with me, with us. Bumpy journey or not, it is worth every second. Promise.

Look ahead, look sideways, don't look back, don't look up too much, always look down to your people with generosity, trust and a sense of possibilities.

IMPERFECT DATA, IMPERFECT INSTRUCTIONS, LOW PREDICTABILITY, HIGH TRUST: JUST A MODEL FOR BUSINESS (FROM BOAT RACING)

My very good, past client, BTG plc created a habit of getting leadership teams together to race boats for a day, in serious waters, to race, of course. The coaching team are of Olympian level, indeed some of them are now part of the British Olympic Team. They get the instructions first thing in the morning, get to do some training in the water and then race for the rest of the day. Some people may be sportive, some may have never been in a boat before. After the long day, the dinner, the social aspect and a good night's sleep, the next day the team is confronted with their own business situation to apply any learning from the day before. It works brilliantly.

There is an extraordinary immediate (organizational and leadership) learning from the model, which I'd like to unpack. The whole experience can be broken down into 4 components. I will explain and at the same time, I will make the comparison with what is more or less standard in our business life.

1. Minimal instructions. The early morning class on racing is beautifully done, but it is one hour, max. There you have 'all you need to know' from safety to rules of racing; from winds to manoeuvring; from strategy to tactics. BTG calls this the 'get it' part. Compare that with our obsession with having a perfect briefing with perfect data with all the dots in a row and boxes ticked, before we start doing anything.

2. Minimum sense making. Nobody receives the total wisdom on racing in an hour, there is no room for absolutely everything to make sense. It just makes enough

sense to assume that other things will emerge. Enough sense to act. Compare this with our usual need to obtain maximum comfort. Is everybody on board? Everybody aligned? Does management support this and that? Are we sure that this is what the CEO wants? Have we double checked with the US? We spend our organizational life creating 'packaged comfort' before we act.

3. The magic trust comes in.

If the team has a decent level of trust, between their members, the magic sparks. You trust that others will have understood, that others will know what to do, that others will help and jump in if needed. No trust, this is where it all breaks down, or at least starts showing some cracks. In our organizational life trust is also the fuel. Nobody quite knows how to create it but you'll see it when you see it, or you won't. In BTG racing sessions, teams with intrinsic low or poor trust in real life, perform significantly worse in the waters. Interestingly, the coaches who may not know about the teams themselves in real life, can spot and predict a bad business execution by seeing what happens in those boats. And they are always right.

4. Then you go, go, go.

And recalibrate and execute. BTG calls these in several ways: to be 'on it', to 'look out' and to have the 'appropriate bandwidth'. It is an imperfect world. As a guest, I have attended sessions where in the morning and during the training bits, we have dealt with all possible winds and associated manoeuvring, to get into the race itself and find zero wind, nothing moves whatsoever. Prepared for high winds, what do you do with the lack of it. Does it sound like business as well?

I am incredibly sceptical of 'sports analogies' for business. This one works, because it is not an analogy, it is real experience of a full imperfect world, in a day with immediate, transferable. unavoidable learning.

Dealing with the imperfect, the unpredictable, the ambiguous is part of today's business life. Part of my serious leadership development toolkits.

And for the imperfect, the unpredictable and the ambiguous, people still seek perfect training, perfect guarantees and perfect comfort. That is old school.

'I AM THE CAPTAIN. WE ARE ON A COLLISION COURSE'

This is a great story of focus, determination, appeal to progressive levels of authority and some other things. We leaders can learn a lot.

The lookout on a battleship spies a light ahead off the starboard bow. The captain tells him to signal the other vessel, 'We advise you change course twenty degrees immediately!'

The answer comes back, 'we advise you to change course twenty degrees immediately!'

The captain is furious. He signals, 'I am the captain. We are on a collision course. Alter your course twenty degrees *now!*'

The answer comes back, 'I am a seaman 2nd class, and I strongly urge you to alter your course twenty degrees'.

Now the captain is beside himself with rage. He signals, 'I am a battleship!'

The answer comes back, 'I am a lighthouse'.

This excerpt, from the *New York Times* bestseller by the inimitable duo, Tom Cathcart and Daniel Klein: *Plato and Platypus walk into a bar...* is a delightful reminder of the dangers of omnipotence in a leader and the need to listen.

In fact, he was lucky that the lighthouse was manned (by no less than a seaman 2nd class). The collision point is not necessarily manned in many businesses. Sometimes maps are not that good. Who knows, maybe maps do not exist but we are using an old one anyway, just in case. Or the navigation tools have been produced by old Business Schools when they were doing 'research'.

THREE WAYS TO GET APPROVAL FROM YOUR CEO OR YOUR LEADERSHIP TEAM

Way number 1: My team has come up with these three options, A, B and C. Which one do you want us to do?

Way number 2: I need you to approve A. We also have options B and C, but we would not recommend them.

Way number 3: Just to let you know that we are doing A. We explored B and C but they did not rank as high as A.

These 3 ways describe 3 different concepts of empowerment, 3 different styles of leadership and, also, 3 different organizations. The 3 are legitimate, but they are very different. Don't kid yourself, they are not simple variations.

Many people still ask for permission for things that the leadership does not expect to have to approve. But they may do so, because it's now on their plate, in front of them. Many Boards complain that decisions are 'pushed up' too much, but do very little to change the situation. On the other hand, many leadership structures expect to be presented with options, for the latter to make a final decision.

Knowing whether 'you are' 1, 2 or 3 and, more importantly, whether you'd like to be 1 or 2 or 3, or which one of them your senior leadership expects, is fundamental. These questions are, more often than not, simply not posed or articulated. In these cases, decision making runs in automatic pilot mode, creating default positions, that are never validated properly, that, sooner or later, will drive people, top or middle or bottom, for different reasons, simply mad.

THE INDECISION IS FINAL. KEEP CALM AND WAIT FOR THE NEXT.

A recurrent problem with decision making is often The Follow Up Problem, which can be described as 'the decision has been made but it does not seem to be implemented'. If I had a pound or dollar for every time a client says 'we are not very good at following up', I would book a long holiday.

If you are a kid in school and you 'don't follow up' (the homework has been set but you don't do it) there will be consequences. In some companies, there is no consequence whatsoever with a decision that is not fully implemented, or not implemented on time. Interestingly, in those companies, the machinery of making decisions does not learn, and more and more decisions are made to compensate for the decisions that were not followed up.

A variant of this situation is Passive Aggressive Behaviour meets Cynicism. Translation: 'let's just hold on for a bit and see if this decision sticks. The track record says that it won't/will be changed or superseded by another one in place of this one. If we just sit back and keep calm, we may see a stream of decisions with different sticking power

SPAIN

FLIGHT: 1·565·7

SOUTHERN AIRLINES
GATE 2
HAND BAGGAGE ALLOWED

BARCELONA, SPAIN
FLIGHT CODE:

56-453

and then we will go for the unavoidable one'.

No decision here is truly final. Keep calm and let's see the (decision) river flowing. A 90's book by Barry Gibbons of that title reminds me of this.

You need to dig deep into the final indecision and understand the cause. You may just find that the issue is not that the decision was good or bad, but that the leadership is not credible enough, or not serious enough, or changing their minds so frequently that it is impossible to distinguish the real one and the ephemeral. This leads to a Broken Windows syndrome in the organization, which increases the possibility of more indecision even further.

Don't close your eyes. Consider the question: what if people are just waiting to see the longevity of this? If you want to decrease the mortality rate of decisions, don't compromise and dig.

You may not have a decision making problem. You may have a credibility problem. Which is a leadership problem. Decisions are just fine. You are not.

THE LEADER WHO SAID, 'MAKE YOUR NUMBERS' INSTEAD OF 'HAVE A GOOD TRIP BACK'

A friend of mine remembers one of his bosses very well. 'Make the numbers', was apparently his way of saying goodbye, thanks, see you later, thanks for coming and have a good trip back to your country base. And the worst part was that he thought that he was very clever, funny, and elevated.

My friend is long retired and, with age, he has gained a clear sense of detachment. His life has been full of challenges. Often hard times. Good times as well. Yet, he is quite content and would come across to you as the least bitter of human beings. He can look back at bad times and find good angles. But, to this day, he hates that boss.

Talk about 'him' and a sudden adrenaline rush is almost visible at skin level. From the way he refers to 'him', the following can be put in writing: robotic, macho, arrogant, un-human (I suppose it doubles as robotic) and definitely not clever.

I am always surprised at my friend's vivid memories and how different and judgemental they are compared with the rest of his life. However, it's not that difficult to imagine my friend's boss. I've seen some versions of it. These people consider the organization they lead in this way:

1. A piece of machinery; leadership is a question of having all the bits and pieces in the right place, with some oil.

2. An input and output system. I'll give you money, you give me results. I'll pay for training, you do X better tomorrow.

3. An amoral entity where operational outcomes are the only thing that matters. The rest is commentary.

4. Their personal playground.

5. A container for their ego. Unfortunately, the oversized nature of the ego finds the container very tight.

You would have thought that in this time and age, these *robosses* are gone. You would be wrong. Many have been promoted; others may have checked out with a pile of stock options. The species still exist.

The worst of this kind, I have written somewhere else in a different context, are the ones who:

1. Comply with the above 1-5 criteria.

2. They think of themselves as humane, charitable, on a religious basis, righteous and caring.

As far as I know, my friend was pretty good at making the numbers. But he can't help it. Having that boss created a permanent disability in his soul.

HISTORY IS CONSTRUCTED

The leader's legacy is not retrospective. We build it daily, so we'd better test it.

In another context, I wrote about company cultures as having a glue. The Company's, One Global Culture does not exist. But pretending that it does holds us together.

The glue is sometimes, but not always, the history narrative, its own history, that is. History is accessible. In recalling it, we construct it. I said that 'part of this narrative may be a 'root narrative' such as the founders, the struggles, the heroes, and the guys in a garage with a telephone'. Also that 'the validity of this root narrative may not be terribly relevant; after all, entire tribes have been created and sustained under the root narrative of ancestors crossing rivers that did not exist, fighting wars that did not take place, or for years wandering deserts that nobody has touched'.

Nationalists know about constructing history. Independence movements often need the nationalist glue, and, in seeking it, they sometimes create their 'against narratives'. Being against something, or somebody, is the glue. Often to the detriment of deciding what it is that they are 'pro', if anything.

(By the way, the victim-oppressor, for example, is a good one, because it does not have to be true, it could be constructed. Victimism is good populism. At macro level, we see it every day in the news. At micro level we see it in our teams, our daily routines and our hierarchical 'us and them').

What's the role of the leader in the construction of the history of the organization? This is in part the legacy question. One that can be addressed from a purely egocentric perspective or not. What's my legacy? It's a question that could also be put in terms of 'what history am I creating?'

It's a powerful question because, although we can always dismiss these things as soft stuff, it forces us to define the building, the one that leaders are supposed to build. And leave behind at some point, of course. But, don't wait til the end and the retrospective. Others will judge. Construct the history as you go along. In trying, at least, you'll have to see if what you do write down makes sense or not, whether you are proud or not.

I have said many times that my favourite test is the 'what will you tell the children?' question.

So, here we go. What's the story? A war story, of winners and losers? (Business as a war) A struggle story? Conquistadores? Terra Incognita? 3.5% increase in market share? Transforming lives? Phenomenal shareholder value? Top of the X list? OK, we could go for hours here.

Then, am I building this on my own? What's the role of others? And how am I building it? Ah, the how!

Dont wait to the end. Build the picture. Write the script. Look in the mirror. Start again.

MANAGEMENT IS POLITICAL CAMPAIGNING INSIDE. LEADERSHIP IS WINNING CAMPAIGNS.

Warning: this statement will be dismissed.

> But, before you do that, I'd ask you to consider the differences between 'organizational business management' and 'political campaigning'. I will try to avoid a value judgment. Just invite you to consider the differences and your mind may do the rest.

Warning 2: my 'political campaigning' is modelled on Obama's.

Warning 3: what follows is an inevitable caricature and extreme; if you play lots of 'yes but', you will soon get bored.

1. Business management, largely, has one message for all: a homogenous mission, vision and directions. Political campaigning is highly segmented; a 60 year old retiring does not get the same message as a 23 year old seeking employment.

2. Business management tends to be quite obsessed with 'alignment'. Political campaigning is comfortable with hosting many motivations.

3. Business management talks a lot. Political campaigning talks a lot as well, but acts more. Their people are called act-ivists for a reason.

4. Political campaigning is very time limited. Business management is a piece of string.

5. Political campaigning understands and masters (social) influence. Business management has a narrow view of influence, largely hierarchical (and when it does accept that there are other types of influence in the organization, it does not quite know what to do with them).

6. Business management thrives in formal structures. Political campaigning focuses on grassroots.

7. Business management emphasises 'people engagement'. Political campaigning emphasises 'people mobilization'.

8. Business management is vertical (communications, command). Political campaigning is horizontal, transversal, peer-to-peer, tribal.

9. Business management goes to Harvard. Political campaigning goes to campaign headquarters.

10. In business management, bad management is not meeting targets. In political campaigning, the opposite of winning is being defeated.

I"ll let you cook this.

TOP LEADERSHIP NEEDS TO ROLE MODEL, LEAD BY EXAMPLE AND LIVE THE VALUES

Now that we have said it, can we please stop talking about it?

Yes to all. All of the above. Who could disagree? Certainly not the leadership development sub-industry.

We want the good guys, well-behaved, morally sound, positively visible and value speakers/value presenters/ value behaving, at the top. I have no problem with this. When I have a problem is when we stop the conversation there and we all go for a walk, as if the engagement of the other 14,980 people in the company depended on it.

Stop looking up. Look sideways, a bit down. What matters is the social copying of each other in the day to day, transversal, horizontal, peer-to-peer, tribal organization. And that may or may not correlate with 'life at the top'. Nobody says the top does not count. What I say is that it is often an alibi for management inaction. A not terribly functional top leadership is often blamed for not terribly functional operations even if these two do not have anything to do with each other.

A healthy organization is one where the top is a model, yes, but life does not depend on it. Usually, in a large or medium organization there will be several layers of leadership and management. All of them count as much, if not more. How 100 supervisors behave may be more crucial than the 10 guys at the top.

What happens at the level of what the Edelman Trust Barometer calls 'people like me' is what shapes organizations. 'People like me' (peers, colleagues, mates, tribe members) represent the highest source of internal trust. It's the day to day interactions at all levels that shape a culture, not the PowerPoints from the leadership team.

Looking up all the time is a distraction, a diversion, a convenient out of focus that is used to explain everything, even if 'the explanation' is here and down, say, at managerial and supervisory level.

And another thing, looking up too much will also give you chronic neck pain.

SHIFTING THE NARRATIVE: ONE OF THE FINEST ROLES OF LEADERSHIP

One of the fundamental roles of leadership is to frame the narrative of the organization. This is easy to say but not many leaders are conscious of the importance of having an overall mental frame and overall compelling narrative that serves as an umbrella for everything. Worse, many leaders in organizations could not, perhaps, answer the question of 'the narrative'. They may recite mission and visions but this is far from describing that overall big story.

There are decisions to be made about those narratives and, even more important, about shifting the ones in place.

Here are three examples:

From a performance/execution narrative that is pretty much one of the efficacy and effectiveness of the organization, to a narrative of ambition, which goes well beyond high performance to high(er) and high(er) goals and possibilities.

From a fixing/problem solving narrative in which problems and deficiencies are the focus, to one of building something new, creating some new culture, a new organization (in which those problems are addressed or solved).

From a 'management of change' narrative, to one of

changeability, permanent state of change and shaping a cultural DNA where change is not a project anymore.

We could go for hours on the listing of possible shifts. It does not mean they are obligatory but the conversation about which narrative is in place and whether it is fit for purpose and for the future, may force us to look at alternatives. It is a vital exercise that impacts on language and action.

I suggest we unpack this carefully. The glasses we have to see the world, creates our world.

The historical language of the organization may have intrinsic liabilities now. New, younger generations, for example, may want to hear something different. Do we always know what?

THINKING LEADERSHIP IN TERMS OF LEGACY. THERE WILL BE ONE.

Big L, small l, legacy is the long term outcome of leadership. There will be a legacy. You're better off shaping it.

This is not something leaders ask of themselves very often. In some cultures, it even sounds presumptuous. Or something just for CEOs and Big People. But we all leave a legacy, good or bad.

You could see a leadership legacy in numerical terms: the market share increase, the share price increase, the number of acquisitions, or any other output of the machine. But it would be much better to see legacy in terms of place and space: what kind of organization has been left behind, what kind of place, what spaces? Is it a magnet? A cool place? A perfect machinery? Darwinian land? A knowledge worker sweatshop? An unmemorable territory? A middle-of-the-road-nothing-wrong-with-it place? What's the story, anyway?

If you ask yourself these questions early enough in your leadership, small l or big L, you'll have a chance to shape a particular legacy, small l, Big L.

CADAQ
(ALT EMPOR
SOTA ES
FONDAL
PLATJA
PORT-ALGUER
PUNTA DES
BALUARD
MOLL D'EN CASTELL
MAR MEDITERRÀNIA · COSTA

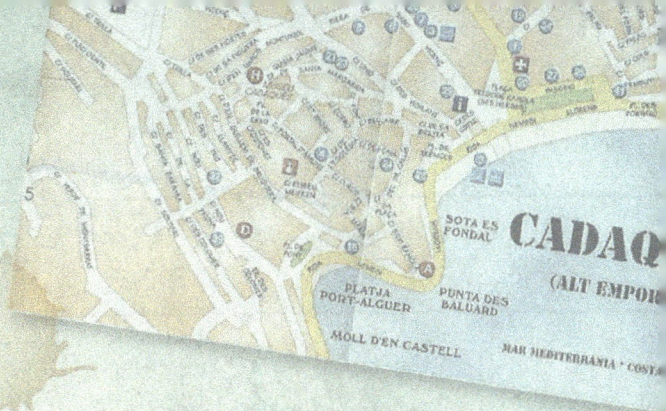

Sometimes I wish leaders could have the equivalent of a near death experience or out of body experience, so they could see the world left behind. Would you be pleased? Satisfied? Honoured? Proud? Embarrassed?

In fact, in the very short term, the idea still applies. What was my micro-legacy of today? A better place? A more elevated, humane, enhanced one? An unmemorable day in the lives of people around me?

Questions, questions. There should be more in leadership programmes. Or establish a kind of questions tax: for every question answered, there must be five or so new questions.

And the collective legacy question is: are we ending the day leaving this in a better place? But, forget the collective, stay an individual; otherwise I am elevating the confusion to a higher level. So, what does it look like, so far?

'WHERE THERE IS TOO MUCH VISION, PEOPLE PERISH FASTER'

'Where there is no vision, the people perish', says the Bible in the Book of Proverbs. This quote comes in handy when you talk about leadership.

But I tend to add a second line: 'Where there is too much vision, people perish faster'. Leaders with absolute clear vision of the future and a perfect plan, scare me. I think they are dangerous. Give me a leader with uncertainty but determination to succeed and I feel safe. Strong visionaries need opticians, not followers.

My best client leaders have willpower, resilience and contagious properties in their DNA. They speak the language of possibilities, not fixed destinations. They also like to be judged by their present deeds, now, not by history. They feel the need to serve and respond to their people, not to a Supreme Being, which, together with 'history' form a convenient, non-reachable duo, out of the scrutiny of fellow travellers. In short, politicians of the genre 'History will judge me', should be banned permanently from any office.

I know of a leader who had a very strong vision, a great Strategic Plan, absolute clarity of where to go, commanded great authority and trust, mastered people engagement, was determined, focused, driven, results oriented, and forward looking. Last time I checked, he died in a bunker in Berlin.

SEDUCING MINDS VERSUS HIRING PEOPLE. JUST IMAGINE.

I like the word seducing when referring to working for somebody, a company, a person, a cause, an organization. If you can't seduce them, then at best you hire, incorporate, bring to the company. But all these may happen without the seduction. And this is not the same.

My 2007 little book *New Leaders Wanted Now Hiring* had the subtitle, *12 kinds of people you must find, seduce, hire and create a job for*, and I said that was the right order.

Seducing is the right concept for leadership and for the HR function when attracting talent. From outside the company and from other parts of the same company. Both.

I invite you to reflect on this concept. The seducing department? That's you, if you're a leader.

What if the next time you review your intake of people you look at this as a seducing exercise?

Not a semantic trick,
not just a language twist.

Shall we try?

AUTHENTICALLY DISRUPTIVE

Pope Francis has introduced disruption. The head of the 1.2 billion Catholic Church lives in a one bedroom apart-hotel, produces off-the-cuff daily comments, does not speak English and gets really angry with the retiring top Vatican Official who has arranged a nice penthouse for him. He drew three times the number of visitors to his audiences, compared with his predecessor.

In Israel, he breaks with protocol (and security) and prays not just at the Jerusalem Wall, the holiest Judaic prayer site, but also at the other wall: the not so holy, separation wall that divides Israel and Palestine. He ends up inviting the Israeli and Palestinian Prime Ministers to the Vatican, not for peace talks, ('that would be crazy on my part', he says), but to pray together, at his place.

He has managed to appear on the cover of *Time magazine* and also in a prominent gay magazine, as 'Person of the Year'. Graffiti on the walls of Rome picture him as a flying Superman in white robes.

The English version of his first *Letter to the Faithful*, which is the length of a manifesto pamphlet and does not even bear the rank of Encyclical, (the recognised, 'official' pastoral document) has sold more copies than the entire collection of Encyclicals of all previous Popes (to the delight of the ailing UK publisher).

He drives the conservative arm of the Catholic Church completely nuts, because Popes are supposed to be very careful about what they say and they are expected to use a deep theological language, not speak like your local priest in his Sunday service. The liberals don't know what to make of him either because he is not going 'as far as they expected'. Atheists say that he is somebody worth talking to and they call him 'awesome' in their twitter feeds. The Cynical, a category in abundance, thanks to the modern history of spin and the erosion of trust in politicians and public life in general, say that 'surely, he must be fake'.

I have two hypotheses. Number one: he is all spin, calculated, media manipulator, Machiavellian extraordinaire, a great salesman, a natural PR guy. This is what some people say. The trouble with this hypothesis is that spin, as we know it, as practiced by politicians and public figures, needs good PR machinery behind it. The Vatican has the worst PR system on the planet. The Vatican's Head of Communications, a fellow Jesuit, seems to sometimes be the last one to know what the Pope plans to say. So, either Pope Francis has supernatural and divine PR skills, in which case he is de facto a One-Man-Spin-Band – a very unlikely scenario – or this hypothesis simply does not hold water.

Hypothesis number two. The man is authentic. He speaks and acts according to what he thinks and believes. What you see and hear is him! And because he is 100% 'The Real Thing' himself, this turns out to be very disruptive! Authenticity is disruptive because our expectations are low. In a fake world, the authentic is unexpected and sometimes troublemaking. The true disruptive idea is Being Oneself.

I believe that in Leadership, authenticity wins the battle. It may be hard to believe, but the truthful, the genuine, the authentic, the honest and the humble have an advantage in today's world. In organizations, having the courage to be oneself, not the corporate man, not the 'yes' man, not the 'no' man, not the fake citizen, but just oneself, may be the kind of disruption we need.

Leaders in business could do with disposing of their uniforms, their costumes, their layers of protective social make up, and try the Francis way. Who knows, that may well deal with a lot of the leadership development that is needed.

ICONIC LEADERSHIP: THE ILLUSION OF COPYING A ONE-OFF

Picture this organization. Closed culture, culture of secrecy, dictatorial CEO. Perhaps a bit unkind, but I have said before, speaking to a large audience of technology executives (and pushing my luck), that the Soviet Union was never fully dissolved since it reincarnated itself in Cupertino, California, with an apple as a logo. Would you like to work in a secretive culture under a dictatorial CEO? Well, the dictator has left us with an enormous legacy and the company is today the biggest in the world as measured by market capitalisation.

How do you fit the Apple case in the organizational and management world? A model of management? Of organizational culture? Which bits do you want to copy? The market capitalisation? The culture? The dictator? Their world leadership in innovation? The Secrecy? The personality cult? All of the above?

The trouble with iconic leadership is that it is not usually transferable. There was only one Steve Jobs and one set of circumstances around him. You can try to wear black polo neck shirts and jeans but that will not make you his clone.

Banking on those one-off, heroic leaders to come to your rescue is not a good idea either. As somebody said: 'If you don't have a Steve Jobs, have a plan B'.

Interestingly, any simple digging into the circumstances around the one-off, hero-leader, often offers some more complex findings. For example, the frequent uncovering of the 'second' in command. A person sometimes equally important who did not attract the same public treatment. In the case of Steve Jobs, this person was Steve Wozniak.

As put in the 99U.com blog (*The Narrative Fallacy: Why You Shouldn't Copy Steve Jobs*), 'Steve Wozniak created Apple. Steve Jobs was a paper pusher and marketing guy. He never created and designed anything. Without "The Woz" it's likely that Mr. Jobs would have simply been the most annoying waiter in California'.

And as a commentator put it: 'And if "The Woz" didn't have Steve Jobs he would have been a really bright, lifelong employee of HP that only people within HP would have heard of'.

But, even if non-transferable, iconic models are useful as a source of inspiration (or the opposite). This is inevitable. Before Jobs we had the late Jack Welch at the helm of GE. He was treated as a saint in management thinking. I personally disliked his 'contingency leadership' style, switching ways of treating people 'depending on what was needed'. We have of course the ubiquitous Richard Branson, who discovered the Elastic Brand. These figures command a whole industry of books, business cases, and their own 'place' in business school programmes (examples, quotes, benchmarks). At the time of Welch in GE, it was impossible to attend a conference, leadership seminar or business school presentation without numerous references to him.

Iconic, one-off, perhaps larger than life leaders and their organizations, are a good place to visit, check-in, see the panorama, and return home in the same day. Dwelling there has little benefit. The real world is somewhere else. Get your souvenirs, write your postcards, post your pictures, take it all in and then get on with shaping your own life.

THE 3 GRAND 'D's ('DIRECTION, DISCOVERY AND DESTINY'), ALSO HAVE THEIR 3 LITTLE BUT POWERFUL 'd' SISTERS

In the book by Gary Hamel and C.K Prahalad, *Competing for the Future*, the authors launched what since then I have called the 3 'D's referring to a Sense of Direction, a Sense of Discovery and a Sense of Destiny. Although they explained these 3 'D's in quite ambitious business performance language, I always thought that the 3 'D's had their own little sisters in the form of a small 'd', perhaps less grandiose but incredibly powerful. I have used them in my leadership programmes since.

direction: not necessarily in the sense of conquering the Himalayas (or taking over a competitor or ruling in the kingdom of market share) but 'direction' in knowing where one is going and, in a rather prosaic way, taking others with you.

discovery: not the discovery of the breakthrough and then the new cure for the incurable illness, but a sense of 'discovery' of curiosity, challenge, perhaps seeing alternative worlds.

destiny: not the grandiose 'Save the World' or 'feeling the burden of history' (à la Tony Blair) but a sense of 'destiny' in achieving something nobody else can do.

I use the Pub Reunion test in my leadership programmes. An old management team gets together again after 10 years. Nobody is in the same position. Perhaps most, or all, have left the company. Write down your 3 small ds, I say, starting the sentence as 'We were the ones who...' What would you like to see or hear? I constantly get extraordinary accounts of small ds'. We were the ones who changed the way X was done for ever'. 'We were the ones who did Y collectively, who engaged everyone in Y, who took the organization in a completely new direction, Z'.

Remember your 3 small 'd's and play with them, with your team. Ask everybody to give some serious thoughts and bring their answers to your next management team meeting. You may hear something remarkable from people who would not have shared their 3 'd's, had you not asked them.

MANAGE THE INEVITABLE, LEAD THE UNPREDICTABLE, ALLOW YOURSELF TO DO BOTH

I've written several times about the tired distinction between management and leadership. It had its logic and purpose, and made the point many times. But never quite catered for real life. In real life, leaders have to manage a few things as well, and managers, perhaps, when they are innovative, maybe leading the way.

I prefer management as the practice of making sure that the pieces of the car work, the oil is in the engine and the drivers are trained. What happens, or needs to happen, or is about to happen, is perhaps inevitable. It is part of being alive as an organization. You need to take care of this and do it to high standards. But the inevitability of daily life may cloud the collective thinking and imply that this is all there is.

Growth, differentiation, transformation, aspiration, perhaps reinvention, and certainly going to the next stage of complexity and possibilities, requires us to seek the

unpredictable, the new frontiers, small font or big font Frontiers. And this is where leadership comes in.

I don't have a philosophical problem with the dual hat management/leadership. After all, the duality would only be a reflection of our social persona. We do that all the time in the family, in the social arena, the civil society. I don't see why business should be so fundamentalist, other than insisting on a semantic convenience and prolonging the inertia of the terms. If you can be a father, a husband and a friend without being labelled schizophrenic, I don't know why we can't all be Managers, Leaders, Followers and Fellows.

In the end, the fundamental question is: what do I need to manage in the inevitability of tomorrow and how can I imagine a day after tomorrow that is not a simple extrapolation of today?

THE BEST ORGANIZATIONAL MODEL IS THE ONE THAT HAS MORE THAN ONE UNDER THE ROOF

Command and control management has less and less friends, and it's quite terminally ill as well. The heirs are fighting for a piece of the estate, not quite sure what to take. It's the time to replace the organizational model, but not with just another one.

The history of management is the history of managing time, effort, and outcomes. It's a history of control that started with very good intentions. In the beginning, it was a case of making work more 'scientific' which was a premise to make it efficient, predictable and replicable.

Cultural shifts, technological tectonic plate movements and dissolution of a standard classification of skills in favour of mixed, unpredictable and constant new ones, have made command and control not a bad or terrible thing but simply something not as effective as before. Even traditional full-blown command and control structures such as armies have to embed some non-control and non-command mechanisms, such as the VUCA (Volatility, uncertainty, complexity and ambiguity) military concepts of the 90's.

In the other extremes of the spectrum, the love for self-management has increased. Self-management is not the absence of management but another form of it, certainly the opposite of command and control, yet not always understood as 'a form of management'.

As in any pendulum in history, the fancy guys now are the extreme self-management, represented by the iconic Halocracy, embraced by the likes of Zappos, and far from plain sailing, shift and implementation. It would be simply naïve to think that this can be implemented anywhere and with no liabilities.

We know that command and control is, at the very least, in an intensive care unit, and it may not make it after all. But we are less clear as to its real replacement. Empowerment, devolution, self-management, all go in the opposite direction. The problem is how much of this is fit for purpose in any particular organization.

The clue is probably close to what I call 'cohabitation' of different models inside the firm, the coexistence of different 'collaborative spaces', form hard to lose management (and control), instead of a single overriding model.

Another clue has to do with experimentation, the trying and prototyping of models. There are areas, pockets, units that could experiment with models of management without compromising the entire 'unity' of the firm. As with 'cohabitation', this requires a bit of courage and a lot of trust.

Leadership today must come with the request for experimentation. There is poor trial and error, and poor prototyping of organizational models in the modern company. We are obsessed with uniformity and with 'the model'.

The best model may be the one that has many models under one model, excuse the semantic trick.

A 3-POINT LEADERSHIP STRATEGY FOR YOUR TRANSFORMATION, SMALL т, BIG T

In caricature, this is a 3-point strategy to develop further. It's a simple mental and practical frame.

1. **Build an overwhelming, compelling, strategic narrative.** Excuse my language. The line contains:

   a. *Overwhelming*: not good, excellent, nice and clever, solid, well thought out, interesting, new. No. Overwhelming. If it does not feel like this, think twice.

   b. *Compelling*: the above needs to trigger 'I want to be there' or 'part of it'. The case for it (whether it is) is now overwhelming and compelling.

   c. *Strategic*: rule out changing the oil in the car for the next six months, as your transport strategy.

   d. *Narrative*: tell me the story, not the bullet points.

2. **Respond tactically.** Don't waste time giving an explanation to every single push back and 'yes but', because you'll spend your life doing it. If you 'respond' and 'tell me the barriers' airtime is bigger than the building of the future, there is something wrong in that culture.

3. **Above all, set the agenda.** Don't let other agendas come in. Be ahead of the game. Resistant people, 'yes but' people, enemies and other people determined to torpedo, need to catch up with you, not the other way around.

None of the above contains 'having all of the answers'. It is perfectly possible to create an overwhelming strategy, a great narrative, respond tactically and, above all, set the agenda and still say, come with me, we don't have an absolutely fixed destination, but I can assure you that you will not regret the journey.

By the way, I have not totally invented the three points above. But they come from the political campaigning arena, not from the MBA.

As I have repeated like a parrot, the answers to modern business leadership come from non-business places. Political campaigning (the good ones) is a good example. It used to be the other way around. 'Business experienced' people were supposed to bring lots of expertise to the socio-political arena. And that was flattering for 'business'. I think that today, this is very naïve.

COMPETING
ON MISTAKES

I have referred several times to Charles Munger, investor, critical thinker, 'librarian' (he reads more books than anybody else): 'we are successful (investors) by making less mistakes than others'. I have also referred to my initiation to boat racing as a learning platform for leadership and my conversion from sceptical to 'you know what? It makes sense'. The instructor said, forget winning each bit, you win the race by making less mistakes than the others.

I also know, and you know as well, that we have the management mantra of 'learning from mistakes'. A good management mantra that in truth nobody likes, but we are supposed to espouse to be cool. (Then in the corridor, the smiling conspiracy: yes, mistakes, really? Do you know what happened to John?).

I propose that we don't make a fuss about the so-called-cool 'learning from mistakes' and instead, starting with senior leaders, people get used to talking about mistakes, per se. My 2 mistakes of the month were A and B; what about yours Peter? This is what I will do next time. (Can you try to avoid the 'this is what I've learned' thing? Nothing wrong with it, but the focus is on what you'll do next time, learning assumed).

Only elevating that language and those narratives to normality, will shape a culture of real 'learning from mistakes', without saying it. The culture will become the kind, where you don't have to say it.

The boat racing instructor had no problem with it. Munger has no problem with it. Why do we, in management, have to look that clever and make the point? We are learning, you see? Just learn.

A while ago, I suggested 'The Hall of Fame of Mistakes' as a disruptive idea, easy to implement.

Given the temptation we all have to corporatise everything that is normal and convert it into hijacked and contrived reality, my only worry is that some people may go as far as over formalising a process for processing the mistakes and their processes. In public. Last time this was done it was the Cultural Revolution in China. I wouldn't like to see Maoist meetings taking over.

BTW, whilst Charlie Munger possesses a modern version of the Library of Alexandria, Mao and company had only one book. Tiny. Red.

Hominem unius libri timeo 'I fear the man of a single book'. It took 10 years in China to get another book. And by then the population was minus 1.5 million.

'GETTING OUT OF THE WAY' AS A LEADERSHIP STRATEGY

Also called, get out of the room and don't interfere. Also asking the question 'may I be, perhaps, actually, the cause of this nonsense impasse?' Also, possibly, 'am I talking too much?' (I need to practice that one).

My favourite model is 'leader as architect'. Leaders create the conditions, the scaffolding.

Scaffolding for assessment of opinions, contradictory views, navigating through alternatives. By definition, if the leader makes statements non-stop, even if he says, 'I am here to listen', he is not leaving room for possible alternative questions. He is providing the scaffolding, and the materials, and the plans, and the walls, and painting the walls.

Simple heuristic: if in doubt, leave the room.

If 'you can't do that' because you don't trust that the team would go anywhere solid, then you have a problem. Statistically, there is a strong chance that the problem is you.

There is a lot of 'you' here.

The reflection is simple and elegant: would these guys be better off if I left them in/with their own space? The honest reflection is what matters, not the answer.

Getting out of the way may be one of your most successful leadership strategies. Also, it's easy to test get out of the way.

'Just-in-time un-management'.

I am leaving you now.

IF YOU NEED TO PARACHUTE HELP, SEND BUILDERS, NOT PROBLEM SOLVERS

Parachuting in help is daily life in the leadership of organizations. It may take the form of sending leaders from outside the division, or internal consultants, experts, or external consultants. Or combinations.

Sending the ones with the answers is relatively easy. Fires are extinguished, anxiety is back to normal levels and the collective sense of accomplishment rules the waves. Crisis over. Next. Until next time?

If you need to send someone, send a builder. The one who takes the opportunity to rebuild something for the long term, to build capacity, to leave the scene not with a problem solved but with a root cause dealt with and fixed.

If you are in 'change management' (whatever that means these days) make sure your change project does not only change something but creates conditions for lasting changeability.

If you are intervening in a dysfunctional division, make sure you declare a sell-by-date and let the parachuted go back to base not a day later than needed, leaving in place a much stronger leadership team.

If you are in dealing with a specific crisis, make sure that the 'crisis management team' helps to solve the crisis and leaves the place with the lowest possible probability of a new one.

Builders are the heroes, solvers are the commodity.

HAVE YOUR BIG WHITE BOARD OF DISTRACTIONS IN FRONT. KEEP YOUR LIST VERY FRESH. THEN, EXECUTE THE STRATEGY.

If you want to execute a strategy, you want to keep cool and move inexorably forward, and you think you do have a clear strategy, the first urgent thing to do is to list your distractions.

List them all including the obvious ones, the small 'just a little deviation but I will get back on track', the 'surely we can't dismiss that topic', the off track, off tangent, the incredibly interesting ones, the fascinating collateral angles, the ones that need to be dealt with before X,Y,Z and anything else.

Have a Big White Board, or a big digital doc, or both, and label it 'Distractions', big letters, and have them in front of your eyes all the time. Look at that board at least once daily.

Add as you go along.

If somebody in your team thinks something is not a distraction, it should be dealt with, but if you think it is, you'd better have that conversation, pronto.

Be ruthless. Rule out compromises such as the 'also important'. If it is important it should be in the strategy. The 'also' is nothing but a red flag. There is no 'also important' in Strategy. If in the box, it's important, the also is redundant. If not in the box, it's neither important nor also.

When Barack Obama was caught in the controversy surrounding his pastor and preacher Rev Wright, the famous 'God Damn America', he tackled that 'distraction' (dominating national news) this way:

'We can play Reverend Wright's sermon on every channel, every day and talk about it until the election. We can pounce on some gaffe by a Hillary supporter as evidence that she is playing the race card, or we can speculate on whether white men will all flock to John McCain. We can do that. But if we do, I can tell you that in the next election, we will be talking about some other distraction. And another one. And then another one. And then nothing will change'.

'And then nothing will change' is our equivalent of nothing will be properly executed, or we will fool ourselves.

Obama's reaction is a good lesson on distractions. He stopped all the crap at that point.

Political strategy here, ours is business strategy.

Incidentally, that Big White Board of Distractions can be revisited any time and something could become a non-distraction. But, if going that way, make sure you have a very good reason and all the critical thinking seasoning you can master.

Rule of thumb, if it is on the Board of Distractions, it is. If debatable, what a wonderful distraction. Believe me, if in doubt, leave on the Board.

WHEN YOUR ORGANIZATION NOT ONLY HAS GOOD LEADERSHIP BUT IS A LEADERSHIP LAB, A LIVE SCHOOL FOR LEADERS, WE ARE TALKING SERIOUS CUTTING EDGE

An organization is super rich in leadership and becomes a Leadership Lab, a School of Leaders, if it has three types in store.

1. Good leadership at the top, is a given. Is there, however, 'collective leadership' within? The ability to function and perform with spontaneous, unsolicited, not dictated by the CEO, 'taking responsibility'. Translation: 'I'll do that', 'I'll take care of this', 'leave it with us, Peter and me', in areas, topics, issues that do not necessarily belong to the (representational) functional hat of the leaders. If this is normal, congratulations, but you are really a world minority.

My test, by the way, is when I see an HR super VP visiting a remote corporate land, presenting the overall company and business strategies to all in a Town Hall, not the HR strategy. Change the function HR for any other: The CFO presenting the R&D strategy, the R&D head presenting the overall HR, etc. In depth, I mean. Many people think this is silly. I think it is a sign of a serious blessing; they get collective leadership. They will be a great Leadership Lab. It's silly until you see it, then you realise its beauty.

2. Distributed leadership: a recognised presence of natural leaders across the board, regardless of their rank and position in the organizational chart. Plus, you do something with them, as opposed to admiring them.

3. A well-defined pool of transferable leaders, of different levels and areas of the business. Those leaders could be called upon to lead any function, any business unit, any affiliate, any new venture or acquisition. And they will be chosen for their transferable leadership capacity. Their original expertise, functionality, tribal belonging is irrelevant. A former technology guy now leads a commercial operation in X. An ex-manufacturing head now leads a technology venture. A former HR director now leads an affiliate. If this sounds crazy to you, you don't know what you are missing. If it sounds impossible, think about how to make it possible. If your organizations don't do this or can't afford to move people

around in top jobs other than at functional capacity level, you are not necessarily in terrible shape, but you are missing a lot.

I often hear, we have excellent technology leaders, or product development leaders, but we cannot give them a top commercial role. Well, sorry for you, but you need to do some serious soul searching as to why you say this. And, by the way, you have just told me that you have a wonderful Talent Management system. Really?

If you have that pool of transferable leaders, and use them as the norm, my second congratulations for the day. You are a minority. Make sure you publicise the existence of this, big time.

If you have 1 plus 2 plus 3, you are a Leadership Lab, a School of Leadership, regardless of your business. It must make your place very attractive. You must be very proud. Make sure people know.

THOUGHT LEADERSHIP IS MAKING PEOPLE THINK, OR THERE IS NOT MUCH THOUGHT OR LEADERSHIP. MAYBE JOURNALISTIC LEADERSHIP?

True thought leadership is not about conveying new ideas, showing directions for innovation and offloading the latest trends. There is a term for that: journalism.

Management gurus, whether from a Harvard pulpit or a Consulting Firm, who pontificate about trends or show their latest 'research' after interviewing 50 CEOs, and even provide tons of valuable data (legitimised by their brand) but do not make people think, think differently, or advance in their possibilities, are glorified journalists. And we have lots of them.

A lot of what comes to us from such prestigious business pulpits is of inferior quality to what can be found in the pages of the *FT* or *The New York Times*.

It made me think 'is this the most rewarding testimonial you can get, whether you are running a 50, 500 or 5,000 people organization, or you consult for them?'.

Mind you, you don't need thought leadership for your intellectual living all the time. You watch the news, read your Twitter feed and subscribe to those trend reports. We need all of them. But let's call thought leadership what it actually is, what it says on the tin.

Although, I understand the temptation, it always amazes me to see those resumes/CVs in the professional pages, digital or otherwise, that start with 'a thought leader, passionate for X,Y,Z'. And I often wonder where the title comes from. Self-attribution of thought leadership is a risky affair.

Personally, I have two other additional attributes to thought leadership, which I don't expect other people to agree with.

My real, personal and possibly untransferable trio of thought leadership is (1) It makes me think; (2) It provides me with some hope; (3) It pushes me to be bolder. Now, that for me is the Thought Leadership Premium Package.

WRITE A SCRIPT,
NOT A STRATEGIC PLAN

'A year from now, you are all standing here in front of the CEO and you say: we screwed up! Write the script for that year, what happened to take you there'. 'A year from now, you are all standing here in front of the CEO and you say: we succeeded! Write the script for that year, what happened to take you there'.

Very often I run these exercises, 'Success and Failure Scenarios', with parallel sub-teams of Boards, top leadership teams or management teams. Literally, I ask them to write those scripts down or at least find all the pieces and assemble them as a script would have been constructed, novel, film, short story... People are incredibly good at writing these scripts (the failure scenario is invariably faster) and can relate to them much better than an account of goals and targets as written in the Strategic Plan.

The storytellers inside all of us seem to enjoy the questions and the production of answers.

For a long time, in my work with clients, I have switched from 'Mission & Visions' to 'Space in the world' and 'Compelling narrative'. It's not a simple change of terms. The questions are different. The emphasis is 'What do you want to be remembered for?' and 'What's the story, your story, perhaps your unique story?' I also insist on writing down the headlines my clients would like to see in the newspapers in year one, or two, or whatever the time frame. A couple of lines, that's all. I have seen more executives surprise each other in this exercise than in many other times of interaction. These visual narratives are very powerful. They bring the authentic part of us to the surface.

Another method I use is to ask people to answer (all in writing again) a question posed by their children (or other children if they don't have children of their own): 'Dad/Mum/Sir, what do you do exactly?' The exercise always starts with some light jokes until it gets really serious. Try to articulate 'maximize shareholder value' to your 5 year old.

It's scripts, narratives, stories; not targets, numbers and earnings per share. There is nothing intrinsically wrong with targets, numbers and earnings per share, but the signposts are not the places themselves.

If you care about the journey and the place, you need a story. If you have a good, compelling one, there will be lots of good people travelling with you.

IF YOU HAVE TWO GUYS WHO THINK THE SAME, FIRE ONE OF THEM

I must have heard this for the first time from Tom Peters many years ago. He was, and is, and will be, the most non-bullshit management guru in history. At the time I thought he was like a hyperactive bright kid that, having done time with McKinsey, had escaped to freedom following the success of 'the book', *In Search of Excellence*. And he is still searching, now more than before, through social media, which he was prompt to adopt.

My take is that, yes, 'If you have two guys who think the same, fire one of them', the question is which one. And if the remaining one thought like you, would you fire yourself?

This is not a game of words.

One of the most unsettling things I hear, usually around 3:45 pm during a day-long meeting is 'I think we are actually saying the same thing, but with different words'. Dammit! 99.9% of cases, no, actually, we are not saying the same. This is just verbal Valium. And it works.

Not many people understand true diversity of opinions. Despite the music against, many hiring policies still provide clones of people on the payroll, just with more experience, or qualifications, or 'having done it before in a big way'.

Corporate life favours groupthink. I am not that worried about the big groupthink, the one so obvious and colossal that somebody will be bound to call time out and shout, seriously? Do we all agree on this? This is benign compared with the insidious Valium of 'I think we are actually saying the same thing'.

We need diverse thinking, audacious thinking, outrageous thinking and normal thinking all together.

In some organizations, if we were to apply Tom Peters' rule, the firing would be viral.

THE JOURNEY: FOR A HIMALAYAN TRIP, TRUST A FEW GOOD SHEPHERDS. INCLUDING YOUR COMPANY HIMALAYAS.

Organizational transformation equals organizational life. Sometimes we add an adjective to signpost a direction. For example, digital transformation. Very often I am not sure what the adjective adds.

My average large company client has at least seven big initiatives running in parallel. There is Six Sigma here, leadership programme there, employee engagement workshops, simplicity, diversity and inclusion, Horizon 2020, quality improvement, innovation programme, talent management programme, you carry on please.

Each of them would have their own sponsor, likely their own budget, their own tribes, their own need to deliver, their own defence mechanisms, their own identity and their own self-inflicted blindness to their neighbouring initiatives.

Ah, by the way, they all compete for the most precious currency in organizational life: airtime.

That the staff are often confused should not surprise us. Being clear would be surprising.

Programmes that are constructed as ABC, steps 1 to 8, number of workshops, number of activities, will be favoured. So, all those trains will depart from the same station at different speeds and avoiding collision, what else?

There will be transformations, however, that don't fit into a 123, ABC engineering style. They are more like a journey, where you need good equipment, a sense of direction and a shepherd if you are trying a Himalayan one. (You don't need a shepherd to go to the grocery store on the corner).

Those real, true transformational programmes are harder because they need a leader (a) who can trust others, (b) who is prepared to accept the unplanned and emergent, and (c) who does not have to have all the answers pre-cooked.

There are these leaders around, but not many. But these are the ones who can exploit the full, real richness of the journey.

195

ALL THE ROADS LEAD TO ROME, BUT MIND THE AXLE OF THE CAR

A friend of mine, Carlos Orozco, uses this analogy. 'If you are driving a car and you have a puncture, you'll try to slow down, maybe go to the side of the road, stop and perhaps change the tyre, or call for help. If you have the car axle (the axis between all wheels, *eje, essieu*) suddenly broken, the answer is not that easy. You may be lucky to go to the side and stop, but you can't do anything by yourself. Car gone. Big problem. No trip'.

He says leadership is the car axle, everything else is fixable.

I love the analogy.

You can fix technology, processes, systems, structures. But if your leadership axle is broken, all those investments go to nothing.

The quality of leadership is the holy grail. There may be more than one way to develop and nurture leaders, but you'd better make sure you have found one that works for you. A tip: it's a praxis, not a seat on a Business School course.

There is a measure of the effectiveness of whatever you do in this area: how many more leaders you have, that have been developed by other leaders.

If your company is a leadership incubator of some sort, regardless of the industry, products, strategy, etc, you have an incredible asset. It may sound obvious but the obvious is often the thing that is overlooked. Mind the axle.

5 QUESTIONS ROBOTS ASK (HOW TO SPOT A ROBOT, SINCE THEY ARE COMING)

1. What's your vision?
2. Where do you want to be in five years?
3. What are the three things you want to achieve?
4. What do you want to accomplish in this meeting?
5. What are the three takeaways?
6. What is the net-net?
7. Give me three bullet points

Robots ask these.

To acid test whether it's a robot language or not, imagine yourself talking to your wife/husband like that. Unless you go back home in the evening and say 'darling, what are the three things you want to achieve tonight?' (so, you are a robot), that thing would not pass the test. If it doesn't, don't use it in the office either (unless you work with robots, that is).

Somehow corporate language has become robotic. We have injected in people's minds a menu of questions that come automatically as default. Situations are even embarrassing. And, still, people carry on.

The CEO has just been in front of the group talking about the future of the company for 45 mins, Q&A comes in, and somebody asks, 'what's your vision for the company?' And it seems normal. The one who asks the question feels very smart. The CEO repeats what she has just said. No shooting. Nobody gets hurt.

We have been told that the robots are coming and they will steal our jobs. Afraid not. The robots are already here. The ones coming are second generation robots and they may even speak human language. Their advantage may be, to be the humans that we are not.

ORGANIZATIONAL DECLUTTERING: A CRUSADE IN WAITING THAT MAY NEED YOU AS LEADER

Einstein said, 'I soon learned to scent out what was able to lead to fundamentals and to turn aside from everything else, from the multitude of things that clutter up the mind'.

Many corporate initiatives compete for airtime in the employees' hearts and minds. Unnecessary organizational complexity and its associated terminology is a significant feature of modern corporate life. You don't need re-engineering, but simple, ruthless and urgent decluttering. Clean up, do less.

Organizational life is cluttered. There are calendars full of activities and meetings fill the day. The internal cycles (strategic plan, business plan, next year's budget) sometimes seem to have a life of their own.

People exclaim, 'I am doing the planning, the budget, the presentations. When am I going to do my actual job?'

People also need to attend training courses, professional development programmes, maybe even a leadership initiative or a work-life balance programme. And perhaps they also need to be part of a Task Force addressing the latest not-so-good results from an Employee Satisfaction survey.

And this is just daily life; just an average random Wednesday in the life of the company. On top of all this, 'higher level' corporate frameworks do exist: there is a set of values, a set of leadership behaviours, a credo, etc. Operationally, the CEO has set the six key objectives for the year and everybody is redrafting their goals and objectives to fit in with these. Many companies seem to be run on the basis that 90% of the focus is on managing internally/inwards and only 10% on the customer side/outwards.

All those initiatives create a corporate 'mille-feuille' with layers that don't usually talk to each other. Sometimes their only commonality is the fact they all compete for airtime. Confronted with this often overwhelming richness of corporate life, the average employee throws in the towel and switches off, unwilling to put some effort into trying to understand the connection between all the different things.

When I look through my client portfolio of the last five years, I could say that the average client has at least five or six major competing initiatives running 'in parallel', cluttering the airtime (not to mention an additional dozen or so minor, local or functional ones).

Decluttering is a truly disruptive 'anti-initiative' initiative that shouts 'Time out!' and forces you to review what's going on and to make sense of it all.

Decluttering can be done now. If you are in a senior management position, you could declare yourself to be the Chief Decluttering Officer and you would do your organization a big favour. It doesn't cost much and the sky won't fall down. Sure, you might upset some people with a vested interest in the cluttering, but that's a small price to pay.

This contrarian do-less will pay off.

If this could be copied by others and if each department or group had a decluttering objective in their goals, the business transformation would be truly signicant.

SALAMANCA, PLAZA MAYOR

SPAIN
AIR MAIL

I'LL SAY IT AGAIN: PEOPLE ARE NOT RESISTANT TO CHANGE

Am I the only voice? 'People are resistant to change' is the silliest statement people can make. I have written about this in many places and expressed it in many speeches. But how can I say this when we all see obvious cases of 'resistance'?

The contentious side of the statement – and this is not just a semantic trick – is the ARE. The 'are' makes resistance an inevitable trait of the human race. Look around: rapid social change, generational change, fads and fashion change, moral changes, and, above all, biological changes from birth to death. Now, try again: 'People are resistant to change'. Does it still feel right?

If anything, we ARE change. We are made of change; materially, biologically, psychologically, spiritually. Our clay is as changeable as the weather, the seasons, the day and night cycle. We are of a highly adaptable nature. In fact, our capacity to adapt as humans is incredible. We were born unfinished and imperfect for a reason, so that we can always change and adapt. We ARE the most changeable entity under the sun.

So, let's qualify, we may object to change, sure. When? When change is imposed on us without us having a sense of relative control or space for manoeuvring. When we don't see the reason, the need. When we perceive change as a threat. When maintaining the status quo is rationally or emotionally preferred. When we feel cheated. When we are attacked and our defences may require stillness. Keep going. Find situations.

But if we look at these situations with objectivity, we will always find not so much natural resistance per se, but reasons where resistance sounds and feels preferable to change. We may or may not be right in our assessment, but that's a different question.

The trouble with most 'change management' approaches is that they start from the premise that 'people ARE resistant to change'. So, when all you have in front is resistance, all your energy will go into overcoming that resistance. 'Here is the mountain, guys; get into climbing mode'.

'People ARE resistant to change'
is simply a bad start for anything that has
to do with change or leadership.

So how about this:
Change your default position as a leader.
Start with:
'People DON'T HAVE to resist this change'.
If they do, let's see why.

Now that's a good start.

THE TRAGEDY OF THE OBVIOUS

'A man was leading a caravan of donkeys and crossing the border almost every day, coming back with apparently the same caravan. Each donkey carried two bags of sand, one at each side.
The border guard got progressively intrigued and suspected that the man was smuggling something, hidden in those bags. Very often he would stop the man with the caravan and would search the bags, only to find sand and more sand. Over the years, this practice continued and the border guard could never find anything in those bags. One day, the border guard retired. Once he had retired, he went back to the border and saw the man with the same caravan. "Look, I am not in a position of authority anymore. I have been watching you, stopping you and searching your bags. I have found nothing. But I am still convinced that you are smuggling something. Would you tell me now? What are you smuggling?"
To which the man answered: "donkeys"'.
(The Leader with Seven Faces, 2006)

The obvious (obvious, from Latin *ob viam* or 'in the way') is sometimes unseen. That rather embarrassing stone in the way that you did not see. Ouch! That friend in the street that you did not recognise. OK, it could be worse.

Also, the obvious is a rather problematic term in organizational life. 'It's obvious' often implies, I don't have to think about it too much, it's clear. Read, a recipe for uncritical thinking.

But I could go for hours here, just to undermine the power of the donkey's tale. I'll leave it to their memory. Just see those donkeys in front, will you?

IN MANAGEMENT OF CHANGE, AS IN LEADERSHIP OF ORGANIZATIONS, 'EVERY DAY IS ELECTION DAY'

'Every day is Election Day' is an expression used in political campaigning and was widely used in the masterful Obama campaigns. The expression has also found uses in many other places to refer to how the winning of 'one at a time', bringing somebody new to the play, every day, all the time, is crucial.

This is a good, symbolic concept for management and leadership in organizations. Management of change is not a programme, or a project, with change happening at events and milestones. It is everyday leadership bringing along new people.

This shift from a programme and a narrative of Beginning and End, to a narrative of Journey where every day counts and every new employee on board counts, is a powerful one.

> Imagine the new day in the organization. Objectives, goals, dreams, desires, imagination, stretches, possibilities. Folks, it's Election Day today. Today as well. Today again.

THE TRAGEDY OF THE OBVIOUS, PART 2. THE OBVIOUS THINGS IN 'MANAGEMENT OF CHANGE' (AND STILL WE CAN'T SEE THE DONKEYS)

(1) It is obvious that top down communication and information bombardment do not create change, or at least not at a scale. Communication is not change. There is no change unless there is behavioural change. However, most of our management systems in organizations and many societal change projects are still mainly based on information. 'If we could just tell everybody, inform everybody, train everybody'. But no revolution has ever been created in a classroom.

(2) It is obvious that even if we admit that behaviours are what matters, still we treat them as pieces of information: we put them in power points and posters (and then we pray). However, behaviours spread by copying, we copy each other, and we are a very sophisticated copying machine. It's homo imitans more than homo

sapiens. If in doubt, look at your television screens.

(3) It is obvious that, if we agree that behaviours are 'the currency', and that this currency multiplies by copying, not by training or an information tsunami, then the question is who has more power to be copied, who influences us more. The traditional view has been to look at the leadership, particularly at the top, and it is hard to blame anybody thinking that way, particularly when we see the consequences of bad examples. However, the strongest source of influence in organizations and societal settings is peer-to-peer, what we see around us. There is plenty of data such as the Edelman Trust Barometer saying this every year for many years. We have largely ignored this, or seen it as a curiosity, or something that is acknowledged, but we don't know what do about it, because top down leadership and visibility and authority seem to be more obvious. However, for the purpose of culture shaping, peer-to-peer has greater power than the hierarchical one. It's tribal, horizontal, 'one of us'. Political marketing knows very well (data, segmentation).

(4) It is also obvious that most of that fluid connectivity of influence from peers takes place in the informal organization: the corridor, cafeteria, men's room, ladies' room, the water cooler, the car park. However, most of the traditional management efforts are focused on the formal organization: the teams, committees, structures, task forces. We have created such colossal teamocracies that people don't know how to interact and collaborate outside the formal straitjacket of the team.

(5) Another thing that is obvious is that stories are a great currency to spread change. But traditionally, organizations have used a lot of heroic stories (examples), it should be obvious that their effect on people is to switch off: 'not me'. They are useless as culture shaping. As opposed to the small stories of success of 'people like me', my peers ('I can do that').

(6) And finally, in these complex times of interdependence (I'd like every division, team, organization, business to write their declaration of interdependence), the top down leadership of before has tremendous limitations and it should be obvious that what matters is how leaders orchestrate things, sometimes silently. This is what we call Backstage Leadership™. It is the art of leading by giving the stage to others and these others are the peer-to-peer groups and communities.

I have described to you a few components or ingredients of the Viral Change™ Mobilizing platform. In Viral Change™ mode, we orchestrate large scale behavioural and cultural change by working in very precise ways with these components and others. It's a true 'operating system' for the company.

So many obvious things in front of us, yet we keep looking for what is smuggled via that caravan of donkeys.

3 INCONVENIENT TRUTHS ABOUT LEADERSHIP AND CHANGE

(1) If the top leadership of the company does not live up to expectations, and doesn't exhibit the values/behaviours that you want to install in the culture, then, you have a problem. If they do live by these values/behaviours, this is great news. Unfortunately, this does not guarantee any cultural change/shaping whatsoever. Looking up (to those leaders) is great for reassurance, but not an engine of change at scale. Looking sideways (peer-to-peer) reassures, reinforces and triggers behaviours. Much better. Stronger. Lots of looking sideways, with lots of people doing great things, shapes cultures fast.

(2) When standing in the car park every day, most people don't look up to the offices of the leadership team every day, when standing in the car park, to see how to behave. What the peer group does and what the unwritten rules of the organization expects, however, shapes people's behaviours and creates cultures.

(3) If you bring in the 'cultural differences' Deus Ex Machina, and assume that the above 'is not true' in some cultures and subcultures, so you continue to assume 'it is always hierarchical in Switzerland' and 'it is always non-hierarchical in Silicon Valley', you may gain some illusion of comfort with your own thinking, but you will miss fundamental and universal human mechanisms of social copying that don't know geographies.

You've perhaps seen examples of uprising and massive social change (including street demonstrations by the millions) in very hierarchical and 'looking up' societies. Last time I checked, those demonstrating and creating change were not Silicon Valley employees. I am afraid so many change practitioners disagree that it's hard to convince people that change management is learned on television screens, not in Harvard's MBA.

If you have a leadership team that is obstructive, does not get it, is uncomfortable with change, and is the cause of all impasses and all ills of the company, I have a strong recommendation for you.

Years of hands-on leadership experience, years of organizational consulting and years of… years, allow me to give you this gem of a recommendation: get out, move companies, move on. Life is short.

NO HIDING LEADERSHIP:
'WE ARE THE ONES WE'VE BEEN WAITING FOR. WE ARE THE CHANGE THAT WE SEEK'

I often use lines from Obama's 2008 speeches to ask leaders about their sense of destiny, small d or big D.

'Change will not come if we wait for some other person or some other time. We are the ones we've been waiting for. We are the change that we seek'.

'We are the ones we've been waiting for' means, no hiding, no postponing, no rehearsals.

It means there are things only you can do and if you don't, nobody else will.

It means stop thinking of managing the inevitable and focus your leadership on what will not happen unless you take that lead.

It means the Jewish tradition of the 'if not now, when?'

It means a sense of urgency.

It means full accountability.

'We are the ones we've been waiting for.
We are the change that we seek' is a full PhD
in leading change in one line.

PROLONGED AGONY IN REORGANIZATIONS IS SIMPLY BAD MANAGEMENT

Reorganizations often follow these phases: smell, gossip, announcement and implementation. The period between announcement and implementation is when most emotions are cooked. It's also often one of unnecessary, prolonged agony.

Management of change(s) may be hard enough as to add unnecessary anxiety. But this is what we see many times: a prolonged period of uncertainty when everything slows down and batteries are just about functioning.

If anybody could calculate the monetary cost of the prolonged agony period, the perpetrators of the gap announcement-implementation would be horrified.

But there is perhaps something powerful about announcing and opening the doors of collective anxiety. And power is addictive.

Prolonged agony is simply bad management. Full stop. Reasonable periods of unsettlement and reasonable doses of uncertainty have nothing to do with that, toxic, unnecessary prolonged agony of months if not years. And asking the organization not to drop performance, and stay 'focused', at the same time, is madness.

Unnecessary, prolonged agony in reorganizations is unacceptable. A terribly bad deal for owners, stake- and shareholders, let alone for employees.

And then we say 'people are resistant to change'.

LEADERSHIP IN ORGANIZATIONS IS ABOUT MOBILIZING PEOPLE. THE LEADER IS A 'SOCIAL ARSONIST'.

'A good organizer is a social arsonist who goes around setting people on fire'.

Fred Ross

Fred Ross (1910-1992), American community organizer, was behind many modern social movements in the USA and also behind the organization of many labour and civil rights activities. Fred was a formidable figure in American grassroots social organization, together with Saul Alinsky (1909-1972), the latter well known beyond his activism by his book *Rules for Radicals*, a left-wing how-to guidebook that no serious political movement, left or right, has ever ignored, either to follow it or to counter it.

I have spent a summer reading about the history of social mobilization, which the USA leads in quantity and quality. As I have said before, the USA, more than anywhere else, has been built on social movements. Most of them follow a well-studied pattern of struggle, success and exhaustion. Others will remain for longer as public platforms aided by the digital world.

History and personal education aside, I found the title of 'social arsonist' fascinating. I was not aware of the term until recently, despite the fact that we routinely use in our Viral Change™ Programmes, the metaphor of 'the mountain on fire' to explain how from a few points of fire (arsonist?) the fire spreads and suddenly the mountain is on fire. That is, cultures, movements, and organizations themselves.

We say, 'once the mountain is on fire, it's on fire'. No point in going back and dissecting ad nauseam whether it was the quality of the trees, the weather or a few arsonists, or combinations. Deal with the fire!

People mobilization is, by definition, at the essence of leadership. Happy to adopt the 'social arsonist' concept, for the Viral Change™ glossary!

I'M NOW OF AN AGE WHEN I ONLY WANT TO WORK WITH PEOPLE WHO WANT TO CHANGE THE WORLD

And still I get lots of people who raise eyebrows, people who look at me with a conspiracy-like smile 'you don't really mean that, but it sounds big', and people who would filter it all, going straight into their junk folder in their brain.

But I am not a politician, a Policy Guru from the X institution, or a professional philanthropist. I don't command armies, or run a Footsie, or am invited to Davos. Or will make it to Mar-A-Lago, or will be given an OBE by Her Majesty, or will be called to mediate between warriors, or run a global NGO.

And if you are reading this, chances are you fall into the same category. So how come?

When I was younger, I used to buy the story of the 'one thing at a time', the 'small change leads to big change', and the 'first change yourself' logic.

I was told to be patient, which is the equivalent of explaining the merits of sprinting to a tortoise. I was told not to put the carts before the horses, but the advice always seemed to come so late that carts and horses had already left. I was told that those ambitions were only for the superheroes, the writers of Hollywood scripts or the visio-luminaires à la Steve Jobs, and, by the way, that category was very small.

But, now that I am older, I don't see the point of aiming low and achieving, versus aiming high and possibly failing (Michelangelo dixit).

When you look around and see the truth and the lie being treated as equally moral; when you read the low employee engagement figures across countries and industries;

when you see trust at its lowest (pick a concept, pick a country, pick a profession), what is left that deserves 'small change'?

'We don't do small change', I put in some of the new company slides (more eyebrows raising). My company does not aim at incrementalism, yet that may be a very legitimate goal. We have painfully walked away from clients who did not understand that we did not want to sell our time, but share our expertise; that we were very asymmetrical with them in terms of P&L, but expected to be very symmetrical in collaboration.

If radical means to be back to roots, maybe we are.

And I know that we are not alone in this thinking. Far from it. There are many, who don't want to do small change anymore; who seriously question the little tweak here and there, whether in HR policies or organizational development, or L&D.

We live in times of scale. Large scale behavioural and cultural change (Viral Change™) for example. Not small scale management team alignment, with zero implications for the rest of the organization.

'Changing the world', for you and for me, may start with changing the rules of the game in the organization, the way people collaborate (for example from teams to peer-to-peer networks), the building of collective leadership. Maybe it is 'a world at a time' after all. Wait a minute? Did I?

When listening to the news, or looking at the twitter feed, I just have this urge to use the Michelangelo test all the time: 'the greater danger for most of us lies not in setting our aim too high and falling short, but in setting our aim too low, and achieving our mark'.

Will we? Who else is there?

Michelle Obama's line in the US elections, 'when they go low, we go high', was for me a Michelangelo-like moment, I confess.

When we see all going lower and lower, whether in the politics of selfishness or the disrespect for truthfulness, or an increasing *Homo Homini Lupus* fabric of society, that 'man-is-wolf-to-man' world, I am left with only one option: higher and higher. Change the world, I suppose. You?

FRAMING IS A LEADERSHIP MUST

1. Your mini revolution starts with simple behaviours

I put framing at the top of the list of 'leadership tasks'. One of those 'it's not rocket science' around us that we refuse to pay attention to. Because it's not rocket science and apparently, in management, we need to reach the rocket sciences qualification to be able to wake up.

Yes, I think that we, in business organizations, completely underestimate the power of (mental and behavioural) framing to trigger and sustain behaviours, emotions, ways of doing etc.

For me, there are 3 aspects of framing that are very simple, and perhaps because of this, we take them for granted, or simply dismiss them. These are my 3:

1. Framing of behaviours, so that they can be copied and scaled up (creating a particular culture, *Homo Imitans*)

2. Framing of the overall narrative of the organization

3. Framing of the use of data or insights

Let's start with the simplest components on the behavioural side.

On the behavioural side, there is plenty of repeated experimental data showing for example how being helped (for example to fix a computer problem) increases the level of collaboration of that particular group of people, who have been helped by the people helping them. Collaboration for completely new different goals. So far you may think, big deal. But here is the trick. The group that received help, increased collaboration with other groups afterwards, no matter what, versus a controlled group that had not received help. 'Helping' is copied and spreads. It frames the future.

There are lots of studies on the difference between people in a group that receive a clear 'thanks', versus a control group that receive a neutral acknowledgement. Similarly, the thanked group behaves differently afterwards on a number of parameters that have no direct connection with the previous reason-for-the-thanks.

Studies on altruism in neighbourhoods show similar patterns. Somebody starts, others copy, a critical mass is created, many other houses in the neighbourhood do the same. It becomes normal. No manual on how to be altruistic. No team, no committee.

Corollary is, start your mini-mini-behavioural revolution somewhere and be persistently focused on a couple of very granular behaviours. You don't have to explain much. Just do it. The more you explain why, the less power. Make it the norm. One-off shows don't work. You will be framing the conversation and seeding behaviours that may even seem small or trivial. If you get used to the technique, you'll see the benefits grow.

It's not a particular behaviour because it's good in itself (I am sure it is), but because you are framing what comes next.

2. Frame the narrative before it frames you

I have said that I would put framing at the top of the list of 'leadership tasks'.

I also said that we, in business organizations, completely underestimate the power of (mental and behavioural) framing to trigger and sustain behaviours, emotions, ways of doing etc.

What about the framing of the overall narrative of the organization?

Well, here are some frames:

Enhance shareholder value

Solve health problems

Improve quality of life

Transform the way medicine works

Enhance life

Provide innovative medicines

Discover new treatments

Make drug treatment affordable

Save lives

I have deliberately taken an example of a pharmaceutical company to make the point that

1. All of the above are theoretically compatible

2. But the frames are different, what you do is different, your priorities are different, the people you attract are different. All the frames are like roads taking you to different places.

It's not a simple question of 'language'. It's a view of the world, a concept of the world, in fact, a 'space in the world' (my preferred frame) that is different. Use the excuse 'it's all the same' at your peril. It's not.

Using the same example of a pharma company, I personally would like to hear how many lives you save, how many people are treated, how many kids are vaccinated, for example, as opposed to, say, how many R&D plants you have and how many people worldwide you employ. But that is just me.

These frames are completely different: solving, creating, building, modifying, inventing, providing, reforming, reorganizing etc. Choose your frame before the frame (by default) chooses you. Then you are stuck with it.

That words matter is not a novel idea. However, we treat narratives as aesthetic statements in their own right, not as triggers of behaviours.

For me, 'building' always wins. I am genetically unable to get up in the morning to 'reform' or to 'increase shareholder value'. Yet, these may be serious needs for many.

I respect that. But don't wake me up.

3. Intention and outcome

My third framing comment, after (1) framing new behaviours, and (2) the framing of the overall narrative of the organization, has to do with the purposeful use of data and insights.

The mode I use is very simple. I have encapsulated it into a meme: 'intention and outcome'.

Data is data. What you do with it, however, requires an intention (why you are saying what you are saying) and an outcome (what you are trying to trigger).

Let's say that 35% of employees do X.

'Only 35% of employees do X' has one clear 'intention and outcome': we are not doing very well; we need to step up our efforts.

'35% of employees already do X' means we are advancing, this is good news, would you not join that crowd?

In both cases the facts are the same: 35% of employees do X.

The strength of the 'intention and outcome' is even greater if you abandon the numbers in favour of:

Just about a third of employees do X.

Already a third of employees do X.

It's astonishing how, corporate language ignores the true power of the nudging frame and uses 'cold numbers' leaving the receiver complete freedom in interpretation.

I don't buy the usual charge of 'manipulation' occasionally attributed to my 'intention and outcome' model. As business leader or social change agent, for example, I am not neutral. If I am in a hospital and want to boost the 'wash your hands' behaviour (to quote an example we are involved in), I do care about what the data is going to trigger.

If I started from a very low baseline of people doing it, **'already a third of health care workers wash their hands'**, intends to signal progress. Even better if it's followed by 'join that crew, we need to get to at least half by next month'.

If I started from a baseline of people dismissing the call to action, or simply assuming (wrongly) that this is common practice, **'only a third of health care workers wash their hands'**, means not really, it's not the norm; we have a long way to go, don't be complacent.

Along all those scenarios, the facts have not changed: 35%

From internal/corporate communications to 'change programmes' of some sort, framing, exercising and testing should be mandatory. And, by the way, you can dress it all up with a lot of elegant cognitive sciences theory behind it, to sound scientific. Or you could just ask yourself 'intention and outcome' next to any statement.

MANAGEMENT TECHNIQUE: THE TRANSPLANT

The answer to individual negativity is group positiveness.
Fighting individual negativity at an individual level is a risky fight. If you are the manager of the chronically negative person, you may use threat (OK, up to you), may engage in a rational discussion about the negative impact of being negative (good luck), you may want to put up with it, you may pray, you may say, OK, but it's Jim, everybody knows Jim.

You may also consider this path:

1. Question. Is Jim influential? You'll need to define this for yourself. If the answer is remotely close to a yes (so he is an environmental health hazard), follow step 2.

2. Is there anybody who can influence Jim? If you are lucky and find more than one person, use them all. A group effect is needed. Individual confrontation, gentle or otherwise, is unlikely to work. Super negative people are not solitary hermits. They love audiences. So, give Jim one. One made up of people who can't put up with negativity. The closer you can get to gathering a bunch of peers, the better.

3. If all fails, the management technique to use is called transplant. Transport Jim to a completely new set up where people have no time for negativity, and one in which it may take ages to build a new audience from scratch.

Human beings transported to an entirely new environment respond by
deploying strategies and behavioural routines, whose own existence
is sometimes unknown to them. The new environment destabilises
old defences. This can go really wrong with weak people, like an old
person suddenly transplanted from home to a hospital or a care assisted
home. In my medical times, I have seen sudden deaths (I repeat, death)
immediately after a transfer of old people, otherwise with no particular
immediate health risk, from their cramped, not very clean, 'unsuitable
home', to a five-star 24/7 care assisted, residential accommodation.

It could be very good, like a student gap year in a new country.
Or an immigrant settled in a new country after an initial struggle.
Or change of schools, or moving abroad, or change of career.

Success is not guaranteed but it's worth
trying. In my old days as a clinical
psychiatrist, some of my greatest successes,
in some cases, particularly eating disorders,
were transplant driven. Short of a miracle.
Those steps 1,2,3 of social engineering work.

WE NEED THE ALIENS. EVERYBODY NEEDS ALIENS. SMART ALIENS WHO CAN ASK QUESTIONS AND OPEN PANDORA BOXES FOR US.

The best swordsman in the world doesn't need to fear the second best swordsman in the world; no, the person for him to be afraid of is some ignorant antagonist who has never had a sword in his hand before; he doesn't do the thing he ought to do, and so the expert isn't prepared for him; he does the thing he ought not to do; and often it catches the expert out and ends him on the spot.

Mark Twain (1835 – 1910)

Mark Twain had surely just had a bad day at the office when he wrote the above. Surely, he was irritated by those people coming along knowing nothing and disturbing everybody. Perhaps he had just been told that his new boss had been parachuted from a completely different part of the company dealing with business 180 degrees from his. I don't know, but, boy, he was irritated.

Actually, that quote starts with a paragraph before: 'There are some things that can beat smartness and foresight? Awkwardness and stupidity can'.

But with all respect to Mr Twain, we, in management today, need some version of the 'ignorant antagonist' coming to the party, because we spend most of the time worrying about the next best swordsman, and when he comes along, we continue as before with zero imagination.

If I had to choose an 'ignorant antagonist', I'd like the following:

- I'd like him/her to be smart, so the ignorant bit applies to the topic of the business but not to anything else

- I'd like him/her to be respectful

- I'd like him/her to ask, of course, lots of 'why', like a 3 year old

- I'd like him/her to challenge the status quo, but not for the sake of doing it, but to uncover the hidden possibilities

- I'd also like him/her not to be politically correct, so that he/she does not need to go around splitting the him/her stuff.

Bring the aliens. Ask them to look and see and feel and smell and make a judgement. A good, good, expert is the one who welcomes the aliens, not the one who is afraid of them or irritated by their presence.

In politics, we have the impossible hope of 'turkeys voting for Christmas'. In management, we have many cases where those people responsible for messy processes are now the ones who re-engineer their own, upsetting old roles and jobs. Will they vote for Christmas? Sometimes I wonder.

We need smart aliens to join the (management) party.

HAVE YOU HEARD THE ONE ABOUT THE THREE ENVELOPES? THERE IS A WHOLE THEORY OF MANAGEMENT BEHIND IT.

This is an old joke and a current non-joke. Here is the story copied from one of the multiple write ups available.

The story of three envelopes is a business classic for dysfunctional organizations. It starts with an incoming manager replacing a recently fired outgoing manager. On his way out, the outgoing manager hands the new manager three envelopes and remarks, 'when things get tough, open these one at a time'.

About three months go by and things start to get rough. The manager opens his drawer where he keeps the three envelopes and opens #1. It reads: 'Blame your predecessor'. So, he does and it works like a charm.

Another three months passes and things are growing difficult again, so the manger figures to try #2. It reads, 'reorganise'. Again, his predecessor's advice works like magic.

Finally, about nine months into the new job, things are getting really sticky. The manager figures it worked before, why not try again. So, he opens the envelope drawer one last time and opens #3. It reads… 'prepare three envelopes'.

But it is not a joke. It is a whole Theory of Management.

Here are some alternatives for the content of the envelopes.

Number 3 is always 'prepare 3 envelopes'. But number one and two work as well with:

- Centralize – decentralize

- Reorganize – keep reorganizing, you have not gone far enough

- Call BIG (Big Consulting Group) – Fire BIG, call SBIG (Second Big Consulting Group)

- Go back to your roots – get out of your roots, disrupt

And many others

The sad part of the joke is that it represents real life in many places.

I could imagine a start-up that creates pre-prepared envelopes and sells them to management teams but in bulk: three buckets of envelopes, number one with a variety of options, number 2 with another random set from books on 'strategy' and number 3 with envelopes with the (unknown) same content: prepare 3.

Kickstarter, I am coming...

THE SOFT STUFF AND THE HARD STUFF. CONVENIENT SPLIT, BUT UNREAL. LEADERSHIP IS NEITHER HARD NOR SOFT.

There is business and, then, there is all that stuff about leadership and teambuilding. This seems to be the worldview of many top managers and leaders. We have the value system and all that stuff, mind you, very important, indeed, and then we have the Strategic Plan. We have the hard days and the soft days. In the soft ones, HR performs. A performance that, although inevitable, is not necessarily too entertaining. That is why Peter can miss day 2.

We still think that leading and leadership is a layer on top of the other real stuff, real business layers. It's still a Manichean world of soft and hard, human stuff and business, HR and the real objectives for the year.

This form of Manichean leadership is still very alive. That is why when I see the real embedment of one on the other, a sort of Unitarian leadership; when leadership is part of the conversation about numbers, when numbers are part of the conversation about leadership, when operations and leadership overlap, it's a joy. I am privileged to have some clients who live like this.

When I am asked to speak to large corporate audiences, which I do several times a year, over a two day 'business programme', I make the point of suggesting my keynote on leadership, or change, or both is upfront on day one, so that the music of leadership and change can frame the rest of the gathering. I don't always win. It's quite common to see a split agenda where the hard stuff and the soft stuff do not contaminate each other.

The key indicator of good
leadership is seeing that it
is not an ad hoc, an extra,
a relax-and-talk-HR-stuff.
There's a long way to go, still.

LEADERS, DEALERS AND DREAMERS

Leaders. They drive the agenda, the agenda is not driving them. They drive the agenda even when other people think they don't. They want to make a specific difference, transform something, be ahead of the game on something. Leaders want to be at the core of key decisions, key strategies. By definition, leaders do not miss any boats. They drive them. Leaders have followers.

Dealers. They want to obtain something. They may aim at A and obtain B. B may be a good deal or a bad deal, but it is a deal. Somebody has something to give, dealers are there to get it, for themselves, for others. Dealers negotiate. They think of themselves as great negotiators. When they obtain something, they feel very good, often to the extent of consciously or unconsciously forgetting the value of what they have not obtained. Dealers have counterpart negotiators. Perhaps partners, but not followers.

Dreamers. They have imaginary views of worlds. They create stories about them. They believe those stories regardless their solidity. This is secondary to the dream. Whether a good dream or a bad dream, there is always a narrative: A Promised Land, a place to escape oppression, a nation in full control of its destiny. There may not be land, to be promised or not, no oppression other than in their minds, and no nation that can ever be in full control. But it does not matter much. They are very good at the fabrication.

Dreamers have admirers, not followers, maybe partners (in dreaming).

Leaders may need some dealers to get the deals, and some dreamers to provide the music.

Dealers can't do much without leaders. In fact, dealers fool themselves by thinking that obtaining the deal is leadership. Very often the leader is on the other side, giving them a deal that sounds incredibly attractive. It may be attractive, indeed; it may also be irrelevant.

Dreamers without leaders just dream, but they have a fabulous capacity to fool the admirers, again, thinking that they are leading. Dreamers like the dealers have come to believe that obtaining some deals is the same as leading.

If you adopt the working frame above, you have gained quite a lot in the understanding of anthropology in action, whether inside the organization or in society. You will then have to develop good logic algorithms of the type: if this is so, then we can expect X, Y, Z. Then, you will understand what is going on. And it will be fun. Promise.

Forgive me a societal example, a free diversion from my usual organizational focus. The UK Government has just achieved a deal that allows the country to escape from some European Union rules, such as benefits for EU immigrants, never joining the Euro, possibility of challenging financial laws that the City of London may not like, and, don't ever mention again 'further European Integration'. It has created, according to his Prime Minister David Cameron, 'a special case for the UK', a victory of great proportions. He now plans to campaign for a Yes in a 'in or out' referendum in order to avoid the so called Brexit. 'A yes, because we want to stay, because this is a good modification of the way the EU works'. But it isn't. It is a series of concessions to the UK government of the day. Full stop. This comes after months of negotiating with the European Union leaders, and on the back of a very significant part of the UK population that does not want to be part of the European Union, probably more than half of the country.

The United Kingdom is not a leader. It has never been. Not in that context. It has mastered Dealership in a way that suits the dealer. The UK (government) is not interested in creating a better or exceptional European Union. It's not interested in leading the breaking of unnecessary bureaucracy, the boosting of extraordinary innovation and entrepreneurship, creating a 'Commons' of the highest quality and, above all, them being the leaders of this transformation.

The UK is a dealer, meeting all the above criteria, including the one on pretending that they lead, and that their deal is a significant achievement for the 'Commons', for all the 28 EU countries. The UK Commons is not represented by the border of the 28 countries in the Union, but by a line on the ground within the island of Ireland and the cliffs of Dover. Nothing that David Cameron has negotiated and 'won', tackles fundamental issues of the European Union. It tackles fundamental issues of the UK Tory party. It's a deal, not a lead, let alone a dream.

Could the UK be (have been) a leader? Of course! It's a choice. It has great brains, great ethos, great societal fabric and a great deal of critical thinking. [Isn't it ironic that the European Union 'Constitution' was drafted by British lawyers?] But it does not want to be a leader.

It is a crucial time in the unpredictable, volatile and interdependent world affairs. Others will lead the boats, others will dream within the boats and others will make a deal about the size of the life jackets.

PS. For me, what a fantastic alibi to run out of space and not elaborating further and/or bringing other 'examples'.

OH, MENTAL FRAMES!
HOW EASY TO CREATE MISERY!

'Let's be real and aware of the current budget realities' is a warning that leaders should give to their people only if they are unreal people and unaware people. Otherwise, particularly when repeated in every single discussion, it produces two things: lack of imagination and misery.

Lack of imagination because it accelerates our minds towards what we cannot do, instead of what we can do, could do. So, I am told, in a way, to stick to the basics, bread and butter, safe and budgeted, why think further?

I have written before about how 'budget constraints' that leaders think (naively?) will lead to more imagination, often leads to 'mind constraints'. I don't have to think about X and Y, and Z anymore. No budget, not happening, oh dear, that's it. Of course, it could go the other way and spark some cleverness, smart alternatives and creative pathways. But, for each of these, I have seen ten of the opposite: collective anaesthesia.

Misery, because the airtime is consumed with the negative, what is not possible, what was perhaps possible before but not anymore, how sad. Said once, ok. Twice, maybe. Starting every single meeting with 'our budget constraints' or 'in the current budget situation' or 'let's be real about the realities', quite depressing.

In 'current budget constraints' (AKA cuts), the issue is not to ignore them or pretend that there is no pain. The problem is that talking about pain, referring to pain, discussing pain, lamenting pain and reminding everybody of the pain, does not take pain away. In fact, it multiplies it.

LEADERSHIP:
THE WAY OF THE CAT AND
THE WAY OF THE MONKEY

There are two ways to carry a baby – in ancient Hinduism tradition - the way of the cat and the way of the monkey. The baby monkey, weak as he may be, climbs onto the mother and holds on. The baby cat is carried in the teeth of the mother; no effort required. Which one is better, an old tale says, asking the question?

Is there a cat and a monkey school of leadership? The monkey school requires the effort of the follower. The cat school is content with holding followers by the teeth. Which one is better?

(Please don't say both or it depends. Thanks).

Interestingly, the Hindu tale continues by saying that the cat is better. "Yes," Prabhupada said, "that is the difference between the yogi and the devotee. The yogi is trying to climb on the back of the Absolute Truth by his own strength, but he is very weak, so he will fall. But a devotee cries out for Krishna (God), and Krishna picks him up." (Steven J Rosen. *The Agni and the Ecstasy, 2012*).

Question is, how much do leaders think of the follower's efforts? Sorry guys, you think that following is like this, but it's hard work! You need to climb and hold on, and who knows whether you'll fall, or we all will fall as a result. You are a bit heavy, you know?

The cat school of Hindu spirituality may be 'better', but I am not sure the cat school of leadership would be any good for followers or leaders.

Monkeys?

(With apologies for stealing the spirituality piece).

LEADERSHIP IS AN AMORAL PRAXIS. HOW ABOUT THIS TO START A CONVERSATION?

A label that could be equally applied to Mother Theresa, Hitler, your CEO, Kim Jong-un, Mandela, Abu Bakr al-Baghdadi and Pope Francis, is in need of some polishing. That is leadership: the art of making others follow you, forgive me the slightly unsophisticated definition.

Leadership is a praxis. Something that some people practice, more than learn, or teach, or that has a solid, unique foundation.

As a praxis, leadership is amoral. It's only good or bad, positive or negative, depending on what the leader does and how.

As leaders, you bring the ethics to the praxis, the moral jacket to the naked amoral practice. Once you are practicing, the practice is not neutral anymore. You can't get away with preposterous 'It's not me, it's the system', or 'It's not me, I am representing the company'. People using these don't deserve to be leaders.

'The ethics', of course, are not just personal. They include the values of the system, what is expected, accepted, tolerated, or nurtured. By the way, those four words are not equal.

The elephant in the room in Leadership (studies) is that the term is a host for a myriad of interpretations and logic. Perhaps my superficial definition above, 'the art of making others follow you', is as far as one can go when trying to look at commonalities between 'leaders'. Of course, I am in caricature mode here. But it is impossible to continue talking about 'leadership' as a well understood, you-know-what-I-mean concept. In that respect it is like parenthood, the art of bringing up children, do-you-know-what-I-mean? No, actually, I don't, because it includes loving parenting and child molesters.

I am stretching it..

Some labels don't help. 'Failure of leadership', for example, as a diagnosis, is as robust as 'discontinuation of energy based charged particles' is to define a power cut in the house.

So?

In discussing praxis, as opposed to theories or attributes or traits, the key is the behavioural translation: what is it that people did, or did not do and what happened as a result? I know, quite prosaic, but it's a start.

MANAGEMENT UPSIDE DOWN: GLOBAL IS LOCAL, LEADERSHIP GOES GRASSROOTS, TOP IS AT THE BOTTOM AND TRADITIONAL MANAGEMENT NEEDS A RETIREMENT PARTY.

It is perhaps the Age of Inversion. The weights have gone the other way. Globalisation, big G or small g, or just corporate speak, has not gone away, but the value of local is higher. Back is the local expert, the local grocery and the local travel agent. Maybe, even, the local bookshop, dare I say, that has more than books.

Top leadership is weaker than we care to believe. But this is such a sinful admission that nobody dares to say it. Top leadership is progressively less powerful; grassroots anything has great traction. The bottom has power: in the street, in political campaigning, in the health care system, in the peer-to-peer associations. The business organization is next. Employee activism is not employees giving positive messages about their companies. This is a prostitution of the word activism. And it is sad when I see it used as a mere employee with a megaphone. Employee activism is employees taking charge and being more and more self managed, not necessarily in the fundamentalist, extreme way. If you don't have a percentage of your workforce self-managed, even a little, you are not listening.

'Management' is literally upside down and looking for new ways of doing things, more devolved, more bottom up, more self-managed, more autonomous. Old words such as empowerment, delegation and ownership are so incredibly tired that they have lost their meaning. They need a break, perhaps a long break, perhaps retirement.

It is a new concept of the enterprise that we have in front of us, where 'community organizing' and 'people mobilization' skills will be a premium and traditional MBA management may remain but as a commodity. We will send people to understand and participate in social movements, as a way to skill them for leadership positions in the company. We will not send them to a Leadership Course in a Business School. We will hire people who have built something (a football club, a petition, a youth centre, an association) as a premium, and we will have the ones who 'can do a job' as a commodity.

I am not worried about the super-digitalisation, super-transformation taking away jobs from the robots. I am worried about humans thinking that the answers are more skilling of the last Century, or this one, à la Big Business School.

Business will have more leaders coming from charities, from the army, from ex-diplomats in war zones, from social movements, from people who know how to navigate life and bring others with them.

I am convinced. This is not disruptive innovation or innovative disruption or any other clever business speak. It is survival or prolonged agony trying to steer a ship that suddenly seems to have a life of its own. If done well, it's success, an exponential one.

Behavioural Economics, Social Movements, Viral Change™, Network Theory, Political and Social Campaigning, Large Scale Social Interventions, Design, Digital Activism, Voluntarism, all are in, and fresh. Traditional economics, traditional management, linear Kotter-ian change, academic 'research', mechanistic employee (happiness) engagement and old Business School lenses are out. Tired, aged, desperate for a retirement.

We are all very grateful for your contributions. Enjoy the freedom. Well-deserved. We'll call you if we need you. We are busy here figuring out how to look at the world upside down.

WITHIN US, BETWEEN US AND AROUND US. THE ONLY 3 CHAPTERS OF PSYCHOLOGY AND THE ONLY 3 MODULES OF LEADERSHIP DEVELOPMENT.

Trying to make Psychology easy! There are 3 spaces and only 3 that matter:

Within us: how can we get inside us, understand what is going on? Psychoanalysis tried and created an internally consistent super-logic, super-explanation, 'this is how it works' concept of Man. Unfortunately, provision of comfort is not a guarantee of the truth, and the truth is that psychoanalysis is very close to faith. Personally, I don't have any problem whatsoever with faith. Just things need to be properly reallocated to the right shelf in the library. I hate misfiling.

Cognitive sciences tell us a lot. Neurosciences tell us a lot, but we are hooked on technicolour graphics and 'love molecules'. Many things tell us a lot. Google maps tell us a lot (is Geography equal to Google maps?). I can't imagine any serious leadership development that does not include or is seriously based upon, reflection, old fashion introspection. Yet, many leadership development models are about how you deal with people in mode A when confronted with X and, of course, how B is much better if in front of Y. A sort of 'if raining use a raincoat, if on the beach wear shorts'. Contingency leadership is great with advice. It makes sense, I mean the raincoat thing.

Between us. Ah, the space between us! So many things going on there that you could be forgiven for ignoring any other space and using the Social Psychology lenses only. Transactions and relationships sit here. A whole Psychology industry takes care of this space. How much do we know? Well, we do know about influencing others, triggering behaviours, engaging others and so on. A leadership development approach needs to look at this space with the interest of the anthropologist. Just seen a video of people looking into the eyes of refugees, in silence, intensively for 3 minutes, person to person. That space between two human beings. The human transformation at minute 3.01 is simply spectacular, worth a year of Psychotherapy. No Social Psychology manual required. Try at home: executive to executive, executive to staff, looking at each other, eye to eye, three minutes. No manual.

Around us: Sometimes, how little we see or hear or smell. We can go around not noticing, not conscious of the broader context, of our minutia roles, yet uniqueness as fathers or brothers or friends. Old cliché, there is no other like you. Not a duplicate. Not a me-too. I can't imagine a leadership development programme that does not include windows totally open to the world, even remote worlds that we think have little impact on us. Here we are, our only me as me and a world of incredible complexity.

On the whole, my main worry in leadership is the abundance of 'this is how you do it' models and the scarcity of 'what are the questions' models. Introspection, reflection, going inside does not require going back to Psychoanalysis (too late), or Cognitive Neurosciences (yes, those colours and molecules go up and down depending on whether you make love or buy cereals, and?).

What about a mirror? And perhaps a friend, coach, mirror experts? I don't have a good answer. But I just know Psychology is not that difficult. It only has three chapters.

THE PILGRIMAGE TO THE TOP OF THE LEADERSHIP MOUNTAIN TO ASK FOR PERMISSION, BLESSINGS AND A BIT OF GRATIFICATION

Scenario 1: The Leadership Team/Top Management Team is in high control mode. They feel they need to make many kinds of decisions and sanction/approve initiatives. They don't trust people below much.

Scenario 2: The same as above, but they would not agree that they don't trust! It is just 'necessary' to work like this. It's a question of good governance. They don't think trust is an issue.

Scenario 3: The same as 1, but they wish things were not like this! Too many things are pushed 'up to them' that should not be, so they have to react and accept. And they do.

Scenario 4: The Leadership Team/Top Management Team is not in high control mode. They do not feel that they need to make all kinds of decisions and sanction/approve all initiatives. They trust people and let go of control quite a lot. If things are pushed up to them too much, they push back and ask people below to make that decision and reflect on why they felt compelled to send them that particular request to decide.

There are, of course, multiple scenarios other than these four, some above the extremes, some in the middle, some combinations.

What is crucial is to know which one is the one in operation. In my consulting practice as an organization architect, the prominence of one or another does not bother me as much as the ignorance of which one is in place. Many people think that they know, but, in fact, they have created a scenario for themselves that has not been properly validated. Ever. There are unwritten rules around what it is 'assumed that is required' and nobody has asked, is this really, really, how it is?

A situation I have found myself in very frequently, more frequently than just counting as an anecdote, is the one where teams share a strong assumption that they need to 'go up' for permission all the time under the banner 'this is how our culture works'. So they do. But 'the top', in reality, is not a nest of control freak people, at all. Their fault, clearly, is not to push back; they don't have such a habit, so it has become normal. But they have even articulated 'you don't need to come for permission all the time'. However, in this scenario that I am referring to, people still 'go up'. Why? It's not permission, they are seeking. It is (a) reassurance and (b) praise. The latter they may not accept as true; in fact they may be offended to hear such a thing. But the reality is that they play the 'good citizen' game, go up, 'ask for their invaluable input', and acceptance, get the OK, and descend from the mountain full of beans. A successful trip. Until the next calendar day when the mountain is open for visitors again. Then, surely, pilgrimage back to the summit with a brand new set of slides.

It takes some honesty on the table
(and in the water supply of the company)
and perhaps some guts, to stop and think;
unbundle these dynamics and understand what
is going on. But the effort is worth it. And it
may end up saving one or two pilgrimages.

20 RULES OF LEADERSHIP

I review my 20 rules of Leadership every few months. I have published this list regularly in My Daily Thoughts. Very few if any drop out but when they do they get substituted by a new angle mostly as a result of previous months' experience. This is my updated list.

My 20 RULES OF LEADERSHIP

1. Earn credibility all the time. Stocks deplete easily.

2. Act as if you did not have anything to lose.

3. Be unreasonable in your demands, the reasonable ones are taken.

4. Detect bullshit and become proficient at detecting it. Then, protect yourself and others.

5. Exercise provocation with panache and respect. Aim at being appreciated, not hated, for it.

6. Don't be a provocateur, rebel, maverick, contrarian or challenger for the sake of it. Have a good 'because' ready.

7. Infect others, don't do it alone.

8. Be restless, be uncomfortable (and foolish and hungry and the rest…). They're the only things that confirm that you are alive.

9. Watch your ego. Most of the time it is not your friend. Rule of thumb, most of the time it's not about you.

10. Never settle for one possibility only.

11. Don't waste your time managing the 'inevitable'. There is a lot of 'possible' waiting for a leader. Look for what would not happen without you.

12. Seek unpredictable answers. The predictable ones are already seeking you.

13. Don't be against anything. Don't create enemies. The exceptions are mediocrity and dishonesty.

14. Write down your little bit of daily legacy in a secret little book.

15. There is only one test: what will you tell the children? (that you do, you did, you didn't do).

16. More important than what you say is what people hear when you are saying it.

17. Practice 'I don't know', possibly followed by 'and I don't think you know either, so let's figure it out'.

18. Make things happen first, then clean up the process for the next time. In that order.

19. The unexamined leadership, like the unexamined life, is not worth living.

20. Play as many roles as you want, but never a victim or an enemy. Both being 'victim' or 'enemy', requires your full consent.

LEADERSHIP SCAFFOLDING. LET'S TRY THIS MENTAL MODEL

Leadership can be taught, of course, but not in the same way as teaching how to drive a car or how to cook a risotto.

I like the term leadership scaffolding. It means you provide the tools and the models to practice leadership, and to get better at it, with some kind of support system and safety net.

People can't do it for you. Leadership is a practice. Leadership development is no more and no less than leadership scaffolding.

The teaching, the reading, the looking at role models, the overgrown and overdone 360 degree feedback, the assessment, the simulation exercises, the associated teambuilding and the motivational speaking, all are part of that scaffolding. But only you are up on the building site moving around.

Leadership scaffolding is hard because it is not universal. It needs to be tailored to the individual, or the group in the case of collective leadership. When it comes to leadership, some people react well to sports analogies, other people hate them. Some will absorb inspirational reading, others will dismiss that. Some will need and welcome specific toolkits and how-to, others will dislike off-the-shelf, prêt-à-porter models. And yet, all these pieces have a role.

My personal position is that leadership (development, enhancement, scaffolding) needs to be tailored from scratch all the time. In recent months, I have crafted a full plan for one of my best clients. I found myself scrutinizing all I knew about the client and their medium term needs to

drive the next level of possibilities. I also found myself discarding lots of very reasonable themes in favour of what would be unique for the client. When I finished my rounds of research, reflection and thinking, I had built a plan which, on paper, only that client could understand.

There was something pure about the non-transferability of the plan. The scaffolding was, after all, tailored to their unique building. Out of that context, it meant nothing. By the way, I did enjoy it enormously, but also it was significantly more tiring than I thought, although it looked rather unpretentious when put on paper.

I suppose you could say the same about coaching. Coaching is a form of human scaffolding as well. Incidentally, something I don't do, despite everybody assuming the contrary given my psychiatric background.

Funnily enough, our motto is 'building remarkable organizations' and, at The Chalfont Project, we call ourselves organization architects. Maybe this scaffolding model comes from our roots and sits here comfortably.

I suggest next time you think of your team development, you consider 'scaffolding it'. It may be that this frame, in itself, could trigger lots of new ideas.

THE LEADER IS NOT AN ANSWERPHONE OR A HELP DESK.

In our Viral Change™ Programmes, members of the community of (company) activists, invariably ask questions such as, what shall we do with people who are negative? What do we do with those colleagues who are not engaging with me in the conversation? How can I keep my peers motivated? Etc.

In the early days of Viral Change™, we worried about this a lot. By 'we' I mean us as consultants, the sponsor/client, the project team members, all of the above. We felt compelled to have ready-made answers, a library of FAQs. So, we did.

But quickly we learnt that our answers were not as good as the answers of the champions/activists themselves, and, even if they were, champions/activists paid more attention to the answers coming from 'people like them', that is, other champions.

We soon switched the emphasis and diverted those questions to the community itself. Answers came back in the form of 'this is what I did' or 'this is how I would do it', followed by a stream of other people agreeing ('me too') or disagreeing ('that would never work for me, however…').

It was much better!

There is a broader reflection on leadership here. The leader is not a FAQ machine or an answerphone. The leader, however, must have enough insights on what is going on and how people do and solve things to say 'this is how other colleagues of yours have dealt with it'. And then, it is OK to say, 'I would also suggest'. But the power of the peer-to-peer engagement and cross fertilisation is never matched by the mighty leader delivering 'the right answer'.

You as a leader do not have to have all the answers. In fact, I would be suspicious of the one who does. My rule of thumb is 'the answer is in this room somewhere'. Most of the time, this is the plain truth.

WHEN NECESSARY
USE WORDS

Saint Francis of Assisi is a 13th Century figure revered as a Saint by the Catholic Church, and who founded three religious orders. He is considered the Patron Saint of the environment and also of Italy as a country.

Although always a key figure within the Catholic Church tradition, his name has been heard louder recently, because the current Pope, as soon as he was elected, took his name: Pope Francis. As a result, some renewed interest in what Francis of Assisi did or said has seen the light.

The very best quote I know is this: 'Preach the Gospel all the time; when necessary use words'. When necessary use words! I declare Francis of Assisi the Patron Saint of Management! Or at least Behavioural Change, Viral Change™, Leadership and a few other stocks on the shelves of the Management Supermarket. If we could just have this motto at the front of the management house, where we talk and talk and talk and talk.

We are 90% talk, 10% action.
90% thinking of doing, planning
for doing, brainstorming for doing,
deciding about doing, creating
the Doing Strategic Plan,
and 10% doing.

'When necessary use words!'

THE INEVITABILITY PRINCIPLE IS INEVITABLY WRONG. LEADERS MUST AVOID IT.

Years ago, political scientist Francis Fukuyama wrote about the End of History. We all are converging to 'the end': liberal democracy, give or take. It would be inevitable.

Timothy Snyder, Professor of History at Yale, in his little and fabulous book *On Tyranny*, describes what he calls the politics of inevitability. Translation, paraphrasing here, all will settle at the end. Bumps in the road, yes, but the road to that kind of equalised democratic ground is fixed. Inevitable. And he warns us against that wishful thinking. The disruptions we see and the disruptors who govern, or try to, do not give us any comfort for that 'all will be OK in the end'. In fact, he says that the Politics of Inevitability constitutes a fantastic alibi to do nothing and wait.

The Mar-A-Lago School of Deconstruction is so atrocious that surely all we have to do is to wait until the dust settles, perhaps somebody is impeached and the nightmare of crafted historical regression will end. It is inevitable. Well, Snyder would warn, don't fool yourself and, please act as if it was actually evitable.

The spectacle of an entire country thinking that it gains control whilst giving away that control, has baffled many of us (other emotions not quoted here). Yes, Brexit happened.

Frankly, many days look like the description that Hungarian Marxist György Lukács made about the neo-Marxist School of Frankfurt: 'they live in Grand Hotel Abyss, a retreat equipped with every comfort, on the edge of an abyss, of nothingness, of absurdity'. That was 1924, and the Hotel is still open and used by dignitaries who want their country either great again or simply 'back'. However, I am told, the views from the cafeteria are tremendous.

Leadership must fight those 'politics of inevitability', whether in the socio-political arena, or micro social of the organization. Leadership's motto must be 'everything is evitable' so, we are agents of our future and we have an obligation to craft it. OK, death is the only thing in the way, but some people are working on that little problem.

But, otherwise, don't sit down and wait for the inevitable settlement to sanity, common sense, solidarity and the rest. Sitting and waiting, being a bystander, is not on. Whether in the crafting of the future of a country, or in the steering of a future of a company, or the making of a community, nothing is inevitable. You'll get what you make of it. Big or small.

Perhaps the key leadership lesson for the days ahead is that the old-fashioned sociological concept of Agency, our capacity to act, craft and shape destiny, needs to have a big upgrade. Start with education, carry on when on the payroll.

REINVENTING MANAGEMENT IS REINVENTING THE SKILL SET. IT'S URGENT, AND THE ANSWERS ARE ELSEWHERE, NOT IN TRADITIONAL MANAGEMENT PRACTICES.

Reinventing management to deal with the complexities of the world and, therefore, the complexities of business challenges is something that, so far, seems unlikely to come from Business Schools.

Traditional management education has its roots in the past, more predictable and stable times. If you look at the entire encyclopaedia of tools, frames and methods, you'll see that they all look today like a brave attempt to capture a reality that is moving faster than one can handle. It's not that they are useless or inefficient, but that they feel a bit old and tired. They do not sit well in Silicon Valley or many other valleys for that matter. Of course, Deans of Business Schools may beg to differ.

The traditional human capital-oriented functions such as HR, OD, L&D, Internal/External Communications are stuck. Communications a bit less, if anything because the digital toys force that tribe to its upgrade and to play differently.

If you look at the HR/OD/L&D worldwide conferences, you'll have déjà vu. A slightly more elaborate Employee Engagement questionnaire, a sharing of the world ideas to reward employees plus, yet another praise

of the work-life balance world, do not seem to me like 'progress'. The tribe continues to talk to the tribe members. And they feel good about it.

'Specialisation' will have to start considering its own reinvention since no single discipline is any more capable of answering a business or organizational challenge. The Neo-Generalist (Kenneth Mikkelsen and Richard Martin, 2016) with a broad and mature formation, seems a better answer for the skill set that is now required.

Here are two examples of areas where 'the answers' now come from non-traditional business territories.

People's motivation, triggering new behaviours and understanding the balance rationality/irrationality of decisions, can be better served from Behavioural Economics. Yet, not many HR/OD/L&D would know about this beyond the anecdote (and if I infer from recent meetings where I have been a keynote speaker, not even the term).

Culture change and shaping, and large scale change in general, can be better served and understood from the area of Social Movements and other 'disciplines' (praxis, in fact) where people mobilization is the ABC, such as political marketing. This is what Viral Change™ does.

'Look outside' is the motto of New Management. There is no Plan B for that.

THE 'RESEARCH' FOR THE REAL-REAL UNIQUE ATTRIBUTES OF WORLD CLASS LEADERSHIP IS EMBARRASSING

I sometimes think that management thinking, management language and management education (that includes 'research') makes everything possible to avoid critical thinking. The same Die Hard Managers who love the certainty of a spreadsheet and believe in the magic effect of a revenue forecast, who declare themselves rational, critical and good thinkers, are the ones willing to put up with Harvard Business Review 'research' with the solidity of a cream cake.

(Sorry *HBR*, there is nothing personal here, it's just that when something is on your pages, it reaches Biblical validation. In fact, you've gone a long way from unreadable to pleasant to read).

Here is a text copied from somewhere. Forgive me for the censoring of names but be reassured I have not invented anything.

'Based on an in-depth analysis of over 2,600 leaders drawn from a database of more than 17,000 CEOs and C-suite executives, as well as 13,000 hours of interviews, and two decades of experience, advising CEOs and executive boards, X and Y overturn the myths about what it takes to get to the top and succeed.

Their groundbreaking research was the featured cover story in an issue of *Harvard Business Review*. It reveals the common attributes and counterintuitive choices that set apart successful CEOs – lessons that we can apply to our own careers.

What those who reach the top do share, are four key behaviours that anyone can master: they are decisive; they are reliable, delivering what they promised when they promise it, without exception; they adapt boldly, and they engage with stakeholders without shying away from conflict'.

Please note that it is 'ground-breaking stuff' and that it comes with big numbers attached: 2,600 leaders, 17,000 CEOs and C-suite. Big, solid research.

Once we have congratulated the authors for having managed an 'in-depth analysis' of 2,600 CEOs (I'd love to have a publication about those depths), we will be confronted with the characteristics of not-less-than-world-class leaders (title of the piece). These are, let me repeat, decisiveness, reliability, delivering on promises, adaptive and not avoiders of conflict.

Having had my own in depth research, I can confirm that I have also found these characteristics amongst my own sample population: my barber, the florist on the corner, my postman, my daughter's piano teacher (particularly that one) and the head of my travel agency. More ground-breaking, I have also found commonalities between my sample and the authors sample. Almost without exception, all have two legs, went to school, sleep at night and follow sports. As for the latter category, they are sub-classified into those following rugby, those following cricket (I live in the UK, guys) and those following none of the above.

I can also confirm that, without any doubt, I have also found lots of very

decisive people, who punctually delivered on their promises, were incredibly adaptive, never, ever avoided conflict, and are today unemployed, chronic middle managers, bad parents and owners of businesses falling apart. And, also, piano teachers.

Sorry, don't mean to be harsh. But it is exasperating the amount of real estate dedicated to crap arguments and a collection of cognitive bias. If you are not too exhausted, read this entry in Wikipedia:

'The Texas sharpshooter fallacy is an informal fallacy which is committed when differences in data are ignored, but similarities are stressed. From this reasoning, a false conclusion is inferred. It is related to the clustering illusion, which refers to the tendency in human cognition to interpret patterns where none actually exist. The name comes from a joke about a Texan who fires some gunshots at the side of a barn, then paints a target centred on the tightest cluster of hits and claims to be a sharpshooter'.

Management research breeds sharpshooters. Trouble is they also publish.

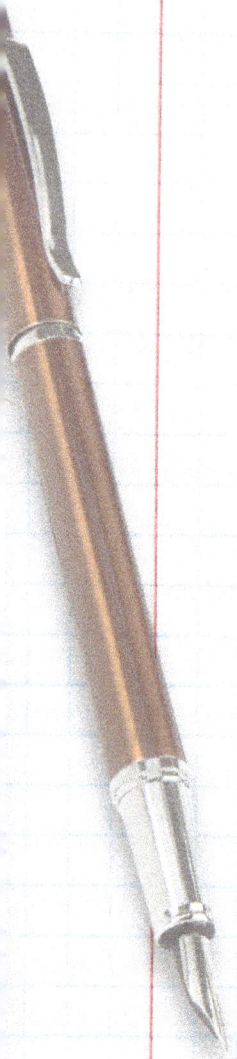

Santiago de Compostela, Praza do Obradoiro

WHEN MANAGEMENT IS OVERWEIGHT, LEADERSHIP MAY BE STARVING

I must confess I have never been 100% comfortable with the traditional distinction by Warren Bennis between leaders and managers which I always thought was too stereotypical: 'Managers do things right. Leaders do the right thing'. However, you read it, 'leaders seem to win'...

But there is a point in distinguishing between management and leadership.

I have my own three distinctions:

Managers make sure that the operational machinery works. Leaders make sure that *there is* an operational machinery that's fit for purpose.

Managers take care of the healthy functioning of processes and systems. Leaders ask the question, why do we need these processes and systems?

Managers push stuff. Leaders pull stuff.

An overweight managerial system reigns when most of the airtime is given over to processes, systems and procedures. Note that I am not saying this focus on processes, systems and procedures is wrong. I am saying it can be given too much weight and steal the entire airtime. When this problem is visible, it tends to correlate with a slim leadership system that does not have enough glucose, enough weight, to stand up and ask strategic questions.

The exaggeration of an overweight managerial system leads to managerial pathological obesity, with 'managing the inevitable' being the main symptom (i.e. all time is spent managing things that would otherwise happen).

Oversized management on a diet, coupled with slim leadership eating healthier and not skipping meals, sounds like a plan. There you are, the CEO as Chief Dietician Officer!

Backstage Leadership™ is key to collective leadership, a cornerstone of the modern organization

I believe that one of the fundamental types of leadership in this Century is Backstage Leadership ™.

This is the art of giving the stage to others, either people who report to you, or those who don't, but are highly connected, have high influence and touch upon vast networks. Backstage Leadership™ is leadership from the back, leadership without PowerPoints, supporting layers of (distributed) leadership in the organization.

When we were working on this a while ago, in the context of Viral Change™, we decided to obtain the trademark for the concept itself, its consequences and its implementation in the organization. Since then, the concept and its application have become a powerful tool for us as Organization Architects.

It's not a management trick to pretend that one gives space to others, but only pretending; in reality it's just false.

Beloved Nelson Mandela said; 'Lead from the back and let others believe they're in front'. Which sounds deceiving. 'Let others believe'. I have no idea of the context in which Mandela said this, but, in its current form, (if I got the quote right), is plain wrong.

It can't match Lao Tzu: 'A leader is best when people barely know he exists, when his work is done, his aim fulfilled, they will say: we did it ourselves'.

This Taoist invisibility of the leader will be hard to swallow in the modern organization, but the principle of 'they will say: we did it ourselves' is priceless today.

Backstage Leadership™ supports, develops and nurtures distributed leadership, therefore collective leadership. The three concepts, Backstage, Distributed and Collective are the Leadership Trio of the Century and the modern organization. Get them right, and you've done well!

Political movements know this, social movements know this, business organizations... Oops!

LEADERSHIP IS NOT AN HR TOPIC. IT'S ALSO NOT OUTSOURCEABLE. YOU ARE STUCK WITH IT.

Imagine this statement: Only 27% of global CFOs say they are well prepared to deal with financial management. Terrible, isn't it? Now consider this: Only 27% of global CEOs say they are well prepared to address Human Capital issues. Terrible? Yes, but a pure anecdote in the business press. However, this is actually what the Global Leadership Forecast 2014/2015 Report from the Conference Board said.

These global leaders (13000 interviewed) also said that they have 4 priorities: improve leadership development programs, enhance the effectiveness of senior management teams, improve the effectiveness of front-line supervisors and managers, and improve succession planning.

It's all that 'people stuff', isn't it? We keep going in circles. We need to de-functionalise the 'people stuff' from HR. Leadership is not an outsourceable function.

Any manager in a (new) leadership position should have a serious reflection time for a deep insight into his/her capabilities. These 'new leaders' need help. Certainly frameworks, and maps, and processes that HR can provide. But HR can't do the work for them.

Also, top leaders need to have 'leadership' at the top of the agenda, not as an 'add on topic' once all the operational conversations have taken place. A seriously engaged (on the leadership topic) top Leadership Team, and a similar mirror of engagement in their direct reports, is just the minimal condition *sine qua non* to function.

Ask HR for help with roadmaps. But don't pass the monkey.

ALL TEAMS WITH A 'SELL-BY-DATE'

> Imagine that any new team comes with a 'sell-by-date'. A label that says: 'This meeting will disband, no matter what, on 12th December'. The team has an initial formation date but also an end date.

One of the problems many organizations have is that they create structures, such as teams, with the hope of providing a platform for collaboration, but these structures are open-ended. There is no sense of when the team will cease to be. Rationally, you would think that this is when objectives have been achieved. However, these objectives may be long term and vague, full of more concrete, short term milestones. Teams tend to drag on in existence. We put time limits on external contracts, but rarely on internal ones.

You'll have many reasons to see this as nonsense. If the team is at its peak performance, do I mean it disbands anyway? Yes, I do. If there is still obvious work to be done, do I disband? Yes, you do. 'This is crazy!' Why?

You can make any provisions you want for a second team to take over (yes, you can share previous membership, perhaps part of it), but you must declare the team finished, celebrate, and start a new team with another 'sell-by-date' the following day.

Perhaps this is an opportunity for a change in leadership, a review of lessons learned, a membership swap, a knowledge transfer that needs to be ensured (because the crew changes) versus languid knowledge, only reliable in its documented form. Perhaps you can have some new crew members shadowing old team members for a few days or weeks.

After counting the reasons why 'this will never work', imagine the benefits of a constantly renewed team structure. If your main concern is 'disruption' and 'instability', I agree with you. This is precisely what it creates, by design.

See the other side: complacency is gone, knowledge transfer opportunities are high, professional development broad, people's minds are fixed on delivery.

Our organizations have become *teamocracies* with a life of their own. The team is a vehicle, not an end unto itself. Sell-by-dates will restore some sense of focus.

INTOLERANCE, DIVERSITY AND EXCLUSION: IT'S BEHAVIOURAL!

'Diversity and Inclusion' (D&I) is becoming a 'policy' that many Boards have decided to adopt. This is good. However, as in 'Corporate Social Responsibility' (CSR), one has to see what the terms really mean. Is it just nice language? Politically correct window dressing? Or real policy?

The answer is in what you see. If D&I is mainly translated into more women on the Board, or CSR consists exclusively of a green quota of some sort, then it is window dressing. If the policies are much broader, then intentions are more serious.

Even with well-developed and broad policies, people tend to get lost in the difference between policy and behaviours. You can impose a quota of women on the Board, yet women may continue to be treated as second-class citizens elsewhere in the organization. Policy can be 'imposed', behaviours can't. Behaviours are copied in the environment. It's Homo Imitans in action. If you have a climate of intolerance, a twenty-page policy document will be unlikely to change that.

Tackling 'intolerant behaviours' in the case of D&I is more important and more powerful than a D&I compliance policy. But intolerance is a defence mechanism. We can be intolerant in order to protect ourselves against a potential attack on our identity, our boundaries. When intolerance is part of the societal DNA, it is very difficult to breed any D&I within the organization.

Tolerance shaped in the schools will deal with intolerance in the community and ultimately the organization. The education system is the key.

Society knows intolerance well. In Belfast, Northern Ireland, back in 2014, you could see pubs with a 'Locals Only' sign, directed at the large Eastern European immigrant communities. Before that, not too many years ago, in English pubs you could see the sign 'No Blacks or Irish'. In my father's generation, immigrant Spanish workers were second class citizens in Germany. When the Spaniards became middle class citizens in Germany, the Turks took over their place. We never solved the question of intolerance, we just traded it off.

Back to Belfast of our days, in the Catholic, nationalist Falls Road, there is a mural of Mr. Gerry Adams, Sinn Fein's Republican politician historically associated with the IRA, that says 'Peacemaker, leader, visionary'. On the other side, Rev. Mervyn Gibson, chaplain for the Protestant Orange Order said: 'Sadly, it's not a memorial mural!'

Deep rooted intolerance will only be addressed by behaviours adopted and mimicked. For the social side, this may require fresh generations influenced by a healthy educational experience, but for organizations, surely we can be more ambitious in putting non-negotiable behaviours in the place of tolerating intolerance.

Top Influencers 2, Top Leadership 1 (Hierarchical power in the organization is half of the 'peer-to-peer' power)

Let me share a piece of our own research that just came out of the oven.

In a 1200 people, pan European company, in the financial sector, we have compared the power of the five person Leadership Team, in terms of messaging and engagement, reaching other people, with the power of the top five Viral Change™ Champions, defined as top influencers and hyper-connected in the organization. The analysis has been done blind and anonymously. All staff were asked a series of seven questions to try to identify the colleagues whom they would trust and reach out to, in order to obtain some real information, or the ones who usually reach out to them for the same communication purposes.

We analysed three steps (or 'degrees of separation') that can be understood as the immediate layers of connections.

One layer or step equals your immediate network, the second step equals the connections of that immediate network, the third step, the connections of those connections.

The results are revealing. By step one, the Leadership Team had a reach of 21 people whilst the Viral Change™ Champions had 104. Step 2 (connections of the immediate connections), Leadership Team 100, approximately, and Champions 3 times more, around 300 people. Step 3, 250 for the Leadership team and 450 for the Champions. By step 3, the five person Leadership Team was able to reach (tap into) 27% of the workforce, whilst the five top Viral Change™ Champions reached 49%, almost half of the workforce.

The power of this data, gathered through the use of Social Network Analysis (SNA), is its inclusiveness (all people in the workforce participated) and its anonymity.

The results reinforce the well established principle in Viral Change™ that hierarchical power is limited when compared to one of highly connected and influential people (Champions or Activists, in the Viral Change™ methodology). Of course, these Viral Change™ influencers need to be found, identified and eventually asked for help to shape a cultural transformation of some sort.

Finding the real influencers inside the organization is vital to orchestrate a bottom-up, peer-to-peer transformation ('change', 'culture', new norms etc.). It does not get better than this. Many organizations naively think that this pool of influencers match existing pools such as 'Talent Management', for example. This is not the case.

In the macro-social world, it has been a while now since 'the death of the influencer' has been proclaimed, for example in mass marketing. There are reasons for that. In many social phenomena, critical masses appear without clear individual influencers. However, inside the organization, the importance of particular individuals, not in the hierarchical system, is clear. Internal influence of the few is well and alive.

Backstage Leadership™ is the art, performed by the formal Leadership Team, of giving the stage to those real, distributed leaders who have approximately twice as much power as the Leadership Team when it comes to influence, messaging and communications inside the firm. Similarly, these influencers shape behaviours and culture.

Our data is consistent with Edelman's Trust Barometer that places the category 'people like me' (peers) twice as much higher than the CEO/hierarchical power.

Burn those organization charts! Other than being a sort of Google map for who reports to whom, they don't say anything about the real organization. Social Network Analysis does. Then, Viral Change™ takes over to shape a culture.

'It's about you,
and between you
(not us at the top,
not the leadership team)'

In one of the multiple accounts of the 2008 Obama campaign, David Plouffe, then campaign manager, wrote in his book *The Audacity to Win* about the importance of the grassroots movement. This may seem obvious and indeed common to many campaign and political strategies. What was different (and remains so today) in Obamaland is the extraordinary emphasis on the transversal, the tribal, 'people like me' connectivity and collaboration. Put simply, the message was a persistent, 'it's about you, talking to other people like you, not about Barack Obama talking to you'. Of course Obama did talk to them, and indeed with superb rhetoric. So they were not short of top-down messages. But the campaign itself de-emphasised that at the expense of the 'you and between you'.

The 2012 Democrat campaign outnumbered that of the Republicans by several factors of magnitude in 'local clusters' and their 'local organizers'. The 'total numbers' were less relevant than the clustering and the sense of belonging. It was about 'them': those local communities, local offices, local groups and the communication and connectivity between them. Then, technology comes in, of course, to facilitate things, and indeed it did.

We, in organizations, tend to dismiss this tribal ('it's all about you') element, perhaps in favour of 'it's all about the objectives, or the strategy, or the guidelines from the top or even the vision'. Obama and Co. also had

objectives, strategy, guidelines and vision, but they seemed to say, 'don't get distracted, focus on that vision, but it is really, really, really about you: how you discuss it, what it means for you, what you can do, how you can involve others'.

This resonates with our Viral Change™ programmes where we focus 75% of our time on the grassroots, bottom up, 'people like you' and 'it's all about you' engine of change, and 25% on the top down messaging. Messaging is very important indeed, but it is very easy to kid yourself and steal airtime with messaging, forgetting everything else. Messaging is the 'push'. Viral Change™ orchestrates the 'pull'. The more protagonistic the grass roots movement is, the greater the scale up of behaviours.

A good learning from the political strategists of Obamaland was that no matter how much top-down communication they could provide (and of course, Mr Obama did!), what really mattered was that transversal, local clustering, 'it's really about you', grassroots penetration. The Obama campaign was extremely successful because it was not a campaign but a social movement. Viral Change™ orchestrates these social movements within the organization and in the macro societal world.

Viral Change™ was published in 2006. Oh well, Obama did not call us, but then maybe somebody could have called the White House!

GREAT PLAYERS, GREAT TRAINING, WRONG GAME

It's a new world out there. You'll realise this truth if you open the windows of your organization and let in the sun. (You'd be surprised how many companies are run with the windows closed or with some sort of shutters, just to avoid this pernicious flow of sunlight).

The current organizational climate is very different from the one of just a few years ago. This should be stating the obvious and shouldn't need any explanation. But many of the changes and their impact have come to us at the speed of light – for a great part thanks to technology – compared to other economic, technological and political changes of the past. These days, people sometimes seem to be caught between the realization of the change and the semi-automatic reaction, all at once, all in one afternoon. This speed of change has left us little time to reflect. The new has taken over in the blink of an eye, erasing the memory of the old almost instantly.

Having agreed that this is indeed a different game, the next question is: what kind of new skills and/or 'new people' are needed for this completely different story? Over the last few years, organizations may have done well in preparing their people, developing skills and competencies and building their own pool of 'key talent', as people like to call it these days. The football players are strong, well cared for, well-trained, well-dressed and well paid. One day, they run through the tunnel onto the pitch, with all the new hires in a line and all their new gear, the excitement, the energy and the absolute will to win... only to find that the pitch is a basketball court. Great players, wrong game (or great game, wrong players)! This is my two-second diagnosis of many organizations where I am called in to help as an organizational consultant.

An alien just landed from Mars would be forgiven for thinking that there is an epidemic of blindness in many of these organizations. On one hand, there is an acknowledgement of the 'big changes occurring', but on the other hand, there is little change in the hiring practices, the organizational architecture or the development of people and skills. We carry on looking for the same sort of people, preferably somebody who 'has done it' before somewhere else. 'Somebody with experience'... that is: another great football coach to launch into the basketball court.

In the now ancient re-engineering era, the following joke was often heard. Joe's just been fired after 18 years of service. A manager says to that: 'There goes Joe... just made redundant, 18 years of experience out the window'. To which the re-engineering consultant replies: 'There goes Joe... just made redundant, one year of experience repeated 18 times'. Despite many toxic aspects of the re-engineering era, there is some truth to the joke. The only problem is that that assessment could also be applied to Mary and Peter and George, who stayed in the organization. The re-engineering movement did not direct people to the basketball court; it only reduced the number of stewards, cleaners and bar attendants on the old football pitch.

'PATHS, NOT WORKS'. A PHILOSOPHER'S METAPHOR THAT EXPLAINS OUR LEADERSHIP CHALLENGES WELL.

Philosopher Martin Heidegger (1889-1976) requested before his death that the collection of his writings be called 'paths' not 'works'. He had used the word 'paths' several times. It provides, according to some interpreters of his 'works', an image of 'leading' but not necessarily to anywhere in particular; like many paths do in the woods.

Good leaders are good path-makers. Sometimes the journey is not clear. The destination may still be ambiguous. It's the journey, stupid! Pretending that there is a fixed destination and that you know all the highways, roads and pathways, does not make you a good or better leader.

The great Spanish poet Antonio Machado (1875-1939) said it well in one of his most acclaimed poems. It would read in English something like this: 'Walker, there is no path to follow, you make the path by walking'.

The allegory of the Path, whether Machado's path-making or Heidegger's 'paths, not works', is a good allegory for leadership. I have spoken before of the leader as a Cartographer, as a mapmaker (*New Leaders Wanted*, 2007).

Pilgrimage is also a good metaphor for a leadership journey, a journey not in solitary but accompanied by followers. Not surprisingly, the image of the Journey is also frequently associated to leadership. The Journey contains all sort of challenges and discoveries for the pilgrim, as it does for the leader.

All this is crucial to a form of 'leadership thinking' in short supply: the reflective one, the emergent, the discoverable, the non-prescriptive. I make no secret of my mistrust towards 'a set of characteristics' or 'a list of attributes' of the good leader. Yet, I understand those 'sets' (very often of dubious evidence-based origin) as maps in themselves. I respect the maps, but not when they become an end in themselves.

I am in favour of any path, in any Journey, that prompts questions. Questions such as 'what does it mean to be a leader here?', or 'why would anybody come with me on this journey where we are going to make the path by walking?

I am worried about our natural ability to provide answers even without the questions. Off-the-shelf leadership development is not healthy. It is finished 'works' not 'paths' in the making.

POPE FRANCIS' DESCRIPTION OF THE 15 DISEASES OF THE CATHOLIC CHURCH ADMINISTRATION APPARATUS (CURIA) SAYS A LOT ABOUT THE UNIVERSAL TRAPS OF HUMAN ORGANIZATIONS

Pope Francis, spiritual leader to 1.2 billion people, likes to call a cat, a cat. He has gained a world cat-naming reputation, received with an equal mixture of excitement and joy, including non-religious people, and bewilderment and even panic; the latter mainly by his own administrative structure in Rome, or Curia. He likes to make off the cuff remarks, whilst all his predecessors waited 100 years before deciding that it was time to pontificate on something (and this word comes from Pontiff, as used to refer to Popes, which in Latin means 'maker of bridges'). I believe that the most difficult job on earth must be the one of Head of Communications for the Vatican. Francis is Authentically Disruptive.

I am bringing this here because, at one of his Christmas time addresses, Francis, in a well-prepared speech, launched his '15 diseases of the Curia', in front of all the most senior people in the Catholic Church. Leaving aside religious belief and context for these words, these 15 illnesses that he has identified, tells us a lot about the universality of the pathology in any big organization of any kind. Here they are in his own words, and a little comment by me.

1. Feeling immortal, immune or indispensable. 'A Curia that doesn't criticize itself, that doesn't update itself, that doesn't seek to improve itself is a sick body'. OK, so this is self-criticism, critical thinking, and a bit of humility. Corporates? Yes, please. We know about this. Groupthink? Yes, we can.

2. Working too hard. 'Rest for those who have done their work is necessary, good and should be taken seriously'. OK. Work-life balance, Vatican version, equally applies to the average business organization.

3. Becoming spiritually and mentally hardened. 'It's dangerous to lose that human sensibility that lets you cry with those who are crying and celebrate those who are joyful'. Here we have a version of social and emotional intelligence. Leadership 2020 needs this at the top of the agenda.

4. Planning too much. 'Preparing things well is necessary, but don't fall into the temptation of trying to close or direct the freedom of the Holy Spirit, which is bigger and more generous than any human plan'. OK, we in corporations, sometimes have over-analytical processes and systems that become ritualistic and suck most of the energy, shaping an inwards culture. Airtime is limited. 80% inwards looking, only leaves 20% outwards. Some parallels? Yes, Sir.

5. Working without coordination, is like an orchestra that produces noise. When the foot tells the hand, 'I don't need you' or the hand tells the head 'I'm in charge'. This is the 'big company syndrome'.

6. Having 'spiritual Alzheimer's'. 'We see it in the people who have forgotten their encounter with the Lord ... in those who depend completely on their here and now, on their passions, whims and manias, in those who build walls around themselves and become enslaved to the idols that they have built with their own hands'. These words have a precise religious context, but they apply equally to other types of 'Alzheimers' in which management practices become insensitive to the nature of a 'human being'.

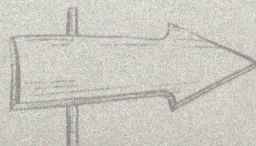

7. Being rivals or boastful. 'When one's appearance, the colour of one's vestments or honorific titles become the primary objective of life'. OK, this is corporate and leadership egos. You and I see this all the time.

8. Suffering from 'existential schizophrenia'. 'It's the sickness of those who live a double life, fruit of hypocrisy that is typical of mediocre and progressive spiritual emptiness that academic degrees cannot fill. It's a sickness that often affects those who, abandoning pastoral service, limit themselves to bureaucratic work, losing contact with reality and concrete people'. I don't know how to put it better in corporate speak.

9. Committing the 'terrorism of gossip'. 'It's the sickness of cowardly people who, not having the courage to speak directly, talk behind people's backs'. One of my 30 Disruptive Ideas from the book of the same title, and our Accelerators at The Chalfont Project read 'Go to Source, decrease the noise'. In any organization, there are noise Amplifiers and Noise Cancelling people. That he has chosen to use a dramatic term such as 'terrorism' to refer to gossip, says something about his brave stance.

10. Glorifying one's bosses. 'It's the sickness of those who court their superiors, hoping for their benevolence. They are victims of careerism and opportunism; they honour people who aren't God'. Mmm, should I bother to comment?

11. Being indifferent to others. 'When, out of jealousy or cunning, one finds joy in seeing another fall rather than helping him up and encouraging him'. This is a serious sign of organizational toxicity.

12. Having a 'funereal face'. 'In reality, theatrical severity and sterile pessimism are often symptoms of fear and insecurity. The apostle must be polite, serene, enthusiastic and happy and transmit joy wherever he goes'. This is a favourite theme of his: in his view, religious practice

does not need to be like going to a permanent funeral. Some organizational cultures are a bit like that, a type described by the great and late C.K.Prahalad as the 'Calcutta in summer' situation.

13. Wanting more. 'When the apostle tries to fill an existential emptiness in his heart by accumulating material goods, not because he needs them but because he'll feel more secure'. Much has been written about the corporate culture of greed. When is enough enough?

14. Forming closed circles that seek to be stronger than the whole. 'This sickness always starts with good intentions, but as time goes by, it enslaves its members by becoming a cancer that threatens the harmony of the body and causes so much bad scandals especially to our younger brothers'. In my consulting experience with organizations I have very often found the desire by leaders to create 'One company', where 'the whole' is priority, and where sense of belonging goes beyond your function, or area, or division, or country. Needless to say, we all, you and I, tackle this with different degrees of success.

15. Seeking worldly profit and showing off. 'It's the sickness of those who insatiably try to multiply their powers and to do so are capable of calumny, defamation and discrediting others, even in newspapers and magazines, naturally to show themselves as being more capable than others'. Comments unnecessary!

Although it all makes sense, it should not be 'unexpected' by somebody in my profession. It did surprise me to have this diagnosis in front on my eyes. It seems that putting people together, growing to a certain size and spreading titles, jobs and role descriptions, ends up in some sort of common pathways.

I would really welcome seeing any CEO of a sizable company stand in front of his top 200 and call a cat a cat in the same way.

BUT WHAT DO THEY THINK? WHAT DO THEY WANT US TO DO? WHY DON'T THEY JUST TELL US?

In my consulting work, it is incredibly frequent to see people stuck with a question: 'but what do *they* want us to do?'. Or, 'we need to know what *they* want so we can do'. Or, 'should *they* not tell us what our role (mission, remit) is, first?' *They* are the execs on the top floor. Or the exec suite. Or the ones with the closed office next door.

This is particularly frequent for groups and corporate functions often sitting at the crossroads between other functions or Business Units. I have in my mind Internal and External Communications, Branding units, Franchise structures, Project team structures etc. They all seem to need a clarification of frontiers, a declaration of borders, even better if that comes with Border Police and a Manual: this is mine, this is yours, do not trespass. Not unreasonable. Perhaps. In the 19th Century.

There is a hidden, or not that hidden, assumption that there are people (execs at the top) who seem to know the answer, but *they* don't tell you. If *they* just did, once and for all! Of course, in the absence of *them* telling you, a possible path is to guess. Here, the game of guessing, and second guessing, comes in, one of the most futile exercises in organizational life, big organization or small organization.

In my experience, nine out of ten cases when *they* don't tell you, is because *they* haven't got a clue, not that *they* want to keep it secret from you. I am saying this as a partial compliment, not a criticism. Of course, if *they* knew, but decided not to tell you, *they* will be simply deceiving you. Frankly, this is not my experience. The partial compliment comes from the fact that, at least, *they* have not made it up so that '*they* have an answer for everything'.

A good working hypothesis is this: there is no magic answer on the 10th floor. If we are stuck with this, *they* are also stuck. So, there are two options.

One. Wait. Wait for the magic to come down and put up with it if you don't like it. You may have, finally, tremendous clarity, a clarity that you may regret.

Two. 'Occupy the street'. Take accountability, take the space, figure it out yourselves. Chances are, they will very much welcome this. To the surprise of many of my clients, this is generally the case.

The reason why the above partial compliment was only partial, instead of a full one, is this: they should be more open and honest and say, 'you figure it out'.

The dark is not a workable leadership place.

THE TWENTY PERCENTERS

It is said that in any organization, 20% of the people do 80% of the work. I often think that this is conservative and strictly Pareto, but in some places I know it may be just or only 5%.

These, let's call them twenty percenters, are a heterogeneous group, but it contains real, real gems. If you discount the workaholics who grab work and spaces as part of their daily dose, and the ones that don't want to do it, but are forced to. The rest are Rough Corporate Diamonds.

These are people who jump in, you hear them saying 'I'll do that' or 'can I help you' or 'I'll take this one'. Other tribal expressions of this luxury species are 'leave it with me', and 'count on me'.

These people deserve the status of Protected Species and a double bonus, the order is not important.

You see them in meetings taking notes and sharing them with all, when nobody has asked them to do so, and when the risk is that nobody will. They feel duties that nobody else does. They have levels of commitment about several standard deviations from the norm. They are pretty silent about that. They tend to be humble, but not fools; unassuming but not invisible; incredibly helpful without necessarily stepping into well-known other's shoes. Employee Engagement Questionnaires have no questions to identify them.

They are particularly sensitive to the organization's Structural (Accountability) Holes: those grey areas full of orphan topics and actions. They take accountability. They are the Twenty percenters.

If you don't know them, you need to improve your social skills and buy a pair of spectacles. If, as leader, you know them, say a big thanks, tell them that they are not taken for granted, tell them how proud and privileged you are to have them.

As an organizational architect for many years, I see them from a distance. If I have to create a client project team working with me, I want them in. I'll be honest, the main reason is because I know we'll get things done. But the second reason is because I know, it will be a joy to work with them.

THE ORGANIZATION'S COLLECTIVE SELF-BELIEF IS OFTEN HIDDEN. LEADERS NEED TO HEAR THE UNSAID.

Some organizations or groups inside the organization, suffer from a lack of self-belief. You could say weak self-esteem. The belief system there is often contaminated by a narrative of impossibility. We are too small. We are too big. We are too conservative, or old, or too young. Or we don't have the money. Or we could, but the culture will never change. Or it will be hard, slow and painful.

The narrative dominates the thinking that, in turn, dominates the triggers for behaviours and the behaviours themselves. No point taking risks or being adventurous. Not here. For example.

Good leadership can change the narrative of the belief system. Being aspirational and inspirational at the same time as being realistic and honest about possibilities, is a good formula.

Leadership has a choice. It's called setting the bar. My favourite is the Michelangelo bar: 'The greater danger for most of us lies not in setting our aim too high and falling short; but in setting our aim too low and achieving our mark'.

Very often the true conversation on beliefs and expectations does not exist. Leaders need to hear what is unsaid. They need to go beyond what they hear and see if this is said because people try to please you. This is not even cynical or malicious or manipulative. Many people genuinely want to please leaders they consider good ones, made of human DNA, not robotic.

Ask. What do you think? Can we make it? Is this doable? And, by the way, speaking of risk, is this risky enough? For example.

FROM 'US AND THEM' TO 'US WITH THEM'. DON'T KILL THE 'US' ON BEHALF OF A FICTITIOUS 'GLOBAL'

I sometimes think that many global 'one company' initiatives are missing the point. The intentions are good: 'look, we are all together in this, all in the same boat, one family, one set of values and a culture'. It sounds good. And at the same time: 'we are diverse, respect many differences of opinion, sensitive to the markets and the local issues, we are all for local empowerment'. There are two narratives in conflict. I am not saying impossible to reconcile, far from it. But we need to acknowledge the tension. It is up to us to see it as a healthy or unhealthy tension. It is also naïve to ignore the tension and more naïve to try to supress it.

The one company narrative is particularly ill-constructed when it is based upon an ideological position, not on rational needs. I know of a case where the European region of a company managed to create a unique product development structure within the global product development system. The USA headquarters felt very uncomfortable from the beginning despite the fact that the European system was not in conflict, but it represented a high value, innovative add on (incidentally featured in a business school case). The tension continued until the European idiosyncrasy was supressed on behalf of the One Global Team. Read US. The One Global Team concept had no basis other than ideological and power control. And perhaps inability of the so-called Global Leaders to manage a global structure. But lots of people were very happy with the killing and preferred to have a lower denominator, global system. Managerial incompetence was hidden in the closet.

The 'us and them' distinction is often quasi-toxic. It stresses the differences and implies some sort of conflictual relationship. However, if you want some identity and belonging, you are going to need a dose of 'us and them'. The challenge for the leader is not to supress the 'us and them' by decree in the hope that conflict will just evaporate, but make the most of the 'us with them'. Build the with, retain the and.

Differentiation may be very healthy and helpful (may I remind you of the concept of brands?) or may be divisive and obstructive.

There is a choice. And it requires the leader to navigate through what is common and what is not, to find strength in the differences and to collaborate and be part of the bigger picture at the same time.

I have always said that acrobatics should be part of management education. OK, the mental one.

BLASTING MIDDLE MANAGEMENT IS A SIGN OF LEADERSHIP INCOMPETENCE

For years, middle management has been targeted by executives, business leaders, business gurus and so called 'change experts' as the origin and cause of all evils. The nicest things said about them includes, bottlenecks, resistant to change, blockers of information, micromanaging the troupes and, in general, those who 'don't get it'. The problem, that is.

Blasting middle management is a sign of top leadership incompetence. Most likely, all middle managers report to the non-middle ones, that is, upper management, or to the ones who usually criticise them. The criticism is sometimes obvious in leadership meetings when people in the room refer to those, obviously not enlightened enough, outside the room, as 'they'. 'They' don't get it, are a problem, difficult, uncooperative. We, of course, know what we are doing and have complete light descended upon us. It's a show of desperation and, for me, a bad behavioural predictor of the leadership capabilities.

I have made myself many times transitory-unpopular (in the road to permanent) when, in top leadership meetings, I have dared to say: all the problems of the organization lie in this room. I have said this very, very nicely.

As a top leader, ban the sport of shooting at anybody in the middle management field. Perhaps, once upon a time, you were also middle management. If there is a problem, fix it. Maybe the problem is you. Maybe not. But suspend judgement. Having dead subordinates is not a good idea.

Middle management, when there is such a layer, particularly in medium size or large organizations, is also the repository of a great deal of corporate memory. That may be good or bad. Good if there is a continuous learning mechanism. Bad if this is the reason why you continue to do the same as before and are stuck in old practices.

The role of the leader is to make middle management part of the solution, not the problem. Good leadership at the top is more about what happens below, than the maturity, cohesiveness, and alignment of the leadership team itself. That is always the easy part.

NAVEL-GAZING (NOMBRILISME IN FRENCH, SOUNDS MUCH BETTER) IS CONSTANT IN THE ORGANIZATION. THE ISSUE IS NOT TO DENY IT, BUT TO FIGHT IT.

There is so much to fix and manage inside the organization that the task could be never ending. Soon, and easily, one could find oneself 90% or 100% focused on the inside. Inwards management, or whatever you like to call it. It's a big risk and an almost inevitable one.

That is why a constant reminder of the purpose of the organization is needed. Without that, the customer-centrism stuff would be lip service, pharmaceuticals would be run with nobody pronouncing the words health, or patient, or, say, transportation with no mention of customer, other than the number in the spreadsheet. Exaggerating? Perhaps. But the risks of collective ego-centrism are always there and handy.

It's not enough to bring the customer language in, but it's a starting point. It's also about having that 'but what is the purpose?' question very clearly upfront.

With our Viral Change™ Platform, we often have simple behaviours such as asking 'what would the customer think of this?' or even 'wait a minute, why are we doing this exactly?', looking at purpose, high or low. These (disruptive, often in all senses of the word) questions are powerful to redirect the focus from the inside (the navel-gazing/nombrilisme) to the outside.

I am not a fan of Time Management techniques. It's personal! But very often the breakthrough in this switch of thinking has come when I have asked the client to record what he or she does (or collectively a leadership team) for a week, and then realised that close to zero time was dedicated to 'the outside', whether the client or the higher purpose. Although intuitively people tend to know that, being confronted with the 'recorded reality' is always shocking.

If the inside competes with the outside, don't let the self-absorption/nombrilisme win. It's a battle for which you need to be prepared.

Management: by invitation.
Unbundle reporting lines
and management teams.

Corporate grade reporting lines and membership of leadership teams
in organizations, often go together. But unbundling these components
is a healthy exercise and a powerful rule in the maths of change.

If you report to Joe, CEO, divisional director or country manager, chances are you share this with another eight or ten people who constitute Joe's management team, executive committee or leadership team. This is what the organization chart says. Most management teams are formed by what the organization chart dictates; by an 'accidental' reporting line. Everybody reporting to Joe is de facto a member of his management team.

In medium-sized or large corporations, structures are very often cross- or multi-functional. Imagine a Business Unit composed of a large Sales function, a smaller Marketing function and then a series of support functions such as HR, Finance, Legal, IT and perhaps a very small Strategy Team. The Leadership Team of that Unit is bound to be composed of the Director of Sales, the Director of Marketing, the Finance Controller, Legal counsel, the Head of IT and the Head of the Strategy Team. I suggest that this happened by default, by the dictation of the organization chart and that nobody ever questioned it.

But a legitimate question may be, 'does everybody need to be part of that leadership team?' Many people in business organizations would of course say 'no'. But the way we sometimes solve the issue is by promotion/demotion. For example, we may say only directors are really part of the Management Team. This is managing by grade, not by brain and it's not what I am suggesting.

Grade in the corporate structure (VP, director, manager, head) should not be a criterion of membership of a particular leadership team. Membership should be by invitation only. And only those who are in a capacity to add value to the role – whether they are in charge of a large part of the cake or not – should be invited.

It may be that, on reflection, the leadership team of the above Business Unit example should be composed of the Director of Marketing, the Director of Sales, the Head of HR and two country managers who do not report directly to the top leader of the Business Unit, but who are called upon to serve on that Leadership Team.

There may be alternative arrangements, but the principle is one of 'by invitation only'. A principle that forces you to stop taking for granted, the fact that membership will happen automatically or that grade or rank are a form of entitlement. It may be counterintuitive at first, but it is very effective. Much of the counterintuitive aspect comes from the fact that we tend to have pre-conceived ideas about how the organization should work. Sometimes these ideas carry flawed assumptions:

1. We must be inclusive. Yes, I agree but it is inclusiveness by invitation. If people feel the need to have all the direct reports together from time to time or, indeed, on a regular basis, they could have some sort of 'Staff Committee' (of all direct reports) if there were reasons for them to meet. But Staff Committee is not the same as a leadership team.

2. We must be fair. That assumes that all reporting lines to Joe are equal. In the above example, it may have been considered unfair to the Financial Controller not to include him in the Leadership Team. There is nothing unfair about a selection made on transparent grounds. Inclusiveness and so-called fairness sometimes result in gross unfairness to the group, because the artificial composition makes the team ineffective or highly unbalanced.

3. We must be democratic. Democracy is a form of government, not a type of organization (unless you work for a company that ballots everybody to elect a CEO!).

When you question management team compositions for the first time and, de facto, try to unbundle corporate grades, leadership and reporting lines, you will encounter some negative reactions and a few puzzled faces. But once this has been accepted as a legitimate questioning of the status quo, a breeze of healthy fresh air will start to flow through your organization!

Something that you may want to try as a model to follow is the Board of Directors. Though there are some differences between countries, a Board of Directors in public companies is usually composed of a few executives and some non-executive directors, who are either representing some shareholder sector or participating as members on their own capacity, background, experience or particular expertise. We have accepted this kind of designed composition as normal when it comes to the Board, but this is far from common for executive and leadership committees. But there is no reason why you could not mirror this, unless you want to stick to the default position because, 'we have never done it like that'.

THE PROBLEM WITH TOO MANY DECISIONS PUSHED UP TO THE TOP OF THE ORGANIZATION USUALLY LIES WITH THOSE AT THE TOP WHO COMPLAIN MOST

When too many decisions are pushed upwards in the organization, and the top layers of leadership complain about it, often in an almost victimised way, the problem usually lies at that top leadership. It's simple. What people at the top say and what they do about it are disconnected.

You can blame processes and systems, decision rights, low empowerment or any other thing. If the behaviour persists it is because it is reinforced. And it is reinforced not by dealing with it, but by accepting it.

General Charles de Gaulle said that 'the graveyards are full of indispensable men'. You could prevent the Leadership Team and teams at the top becoming graveyards.

I have met a CEO who carries a little spreadsheet with her, with the salaries of the members of the Executive Committee on. When a decision is questioned and comes up at the top table, and perhaps dealt with, she asks: was this decision worth 3K or 4K etc? Harsh perhaps, but it makes the point.

Behaviours are perpetuated because they are reinforced. In this case, attention is the reinforcement. Complaining afterwards adds the little victim colour. The problem is at the top.

If the top wants to empower, it needs to make a list of usual decisions and lose control of some of them. One of them, once a month. The more control they lose, the more control they will have.

> The greatest control is achieved when one does not have to control anything. The ultimate goal of the leader is to lose control.

10 REASONS WHY YOU SHOULD RETIRE 'PASSION' FROM YOUR VALUE SYSTEM

1. Passion is an emotion or set of emotions. You may wish, indeed, that your people are passionate, but you can't simply command it, train for it (have workshops about how to be passionate) or order 'we will be passionate'.

2. You can model it, yes. You yourself can be passionate and then perhaps others will be passionate or behave passionately. If you as leader don't know how to model it, don't ask others. I've seen many non-passionate Leadership Teams in my life, declaring passion as a value.

3. Passion is always portrayed as an input. Insert passion, get good work. But in my (behavioural) view, passion is in fact an output. Do satisfying work, you'll be passionate (I can hear the 'It's both brigade' already). I repeat, do you want passion around? Do stuff people can feel passionate about.

4. Passion as a value in a value system is lazy thinking. Who is against? So that's easy. It assumes that by declaring it, stating it and putting it on the wall, it will happen. It does not take much to write it down in the mission and vision statement or the values. And then what?

5. You can't intellectually force passion on others. You can't force or expect an emotional presence, say, in the same way as saying to employees 'be happy'. If you want happy employees, give them the environment and wait, don't declare the requirement for happiness first and expect people will create an environment for you.

6. If you insist with the word, tell me what you want to see in people that, when seen, at a scale, you can say 'that's passion'. Then we could perhaps start a conversation about the behavioural translation of passion. No behavioural translation, don't carry on. Leave it. Incidentally, be careful with the transcultural essence of passion. The potential for ridicule is enormous.

7. If you think that given the above, I am dismissing or ridiculing passion, nothing is so far from the truth. Also, if so, I am doing a bad job. I love to work with people who exhibit passion for something, versus the alternative. But 'the exhibition of passion' does not equal loud voice, high tone or clapping in the corridor. The quiet writer shaping characters on a piece of paper every morning with a cup of coffee, may be truly passionate about what is coming out, yet we may just see a gentle smile.

8. The mistake I am talking about is the commoditising of passion in corporate life, the acquisition of the language of passion as an alibi for the lack of critical thinking ((a) who could be against it? and (b) what is it?); the appropriation of an emotional space as input, when the effort should be driven to produce an output.

9. Passion as an emotion (see above) is energy, drive, adrenaline. These things are not good or bad intrinsically. High octane passion in the wrong direction will need a few dispassionate leaders to come to the rescue. Naïve change management systems look for passionate people (whilst we in Viral Change™ look for highly connected ones), expecting that they will 'change things'. Yes, this is right, but in what direction?

10. 'Passion for technology', 'passion for customers', 'passion for X' is (1) meaningless and (2) egocentric. The customer says, good for you, let's see it. If you are a technology company and you tell me that you are passionate about technology, I will say congratulations, you seem to be in the right place. Now, tell me who the hell are you? I have another 25 saying the same.

I WOULDN'T HIRE ANYBODY WHO IS LIKELY TO FOLLOW THE JOB DESCRIPTION

The job description is dead. It is replaced by a Lego box, no instruction manual, just a map.

'Welcome to the company. Good to have you. Your business card says Director of Business Development, but this is only in case you meet another Director of Business Development somewhere, so you don't feel too lonely.

Your role is to get this Lego box of pieces called possibilities and build something. And then another thing. Here is the map. We are going somewhere around here, and if you could help us to figure out how to get there safe, fast and profitably, it would be much appreciated. Mind you, the 'somewhere around here' may change a bit, so you'll have to be flexible and prepared to abandon the halfmade helicopter Lego model, and perhaps use some of the pieces for a submarine.

We hired you because you are, or we think you are, an entrepreneur. We don't hire employees with background and skills anymore. We hire entrepreneurs with some background and skills. Which means, entrepreneur as in 'undertaking' something, you know, actually doing something, as supposed to thinking of doing. Also, we love an old version of the term used in France somewhere in the 18thCentury that says entrepreneur is 'bearer of risk'.

So, just for the record. We don't mean busy-ness, we mean business. We don't mean any risk, we don't mean chaos and we don't mean permanent state of blue sky thinking. In fact, we are not much in the sky, but with our feet on the ground.

As you will find out in the next hour or so, your business card title bears no consequence internally, where colleagues do many things that the business card never says.

Here is the credit card, the toilets are to the left and then take a right, build your Lego, get moving, help us on the journey and have some fun. By the way, these are the non-negotiable behaviours in this journey: (specific list to continue here)'.

Commentary. No standard, inflexible, pre-defined job description has a place today in the knowledge economy (grrr, sorry, the term is so old). We are kidding ourselves. I personally would not hire anybody who is determined to follow their role description to the letter. So, whoever thinks like me, can we please stop writing those jobs descriptions as a shopping list for the supermarket?

The push back I frequently get is: surely you don't mean any job description? To which I tend to twist the question and ask them to list the jobs that could not follow the above rule. Usually, the list contains the ones that are most likely to be taken over by the digital revolution.

This position is not anti-skills or experts either! If I have a brain tumour, I want a neurosurgeon, not a paramedic. But, no apologies, I want accountants who can spell passion, passionate business developers who can spell spreadsheet, HR people who can spell R&D and R&D people who can sell something. It's 2020 if you noticed.

> Just get lots of Lego Boxes of Possibilities,
> some maps and good leaders and forget the
> Quantum-Physics-like Competence System.
> It looks good on PowerPoint and impresses the
> CEO, but it's as useful as a little boat in a tsunami.

EMPLOYEE LOYALTY IS A PLURAL. LEADERSHIP IS THE HOST OF THAT PLURALITY, ALWAYS AN IRRATIONAL MIX.

What should employees be loyal to? Ask an average leader: to the company, of course. Loyalty may be disguised. It may be called something else, perhaps commitment, dare I say a form of (here we go again) employee engagement. In any case, as in 'engagement', there is no point to ask for 'loyalty' without more qualifications. But there is a lot of a point to understand that plurality.

People in organizations are loyal to many things:

1. To a cause. It may be the company's cause, or not. It may be an ideal cause that the company may not even have, but people pretend it's there.

2. To people, friends, colleagues. Sometimes, this is a reason to stay in a job that is not satisfying, or to prolong the agony of a dysfunctional working situation.

3. To a place. People may find it difficult to move offices, or sites. It's quite irrational sometimes, but powerful. Place and space have high magnetic properties.

4. To a figure, a person, a leader, such as the CEO. Even if that CEO has perhaps never crossed a personal word with you.

5. To themselves, their own idea of life, or how life should be. Once there, it may become sticky and irrational. You think you fit in, so you do.

6. To your cognitive dissonance. Which is to say to your mind being in charge, and not accepting that you made the wrong decision, such as joining that company.

7. To a product, or idea, or something to develop. Many people work in some R&D or, say, pharma companies, just because of one single idea, or product to develop and put in the market. It's the cure of, not the company that is looking for it.

All loyalties are irrational. All loyalties are a choice. All you can do as leader is to host that rich and irrational plural and provide the conditions so that at least one of them has to do with the organization itself.

Customer loyalty has been studied ad nauseam. It's often overrated. Employee loyalty has been buried in other things such as engagement.

Loyalty unsettles me. I have it as number one in my value set. I am not sure why. Oh, I know, I just said, its irrational. That's why it is so strong.

RECLAIMING THE HUMAN VALUES LANGUAGE FOR THE CORPORATE WORLD

Well known Conservative American columnist and writer
David Brooks, wrote a piece in the *New York Times* entitled
'I miss Obama'. What is going on? That is the land of polarised
political positions with a not very good track record of saying nice
things of the other party or political spectrum.

David Brooks, by all accounts a generous soul who has written about Character many times, describes Obama with words such as ethos of integrity, humility, good manners, elegance, high personal standards (extended to people he has hired), care and respect for the dignity of others time, soundness in the decision making process, grace under pressure and a resilient sense of optimism. Wow! Can I have these on my epitaph, please?

I am impressed with Brooks. I have to say not for the first time. But what strikes me is that that litany of virtues is so alien to the language of business, so divorced from the lexicon of Organizational Development and corporatised HR practices, that makes me shiver and wonder: when did we lose all that in the 'business world'?

We have corporatised the basic human emotions and robot-ised the 'people language' in the corporation to the point of no return, so that a 'dialect' has now taken over 'normal language'.

I wish we could have performance management systems that talk about generosity, courage, compassion, tolerance, gratitude, even joy. Could you imagine what that would look like?

'Reclaiming humanity' may be a bit of a cliché in itself, but I can't think of a better term to describe a pending revolution in the workplace.

I refuse to see this as a soft, naïve, fluffy narrative with no place in the world of the 'business organization'. I developed this a bit further at the UK Institute of Internal Communications Conference where I gave a keynote.

Mr Brooks has been a wonderful reminder of the territory we all should live in. For the record, I will miss Obama too. Not my president, not my country, not a saint. But not a role model I am prepared to ignore, whether I am on the same political planet or not. Character above policy? Always.

IF LEADERSHIP IN ORGANIZATIONS FOLLOWED SOME 'ACTIVISM RULES'; NOT STANDARD MANAGEMENT LOGIC. HERE IS ONE RULE.

One of the key rules of activism (social, political, cause) is not to spend more than the minimum necessary time reacting to the opposition. Reacting to the push back, opposition, barriers, enemies, people who have a problem with XYZ must be contained, or it will take over the whole airtime. A cause is not a permanent discussion with those who don't like it.

Good activism is focused on driving the agenda (political, social), not on reacting to those who have a different one, or don't like yours.

Against a backlash on X, the key is to build enough critical mass (people) for X, so that the 'backlash people' remain a minority; not to discuss with every possible 'backlash person' their reasons and rationale. Indeed, key activist-leaders may spend time discussing and trying to convince (and we see this all the time on our TV screens and in our press), but this is the visible part of the moving iceberg. True activism needs to push forward all the time.

In behavioural terms, I have written several times, you don't combat a behavioural epidemic from within; you create a counter-epidemic that takes over.

This key principle (drive the agenda vs react to an opposition) may sound harsh for us always wanting to convince via rationality and emotions. The point is, we should continue to do that but always be mindful of how much we are advancing. In pure activism terms (no moral judgment attached), the focus is to enlist as many pro-causers. Between the choice of spending time to get 50 more people engaged, or not doing so, because we need to convince a few who 'don't get it', the activist's choice is clear: the 50+ win.

Park this principle here for a second. Let's reflect on how much of this is going on in our day to day management in organizations. I suspect not a lot. In the traditional 'change management' approach, a lot of energy went to full discussion and full intellectual engagement with 'everybody'. Traditional 'change management' never distinguished between people's attitudes; it never segmented the population properly, so that it could focus on a majority that could create a fast, critical mass. It also invented the flawed 'people are resistant to change', which made the whole affair dully masochistic. The Viral Change™ Mobilizing Platform avoids those traps.

What if leadership (and leadership of change for that matter) was closer to 'activism' than 'management'? What would the above rule mean?

'THE CONFERENCE': TRIBES TALKING TO THEMSELVES

Who goes to HR conferences? HR people. Who goes to Communication conferences? Communication Directors, Managers and Heads. Who goes to Digital Something Conferences? Digital people, nerds and digital experts of some sort. Who goes to Next Big Thing Leadership World and Pan Galactic Trends Conferences? People who don't have much to do and don't have to justify company expenses.

The tribe meets. The tribe meets in the basement of the Marriott, the Conference Centre (no daylight but great chandeliers), the big Conference and Events (with Spa) hotel, and that five star resort in the mountains, exquisite place, super views from your room, bad wi-fi and breakfast included (could you believe it? Included!)

And the tribe talks. The agenda is about the new trends for the tribe, the incredibly fast changing environment, (probably as incredibly similar to last year's conference), the new tools (please visit the exhibition floor) and the things that will change life forever. And there is, of course, that keynote about Blockchain (block what?) and Ethereum (Eth?). Because no conference today can ignore these. Whether the Association of Weather Forecast presenters or Rocket Science Unite, that needs to be there. (Trouble is not so much to have these on the agenda, but to find a speaker who can make sense of it).

Tribe members talking to tribe members is not necessarily the greatest source of innovation and cross-fertilisation. But, of course, these are not the reasons for these conferences, but the rituals. And tribes do know about rituals. They provide the glue, a sense of belonging, a reason for existence, and zero efficacy.

The ideal conference, the one that will never be, is the one when accountants talk to psychologists over a few mojitos, HR people talk to people in sales, business development, talk to engineers (more mojitos), finance people talk to HR, (endless supply of mojitos), finance talk to any other human being, Communications to finance and engineers, and many tribes are simply mixed up. Over mojitos, that is.

If you want to talk to your tribe members, by all means, do. Plenty of places. But once you have checked your sense of belonging, your tribal membership, the social life of colleagues and ex-colleagues, find a better mechanism to upgrade yourself, get skilled and informed.

The warm, cosy and safe '(functional) Conference' has a role. But, content wise and skill wise, it is unlikely to provide anything that cannot be found elsewhere, probably earlier and better described.

The 'ideal conference' is multi-tribe, multi-functional, cross-worlds and mutually challenging. At the other end of the spectrum there is intellectual tourism.

The 7 Habits of Highly Effective Killers (in the Organization)

1. Postpone. Some great killers postpone everything. They don't even have to use the language, they simply organize things in a way that it is always better to wait to start something: a new leadership team in place, a new reorg, the full headcount, a series of top-down workshops that will explain everything to everybody.

2. Try harder, keep guessing what I want. From my original set of 10 ways you kill an organization, this is still very much alive. You never quite get it 100% right with Peter the Great, there is always a 'but', a 'too bad you did not do X' (American favourite), a 'let's have another go next week'.

3. Let them fail. Peter the Great knows the answers, has the answers, crafts the answers. The team is going in a different direction. Peter the Great simply 'lets them fail'. So he can be Greater next time. If you think this is a non-existent caricature, I can assure you I have a list of names, big and medium sized leaders I know, who behave like this.

4. Keep very, very, very busy. Busy-ness as a permanent state of affairs is a habit killer. It is also contagious and toxic. It makes you feel a bit guilty for not being as busy as he is. For this killer, busy-ness is a minimum requirement to justify your existence. To him, Peter the Great that is.

5. Have a call to prepare for the conference call that prepares for the face-to-face meeting. I don't need to say more. This is real, everyday life in some organizations, unknown in others. If the habit is in, it is very hard to change. Funny thing is, everybody blames somebody else for the habit, nobody wants to own it, but, hey, this is how we do things here.

6. Refer to the culture all the time as justification for everything. So, it's not you, no, of course, you personally would not do that but, in this culture, people do X.

7. Parachute, intervene, disappear, parachute again. Some leaders behave as the Parachute Brigade landing in meetings, affiliates, town halls or 'customer visits' to pontificate, assert, perhaps smile, provide wisdom, increase the platitude level and then disappear at the point that normal life resumes.

DO COMPETENCE-BASED MANAGEMENT AND LEADERSHIP SYSTEMS CREATE BETTER MANAGERS OR LEADERS? (SORRY FOR THE INCONVENIENT QUESTION)

In Louis Gerstner's autobiography as chairman of IBM from 1993 until 2002, he recalls the company's use of a competency model for leadership and change. He acknowledged that they had too many of those competencies, but that, by and large, they contributed to three things: created a common language, provided a sense of consistency and formed the basis for performance management. As you can see, he did not say that it created good leaders.

And I think there is a profound learning here. Most competence-based frameworks for, say, change, leadership, or talent management are more useful as a language for the tribe than as tools to facilitate change, shape leaders or 'manage' talent.

At that time in IBM which Gerstner was referring to, the leadership competence system in the company had eleven of these, which eventually they 'summarised' into three. Most of the competence systems I know today run into several dozen, a broad supermarket of 'pieces' that one has to 'have' in order to be categorised into a particular box, which is usually related to a particular salary or compensation.

There is a whole industry of consultancies selling these boxes and categorizations which usually look conspicuously similar to those of the multinational next door. They all successfully pass the universal test: they are impossible to disagree with. Teamwork, collaboration, 'drives change', empowerment, proactivity, 'provides clear instructions', results focus, openness and customer-centrism, are 'fundamental to your leadership structure'. (I have just saved you a few thousand dollars or any other currency for consulting fees).

So, there you are. The trick now is the dosage. Lower ranks have less of them; as you go up the ladder, you have more of them. By which mechanism one goes from 'manages change' to 'leads change' and then 'anticipates change', is never clear to anybody. The linguistic injection of steroids seems to be enough to expect the differences between levels. And if you land in a higher rank box by accident of life, body attrition or imposed reorganization, you seem to inherit the competences of the new box. The corporate Father Christmas has just given you abilities you did not even know you had.

One of my tired, recurrent jokes in this area is that these systems seem to have been created by a quantum physicist, but this usually gives Quantum Physics a bad name.

But, the language, oh, the language. That is marvellous. Conversations about people and talent management rituals by HR could not take place without the language and its dialects.

And that is a serious asset, as Gerstner acknowledged.

Don't expect the perfect leader to be the sum of a perfect high dose combination of competences. But expect perfect conversations about career progression and bonuses.

Despite appearances, this is not a rant against competence systems. It is a rant against outdated and past-looking competence systems. I can assure you that if you have one of those systems in place, and are performing well, the chances are your company is fully prepared for the past.

The trick, that many of those 'human capital consultancies' do not seem to provide is how to look at strategic, future looking capabilities. That is much harder because one has to project oneself into the unknown and acknowledge that a copy and paste of the competences that seem to have served so far, equally yourself and your neighbours by the way, are going to be in the best case a pass, a baseline, and at worse, completely unsuitable for you.

However, since language is providing you with a powerful glue, it's going to be difficult to abandon those quantum physics boxes.

But, frankly, I can't see any other option. It will take a brave Leadership Team to look at those boxes and say: seriously?

ARCHAEOLOGISTS USUALLY DON'T BUILD HOUSES. WE HAVE LOTS OF ARCHAEOLOGISTS ON THE PAYROLL.

Over years of consulting, I have realised that the best leaders I know never talk about their previous companies, what they did or accomplished, what it was like to be there.

Similarly, the worst leaders I have come across (should I say, suffered from?) never stopped talking about their track record and their usually alpha male/female saving the world for their previous employers. Which begs the question, why did they leave them? Oh! Silly me, they did in order to come and save this one now.

Years ago, I had to suffer a long dinner with a new CEO who spent the evening explaining the migration from 2.3 to 6.8 market share in Singapore, when he was in charge. A wonderful conversation to have over a mediocre Chateaubriand and a few overrated and overpriced chardonnays. The commensals pretended to be incredibly interested and the intensity of nodding in admiration was only matched by the total amount of the bill.

That CEO, by the way, did very well over the coming years, and a Californian mansion with swimming pool later, he sold the company and disappeared to concentrate on his hardest professional challenge ever: how to spend his money. In between, he was a very poor leader, a thought of course not shared by the shareholders, but unanimously felt by everybody else, from managers to cleaners.

Some of these 'forward to the past' behaviours, to repeat an expression I used recently, are quite toxic.

You can't run an organization, small or big, or a division of it, with a forward-to-the-past leadership style, and, at the same time, order employee engagement surveys.

The most disengaged people are those who are in the payroll but never joined the company.

They live in a rear mirror, comparison world, stuck in their previous titles or achievements, and not bringing much value to the table other than sentences starting with 'when I was in X'.

The past is great, maybe. The past may need to be revered, maybe. The past is personal, mostly. But we don't need archaeologists to build a new house. People who talk about their past employment all the time, usually don't have time to engage in their new one.

An enlightened top leadership is sometimes a fantastic alibi for a non-enlightened management to do whatever they want

Nothing is more rewarding than having a CEO who says world-changing things in the news, and who produces bold, enlightened and progressive quotes for all admirers to be. That organization is lucky to have one of these. The logic says that all those enlightened statements about trust, empowerment, humanity and purpose, will be percolated down the system, and will inform and shape behaviours in the mille-feuille of management layers below.

I take a view, observed many times, that this is wishful thinking. In fact, quite the opposite, I have seen more than once how management below devolves all greatness to the top, happily, whilst ignoring it and playing games in very opposite directions. Having the very good and clever and enlightened people at the top is a relief for them. They don't have to pretend that they are as well, so they can exercise their 'practical power' with more freedom. That enlightened department is covered in the system, and the corporate showcase guaranteed.

The distance between the top and the next layer down may not be great in organizational chart terms, yet the top may not have a clue that there is a behavioural fabric mismatch just a few centimetres down in the organization chat.

I used to think years ago, when I was younger, that a front page, top notch leader stressing human values would provide a safe shelter against inhuman values for his/her organization below. I am not so sure today. In fact, my alarm bell system goes mad when I see too much charismatic, purpose driven, top leadership talk. I simply smell lots of alibis below. And I often find them. After all, there is usually not much room for many Good Cops.

Yet, I very much welcome the headline grabbing by powerful business people who stress human values and purpose, and a quest for a decent world. The alternative would be sad. I don't want them to stop that. But let's not fool ourselves about how much of that truly represents their organizations. In many cases it represents them.

I guess it all goes back, again, to the grossly overrated Role Model Power attributed to the leadership of organizations, a relic of traditional thinking, well linked to the Big Man Theory of history. Years of Edelman's Trust Barometer, never attributing the CEO more than 30% of the trust stock in the organization, have not convinced people that the 'looking up' is just a small part of the story. What happens in organizations has a far more powerful 'looking sideways' traction: manager to manager, employee to employee. Lots of ritualistic dis-empowering management practices can sit very nicely under the umbrella of a high empowerment narrative at the top, and nobody would care much. The top floor music and the music coming from the floor below, and below, are parallel universes.

Traditional management and MBA thinking has told us that if this is the case, the dysfunctionality of the system will force it to break down. My view is the opposite. The system survives nicely under those contradictions. In fact, it needs them.

How many people on your payroll have never licked a stamp?

Beloit College, in Wisconsin, creates every year a
'Mindset List'. It shows a list of facts about a particular
new class or college intake. At the time on the 'Class of 2019',
one read things such as, they may believe that
'Hong Kong has always been under Chinese rule' or 'hybrid
automobiles have always been mass produced',
or if you say, 'around the turn of the century', they may
well ask you, 'which one?'. The list is sort of hilarious.
It also contains 'these people have never licked a stamp'.

Beyond the anecdote, there are serious points. A professor of Sociology there, at the time, put it like this: 'The Class of 2019 will enter college with a high level knowledge of technology, an increasing factor in how and even what they learn. They will encounter difficult discussions about privilege, race, and sexual assault on campus. They may think of the 'last century' as the twentieth, not the nineteenth, so they will need ever wider perspectives about the burgeoning mass of information that will be heading their way. And they will need a keen ability to decipher what is the same and what has changed with respect to many of these issues'. Amen to it, I say.

So, in our organizations, do we really understand the who is who of our segmented work force? My impression is not. We simply default to superficial, unhelpful, anecdotal and infuriating comments on 'The Millennials' as our climax of segmentation. And then, so what with The Millennials? Well, they get the same PowerPoints, the same top down messages and the same Town Hall meeting as everybody else. Oh! But the Millennials are soooo different! Say the mostly male, mostly grown up, Leadership Team.

We need to understand the tribal nature of the organization, the real peer-to-peer networks of 'people like us', where the powerful conversations take place. And once we do, once we have segmented, we need to treat those tribal layers differently. Yep, harder than a top down, single communication tsunami.

The 'what do the ones who have never licked a stamp say?', should be one of the multiple tests. Claiming no idea, is not a good idea.

Some workplaces are 'non-places' and as inspiring as Clinical Isolation Units

Working in a 'non-place place' can't deliver inspirations and aspirations. Ideas need infections, not Clinical Isolation Units.

Marc Augé is a French Anthropologist who coined the term 'non-places', to describe spaces of little or no significance, of 'transitory nature' such as hotel rooms, or supermarkets, or airports. (Non-places: *Introduction to an Anthropology of Supermodernity* 1992 2007, 2009). These 'non-place places' deserve an analysis of their own.

I sometimes feel that some organizations work on non-place mode. The environment is sterile and the all-glass offices have simply replaced the all-panel offices for another material whilst keeping the border close (but gaining in luminosity). In a non-place-company-place there is little room for associability, or the associability is forced into spaces where the only thing missing is a sign hanging from the ceiling: 'you must be sociable here'. Examples are the solitary corner with a small table football, the awkward table tennis table surrounded by sofas, the open plan seating area with a whispering TV screen. Be here and do that: play, rest, eat (or eat, play, love).

Some company offices are closer to pre-operating rooms in hospitals than a work place. As an external observer, I often feel the pain of migrating from a 'you work here' to a 'you play here' area passing by a 'you get your coffee here' corner.

Some modern facilities with pristine space and tons of glass are modern prisons of ideas, non-places of undistinguished clinical interaction, that far from inviting human interfaces, discourages natural communications: silence is heard, faces are hidden behind transparent screens, meetings are orderly, conducted behind the borders of fish bowls. Only the toilets provide some space for liberation, even if segregated.

Don't trade off an old, messy, inconvenient and cramped place for a pristine, deluxe, glass cathedral non-place.

In a non-place office, even the receptionist's ephemeral smile reminds you that you enter into a carefully designed world, a sort of Japanese garden of ideas, where humanity has been hijacked until the 5pm rush to the car park.

SOME COMPANY CULTURES ARE WORKS OF FICTION. SOME LEADERSHIP TEAMS 'HARRYPOTTER' A NARRATIVE THAT NOBODY ELSE RECOGNISES.

The description of some company cultures by their leaders may sound like a work of fiction by people inside.

I have heard 'we don't do politics' in highly politicised environments.

I have heard 'we are not hierarchical' in companies run as a benign dictatorship where hierarchy has just changed geography; for example the project leadership tribe is truly in charge, and hierarchical as hell, but not officially.

I have seen nasty inhuman HR practices in highly 'paternalistic cultures'.

I have heard 'save the world' music in companies with leadership teams only concerned about their stock options.

I have indeed, over the years, gained lots of insights about the world of culture fiction. That fiction is the reality for many, those who have a vested interest in maintaining the fiction. In a number of cases, I have seen those people believe their own fiction. Self-brainwashing is actually not that difficult.

For those leaders, their legacy will be that fictional world.

'Fiction is history that didn't happen'. Those leaders did not make history, they just '*harrypottered*' the whole thing.

The '*trumpanites*' were seriously fed up with 'the system' and politicians. Reality TV seemed the solution. Everybody else was corrupt, according to them. So, therefore, Donald's corruption of character was not a problem.

What we witnessed in US presidential politics was not a classic bipartisan struggle for principles and policies. It was a colossal petri dish of unprecedented toxicity which could be ignored no longer, by anybody, including people like me, non US citizens, not living in the US.

Donald Trump was a bad joke; his followers didn't make me laugh.

Donald Trump lifted a veil and the contents of the Pandora box was very ugly. He didn't worry me, after all I have spent more than 15 years of my life as clinical psychiatrist.

The contents of the box did.

S. 9.

FELISA
HIGOS - AGUA Y AMOR

LOGROÑO

15/5/

CAMINO HISTÓRICO

VILLOVIECO

5.9.

Puerta de Nájera

THE PAWN

A VISTA
AL CLUB

TURING

ERS

BA
HAVANA

FLIGHT: 1-565-7

ER

T CODE:

6-453

LA HABANA, PARQUE CENTRAL

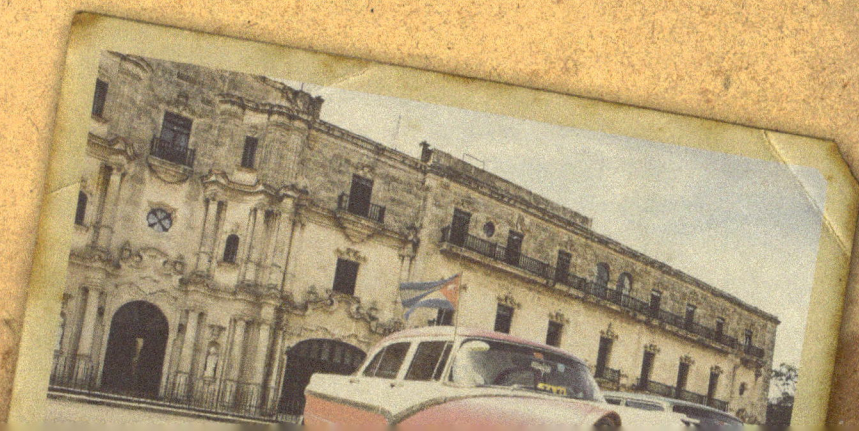

DON'T LET THE EXPRESSION 'THIS IS JUST BUSINESS' BE SYNONYMOUS FOR INHUMAN. BUSINESS? NOT IN MY NAME.

Somewhere along the line in the history of 'business', something went wrong and people took the wrong turn at the bifurcation in the road. The world of 'business' started to speak a funny language and the 9 to 5 man (and at that time it was still 9 to 5 as opposed to today's 24/7) became a species in its own right, eager to show that he was different from the 'the rest of the day man'. Perfectly reasonable people at home, in church, at the kids' football match and in the bars with friends, became 'managers' at 9:00 am, and they not only spoke a different language, but also behaved differently.

SOMETHING MUST HAVE BEEN IN THOSE 'MANAGEMENT' CLOTHES PUT ON AT 09:00 AM THAT ALLOWED PEOPLE TO SPEAK AND BEHAVE ON BEHALF OF SOMEBODY ELSE: THE BOSSES, THE BOARD, THE SHAREHOLDERS OR SOMETHING QUITE ESOTERIC AND NEVER SEEN, AS INVISIBLE AS A NEUTRINO, CALLED 'THE MARKET'.

On behalf of 'business', managers started to exercise power over others and seek more and more control over life. When pain was inflicted, the word 'they' had to be invented: 'they want us to do this', 'they will not like that'. This magical 'they' could justify almost anything. Then, Darwinian forces took over and power, status and ability to dictate percolated 'business life'. In this business life, things that were not acceptable outside 'business life' became very legitimate here. It became possible, for example, to fire people on Twitter.

Modern Darwinian Alpha managers could be rude, ruthless, take no prisoners and do that on behalf of 'it is business, isn't it; we are here to make money'. Also, a convenient, transitory schizophrenia became epidemic: 'it's not me, it's the system, if it was me, I would not do this, but I have to, it's business, it's not personal'. Which is, in itself, the most personal statement a manager can make.

The power dynamics became a force of its own. I will always remember one of these schizophrenic corporate moments that I lived a few years ago with a client, when the head of the division, my client, was told by her bosses that she was doing the most fantastic job, had created the best alignment of people, funded the most innovative leadership development for the top managers, and she was a model of the modern way of doing things in the company, a benchmark for all. Now, unfortunately, the division was to be disbanded the following month and amalgamated with a bigger one (who had been playing Barbarians at the Gate for a year), everybody either absorbed into a different (usually lower ranking) job or asked to leave. Needless to say, our Leadership Development Plan, benchmark of the universe, had to be stopped sadly, now. Hey, but how are the kids?

There was no logic, no sense, no reason, certainly no business or organizational reason. This was magical schizophrenic thinking. The only reason why this happened was because of a capricious request from a Bigger Power Holder to 'reorganize' and give extra troops to somebody else. Pure currency, bazaar transaction, absolutely nothing that 'the business' could gain from.

These kinds of situations are not unusual. The music in the background is the same: it's business, not me. But the situation above had nothing to do with business. It was simply the same as street, neighbourhood, territorial distribution between gangs in downtown Powerville. Whoever thinks that things in organizations, particularly reorganizations, happen because of the business, the markets, the customers or the environment, has perhaps not worked in a major corporation. Stuff happens because of power dynamics. Some organizations are successful despite this.

If every time that something absurd, let alone, unethical, rude, disrespectful, or inhumane, is done on behalf of 'business', Mr Business could come out of the closet and shout 'Not in my name', we would have a different society.

I have painted a deliberately negative scenario.
I am conscious of that. If your business is not like this,
congratulations. You belong to Planet Sanity. Hold on
to it. So, if you see some of this somewhere else under
the 'it's business, isn't it', as coterminous for inhuman,
please join me and shout,

'NOT IN MY NAME!'

COULD THE 'GLOBAL TEENAGER' TEACH US ABOUT 'GLOBAL LEADERSHIP'?

Today, there are more similarities between a teenager in Shanghai and a teenager in Rome, or Singapore and Madrid, or London and Paris, than you might expect, given the transcultural differences between China, Italy, Singapore, Spain, UK, France etc. In our traditional thinking about geographical cultures, the focus is on differences. The reality of the age-related tribes such as the Global Teenager is commonalities. How can we reconcile both?

In the world of organizations, the issue of 'global leaders' comes up all the time. What are they? What are their competences? What does one have to 'have' to be or to become a global leader? There are indeed some answers, not surprisingly mainly from the field of intercultural studies led by consultants or academics. But most of these views are based on fairly retrospective data. Many times the answers feel a bit old and suspiciously predictable. For example, we are told that global leaders must have 'cultural sensitivity', which is the equivalent of saying that an aeroplane must have wings.

I am caricaturising this a bit – at the risk of annoying a great group of expert colleagues in this area – there is something about the set of competences of 'global leadership' that make me feel slightly uncomfortable. The competences are sometimes a sort of mental 'déjà vu'. Have I seen them before? Which ones are specific, if any?

I wonder if instead of looking backwards with analytical tools (as is usual in academic research), we would gain far more by looking forward in time and observing the emergent characteristics of any 'global phenomenon'. I suspect, teenagers are a good start. They did not receive training on how to be global. How did that happen?

JUST WONDERING, IF INSTEAD OF FOCUSING ON DEVELOPING GLOBAL LEADERS WE COULD FOCUS ON DEVELOPING GOOD LEADERS. IF WE DROP THE 'GLOBAL', WILL THE SKY FALL? WILL NEW GENERATIONS OF LEADERS BE GLOBAL IF THEY ARE GOOD LEADERS?

DON'T TRUST ARMCHAIR CRITICS, REFORMERS AND BROADCASTERS OF LEADERSHIP WHO DON'T KNOW WHAT A DRY CLEANERS IS

FOLLOW THE ONES WHO DO, WHO MOVE, WHO TRY, WHO PUSH. THE ONES WHO GET DIRTY (AND SEND THEIR CLOTHES TO THE CLEANERS).

Armchair activists and ideologues have a role, but I am a little sceptical, often even a bit tired of them, although it does not stop me admiring the good ideas and insights. They pontificate from high, but they don't know the price of a loaf of bread or a bottle of milk (a tried test for politicians).

I really love this piece from Teddy Roosevelt's 1910 *Man in the Arena Speech*. And can't see how any extra words from me could add anything.

'It is not the critic who counts; not the man who points out how the strong man stumbles, or where the doer of deeds could have done them better. The credit belongs to the man who is actually in the arena, whose face is marred by dust and sweat and blood; who strives valiantly; who errs, who comes short again and again, because there is no effort without error and shortcoming; but who does actually strive to do the deeds; who knows great enthusiasms, the great devotions; who spends himself on a worthy cause; who at the best knows in the end the triumph of high achievement, and who at the worst, if he fails, at least fails while daring greatly, so that his place shall never be with those cold and timid souls who neither know victory nor defeat'.

COMPETITION GLORIFIED: YOU ARE NOT A STUDENT, EMPLOYEE OR CITIZEN, YOU ARE A CONTESTANT

I have not counted the number of TV shows, either side of the Atlantic, that are based on individual competition, but there must be big numbers. Competing will get you out of a jungle, or will win you a music contract, a best baker award, a bride, a groom, cash, a job, or just a title of Winner of this Year's Whatever.

A fraction of these contests will entail collaboration as a means to winning. Even when collaboration is part of the show, such as in *The Apprentice*, contestants at the end are entitled to blame each other as a means of saving their own skin. (*The Apprentice* is, in my view, the worst public projection of what business is really about).

We are creating a world of 'contestants', always competing on some form of battleground: the TV studio, radio, the school system, the company. It may be soft or hard Darwin, but it is Darwinian. Many people will argue that this is not bad, that this is life after all, and that ignoring 'competition', for example in the school, is not doing kids any favour. So, it's a vicious circle in which we prepare kids to win (more than to know, to grow, to live, to love or to contribute, or to just be), which in turn prepares (some of) them to join a company to... compete, which, I suppose, makes the company... competitive.

No wonder a survey of 2000 adolescents in the UK, run by *The Guardian* a few years ago, showed that the number one concern of this pool was 'fear of failure' (followed by bullying, pressure to be thin and depression).

Slight problem here. This is 2020. The world is interdependent. Nothing that we do today can be done out of independence, no matter where you sit: the company, society, geopolitics, business. The key competence of the Century is actually collaboration, not

SOUTHERN AIRLINES
GATE 2
HAND BAGGAGE ALLOWED

FLIGHT: 1-565-7

HAVANA , CUBA

FLIGHT CODE:
56-453

competition. The laws of collaboration and competition are different. We have a societal bias for one (competition) and we desperately need tons of the other (collaboration). I have used the term 'competing on collaboration' many times in my consulting life. It's not a clever attempt at playing with words. We need to master this. It is the top fundamental organizational and personal competence of today.

Yes, there are attempts to inject collaboration in schools and organizations via training or gamification, but they are timid and powerless compared with the enormous pull of competition.

As leaders, we need to reinforce, reward and recognise collaboration and stop reinforcing, rewarding and recognising the heroic individual contributions and achievements. It's hard when faced with the superhero, the hyper-achiever, with a stockpile of stock options and bonuses, to say: 'Congratulations but you don't get the bonus. You did a great, fantastic, incredibly successful job ...on your own'.

WE ARE HITTING 'CULTURE', AGAIN. THAT MEANS CHOICES,
FOR EXAMPLE, HOW PEOPLE ACHIEVE WHAT THEY ACHIEVE.

THE VIDEO AND THE AUDIO OF EMPOWERMENT ARE OUT OF SYNC

Have you seen those videos or TV interviews, or programmes, in which there is a disconnect between what the person says (as clearly seen by the movement of his lips) and what you hear? Sometimes a delay? Sometimes it simply doesn't match?

We have lots of these in organizations.

The audio says, take risks, be bold, be honest, you're empowered, push the envelope, fight the default positions, you have permission, you need to own things, act as an owner.

What you see in the video is people being, if not fully penalised, certainly questioned for those risks taken or not really promoted, or told off and to be more prudent next time, or told 'next time make sure we know, you ask, discuss, get buy in, be more careful' and all other variations.

I'VE GOT A NEW TOP LEADERSHIP ROLE: CHIEF SYNCHRONISING OFFICER.

OF COURSE, THIS DISQUALIFIES SOME LIKE THE CEO WHO TOLD ME A FEW MONTHS AGO ABOUT HIS DESIRE TO HAVE A VIRAL CHANGE™ BEHAVIOUR DESCRIBED AS 'TAKE RISKS BUT BE PRUDENT'. I TOLD HIM THAT IT SOUNDED LIKE AN ADVERT FOR SAFE SEX. IT DID NOT GO DOWN WELL.

SATURDAY POEM FOR LEADERS WHO DON'T READ POEMS

There is an 'Accidental Literature for Leaders'. I call this my compilation of poems or pieces of narrative that are not intended for management education (!) but serve us well for reflection. They are cheaper than a leadership development programme. This is a beautiful poem from Constantine P. Cavafy (1863 – 1933), an Egyptiot Greek poet with a day job as a journalist and civil servant. Which gives hope for day jobs… It's called *Walls*.

Walls

'With no consideration, no pity, no shame,
they have built walls around me, thick and high.
And now I sit here feeling hopeless.
I can't think of anything else: this fate gnaws my mind -
because I had so much to do outside.
When they were building the walls, how could I not have noticed!
But I never heard the builders, not a sound.
Imperceptibly they have closed me off from the outside world'.

Leader's action plan:

Make sure that you hear the builders.

Make sure that your people hear the builders.

Look out for walls around you that appear from nowhere.

Make sure you are not the builder that builds the walls for your people.

If it looks like a wall, make sure you can open a door and a window.

If inevitable, choose your own walls.

If it's too late, at least paint the walls.

Tell your children about builders that build walls and make no noise.

'IF YOU PUT THE FEDERAL GOVERNMENT IN CHARGE OF THE SAHARA DESERT, IN 5 YEARS THERE'D BE A SHORTAGE OF SAND'

These were, Milton Friedman's (1912-2006), Nobel Prize winner in Economics, unkind words about governments. The leader of the Chicago School of Economics and father of 'monetarism' had little time for them.

His point is an important one when applied generically, as I'm doing here with organizations. Any function, or a firm, can manage resources well, but could also screw up completely and even deplete them. So many times, the thought has come to me when observing some companies: 'These guys are making money despite themselves'.

We have all witnessed companies going out of business despite being pioneers in a sector. They had all the sand they wanted. Many things can go wrong, of course, but killing Kodak, for example, belongs to a higher category of bad leadership.

The Public Sector has a reputation for 'sand depletion' – as Friedman suggested – which, in my experience, is unfair, although some examples are notable.

The Private Sector on the other hand has the reputation of 'sand conservation' (and enhancement of the shareholder value of the owners of the sand), which is similarly unjustified. Just take a look at a list of companies, market fiascos and 'sand depletions', and you'll see most are in the Private Sector.

The truth is that good and bad management, and leadership, runs across most sectors and geographies. With all respect to Mr Freedman, 'If you put some guys, Public or Private Sectors, in charge of the Sahara Desert, anything can happen'.

ONE OF THE PROBLEMS WE HAVE IS THAT PUBLIC AND PRIVATE SECTORS DON'T LEARN FROM EACH OTHER AS MUCH AS THEY SHOULD. DEPLETING SAND IS NOT THE EXCLUSIVE PATRIMONY OF EITHER. THERE ARE GOOD AND BAD SAND LEADERS IN BOTH BIG DESERTS AND SMALL DESERTS. SOME PEOPLE BUILD, SOME DESTROY.

I MAKE MY BEST CLIENTS RESTLESS. I MAKE THE OTHERS COMFORTABLE.

My work as an organization architect entails exploring avenues, not the offloading of a dictionary of templates onto my clients. With my team, we bring organizational design, leadership, change and management innovation expertise. But we don't have off-the-shelf answers. Certainly we don't have 'houses' ready, in search of a spec.

I am more of a jungle guide, an explorer, certainly a cartographer. The 'organizational houses we build' don't have standard plans. Of course, windows are windows and bedrooms are bedrooms. Translated into organizational terms, there are fixed things. We don't reinvent the wheel. Unless the wheel is not a wheel. It looks like one but it's another kind of round thing.

The best clients want and love the building journey. Every bit is a discovery. Growth is fast and exciting. Risks, yes, there are risks. But we live the development of the organization, of its leadership and behaviours, of its processes and systems, fully. I bring ways to accelerate that journey. We are all a bit exhausted at the end, but, my God, it was worth it! When one looks back, you can see that mutual trust rocketed.

The other clients want answers, possibly quick ones. They want to shorten the road to the destination and want to know what exactly that destination looks like. If possible, on Wednesday the 22nd. That does not make them bad clients, just not the best.

These clients want comfort and want to pay for comfort. The best clients want the best, comfortable or not, and they suspect from the start that the journey may be a bit stressful. This does not make them masochists. Simply they don't want to settle for the unexamined comfort.

There is a parallel with leadership. If your leadership makes you very comfortable, you may need to have some extra reflection. It's not that comfort is sinful. It's simply suspicious.

AS FOR ME, WHEN THE BEST CLIENT IS RESTLESS, THAT MAKES ME COMFORTABLE THAT I AM DOING MY JOB. WHEN THE OTHERS FEEL VERY COMFORTABLE, THAT MAKES ME RESTLESS.

THERE ARE OFF-THE-SHELF ACCOUNTING PACKAGES TO BUY AND USE. THERE CAN'T BE SUCH A THING AS AN OFF-THE-SHELF LEADERSHIP DEVELOPMENT PROGRAMME.

Avoid off-the-shelf leadership programmes. Prêt-à-porter leadership development is attractive but unlikely to be a good answer. There are not universal leadership skills. There are not 'four characteristics of the leader', or '10 personality treats of the good leader'. These lists are a myth. I don't care if they come packaged with lots of 'research' or backed up by a database in the thousands of 'peer companies'. They are made up. Or out of date, or out of sync.

Leadership development needs to be crafted case by case. Yes, there are 'universal issues' and 'hot topics', but a leadership programme needs to be cooked out of the right ingredients. Off-the-shelf programmes are attractive, handy, promising, and usually put on your table with the label of a particular management guru or 'well known people' who do this stuff.

Yes, sure, you can put your workforce through one of these and it won't be a waste. There will be 'ahas!' and learning and some benefits. But this is far from a true leadership development programme, because this is something that can only be crafted for a particular company, in particular circumstances, with particular people. Yes, perhaps borrowing pieces from here and there.

In my latest Leadership Development work, we spent a 'disproportionate' amount of time on the issue of control: 'Lose control, to gain more control' (*Disruptive Ideas*, 2008). Why? That was issue number one for those leaders. Their number one need

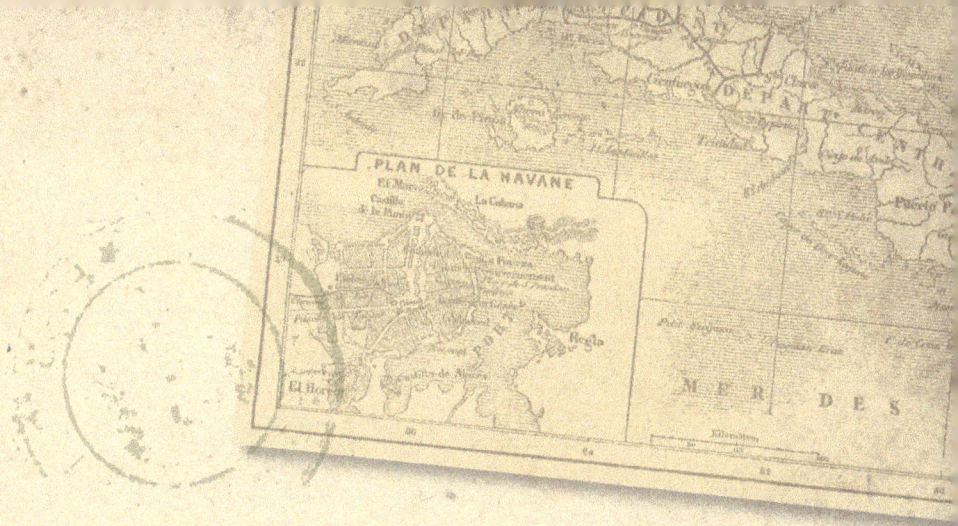

individually and collectively. I could guess that this topic would be rather universal (and it ranks pretty highly on my radar screen), but I don't know. I know what that particular client needed.

No company goes to a library of mission and values and 'buys' the one of peer A, or competitor B, or fashionista C. You build this system from within. Or you should! It's hard to see how pre-packaged sets of Leadership Development competences should be adopted uncritically. But this is what many companies do.

PRÊT-À-PORTER WORKS FOR CLOTHES. OFF-THE-SHELF PACKAGES WORK FOR ACCOUNTING. LEADERSHIP IS AN ART AND A PRACTICE. AS AN ART, IT'S LIKE GOING TO AN ART SCHOOL: YOU DON'T GET A PRE-MADE 'PORTRAIT KIT'. AS A PRACTICE, IT'S LIKE GOING TO THE GYM: NOBODY ELSE CAN DO IT FOR YOU. BUY AS MANY PENCILS OR AS MANY TREADMILLS AS YOU WANT, BUT...

MY FRIENDS, THE MONKS', SECRET WEAPON: THE ASTERISK. I WANT LEADERSHIP WITH TONS OF THEM.

MY BEST FRIENDS ARE MONKS OF THE TYPE THAT DON'T TALK MUCH. SO WE DON'T TALK MUCH. I VISIT THEM A COUPLE OF TIMES A YEAR IN THEIR MONASTERY IN THE SCOTTISH HIGHLANDS. THERE ARE OTHER MONKS EVEN STRICTER IN TERMS OF SILENCE, BUT THIS CATHOLIC BENEDICTINE COMMUNITY STILL LEAVES ROOM FOR SOME TALKING.

I asked one of the monks, a friend for many years, about silence, a theme I have been in full research mode for, in the last 5 years. I am looking for a magic formula to inject it permanently into leadership programmes. Yes, I am trying to sell silence to leaders.

I don't expect the monks to find that formula for me, in my area of organizational consulting and business. But something they are, is world experts on silence. They started that corporate competence around the 6th Century and they are still here, silent. Kind of.

In the middle of an always engaging and, as ever, beautiful, if short, conversation, I asked him, 'so, how much more silence do you think you need?'

I was trying to be a bit cheeky, provocative, but my friend didn't get it. He paused for a few seconds and said, 'well, I suppose, we have the asterisks'. Of course, the asterisks! What? Ok, I

needed some explanation. It turns out that I had seen these asterisks a thousand times, but never paid attention.

The monks go from their quarters to their monastery's church for prayers seven times per day, for anything between 15 minutes to 60 minutes at a time. They sit in layers, facing each other. Half of them on the right, half on the left. The Abbot in the middle. It's like the British Parliament (House of Commons) but civilised. They sing the ancient Psalms. My friends do so in Gregorian Latin. The valley around beautifully amplifies it.

The texts are divided in phrases. One phrase sang by those on the left, the next phrase sang by those in front of them, on the right of the church. This Latin ping-pong has been going on for centuries. If you look carefully in the books, there is an asterisk in each of the phrases. That asterisk means that you have to pause for about 1 second, so you don't rush to the next phrase. This mini pause is really 1 second, a noticeable 1 second. It has nothing to do with breathing, because the length of the phrase is very diverse. It's about one second silence, letting the mind ponder.

They sing the entire collection of 150 Psalms in a week. And repeat it over 52 weeks. My calculation is that there is an average of 50 asterisks per service, give or take. That means 350 pauses of 1 second a day. Or 2,450 pauses a week. Or 127,400 seconds a year. That's about 40 minutes extra silence a week. Or 35 hours extra of silence a year. Or a full extra week of silence.

Of course these calculations are silly! The total amount is not the point. But the asterisk is a constant sign to stop and listen. Producing that artificial stop in a repetitive way creates a habit of the mind. Speaking about habit-making, this is an ancestral one! Do that many times a day and your brain will function in a different way. Perhaps pausing to think!

They also have what they call 'Lectio Divina' (Divine Reading) which is a way of reading spiritual texts very slowly, stopping sometimes on words, as if asking the word or the phrase to talk back to you. It is the antithesis of intellectual reading, the anti-study. This is another little gem invented by Benedict of Nursia, or Saint Benedict, (480 –547), the founder of a monastic tradition, who had a knack for regulations and wrote one of the oldest rules (for monks). Not surprisingly, the first word of the rule of Saint Benedict is 'Listen!'

1. I need to patent the asterisk. Not sure I will succeed!

2. I want leadership with tons of asterisks. Tons.

3. Can we inject asterisks into our corporate narratives?

4. Buy yourself a box of asterisks.

5. What if we scatter asterisks in mission statements?

'WE HAVE NO TIME' PEOPLE AND 'THERE IS PLENTY OF TIME' PEOPLE, SHARE THE SAME SIXTY-MINUTE HOUR

We all know these two types of people. The 'there is plenty of time to review X or finish Y' and the 'We have no time for (the same) reviewing X or finishing Y'. X and Y don't change. It is not always a question of right and wrong. Not about how much time there 'really' is. 2 days? A week? Or whether the time in front is realistic or not.

Many times it is a question of attitude, people who like this term would say. Whilst time is objective, its perception is not. We have all experienced this. In good company, 'time flies'. One hour could be either an ephemeral space in your life or an eternity.

Some form of personal mastery requires the ability to transform the brilliant ephemeral into an eternal experience, and the other way around, to put things in perspective and convert a perceived painful eternity into an ephemeral point in life.

How people use these expressions ('plenty of time', 'lots of time', 'no time', 'no time left for') has always been a key pointer to me for my own understanding of the culture of the organization.

'Journey cultures' use time in a very different way from 'destination cultures'. In journey cultures, the time spent travelling to Ithaca, is as important as reaching Ithaca itself. C.P. Cavafy again, one of my favourite poets.

'KEEP ITHACA ALWAYS IN YOUR MIND.
ARRIVING THERE IS WHAT YOU
ARE DESTINED FOR.
BUT DO NOT HURRY THE JOURNEY AT ALL.
BETTER IF IT LASTS FOR YEARS,
SO YOU ARE OLD BY THE TIME YOU
REACH THE ISLAND,
WEALTHY WITH ALL YOU HAVE GAINED
ON THE WAY,
NOT EXPECTING ITHACA TO MAKE YOU RICH'.
I CALL IT THE LEADERSHIP ITHACA TEST.

IT'S STILL DAY ONE:
THE WINNING PHILOSOPHY OF
DAY TWO AND DAY TWO THOUSAND

JEFF BEZOS, CEO OF AMAZON, HAS A FAMOUS AND WELL QUOTED LINE: 'IT'S JUST DAY ONE' (OF THE COMPANY). AND MORE THAN 20 YEARS LATER, HE REPEATED THE 'IT'S STILL DAY ONE'.

He recently said: 'In fact, I believe that the alarm clock hasn't even gone off yet', he said. 'We're still asleep in our beds, far from having even pressed the snooze button'.

Like all catchphrases it has led to many interpretations. But the line embraces the spirit of constant renewal, of possibilities of reinvention. It's a powerful line no matter what.

If this is not a 'continuous beginning', philosophically speaking, I don't know what it is.

As I reflect on this line, on my days of vacation, I wish we all had a 'Day One' ethos in the way we do things. It's full of possibilities and positive outlook, something we often forget in our Day Two and Three and Four…

MY BEST FRIEND AND BUSINESS PARTNER, UNAWARE OF BEZOS' LINE, SAYS VERY OFTEN ABOUT OUR CONSULTING BUSINESS: WE HAVE ONLY JUST STARTED. AGREE, IT'S DAY ONE OF OUR 21 YEARS.

MY TOP 5 LEADERSHIP QUESTIONS AT THE TOP OF THE AGENDA

Here are my top five from my organizational consulting work. The paraphrasing is mine, the ownership is shared with my best clients. (In fact, I could categorise my clients by the types of questions on the table).

1. How can we mobilize people?

'Mobilize' is a better term than 'engage'. Engage is too passive. I can engage in a great conversation leading to nothing. Leadership of people inside the company (and outside the tent) is people mobilization. We need to think in these terms. Leading companies are/will be people mobilizing companies. The model is the social movement, not Harvard Business School (have I said this before?).

2. How to (re) shape a company operating system? AKA culture.

Yes, that is what it is. This is different from 'achieving an X culture'. You never achieve a culture, as you never hold water with your hands. Well, not all. 'Achieve' as a destination is old linear stuff. Reality is continuous reshaping and moving forward. So, it's a journey model, not a destination model.

3. How do I scale?

If I want a culture of safety; ownership; accountability; agility; customer-centrism; all of the above, how can I inject these, at a scale?

Many initiatives, good ones, Organizational Development ones, Coaching, Team Building, Leadership Development, do not scale well. That does not make them useless. Don't stop them. But things that don't scale or scale only by addition (a bit of this plus a bit of that, one team, next team) are weak when trying to shape an entire culture. If you want scale, it's a *social movement*.

SOUTHERN AIRLINES
GATE 2
HAND BAGGAGE ALLOWED
FLIGHT: 1-565-7

HAVANA , CUBA

FLIGHT CODE:
56-453

4. How to create a behavioural DNA that ensures success and, in particular, strategy execution?

This is the key question. It starts by trying to figure out what that DNA looks like. Not a back of an envelope affair. Values, beliefs, words, need to be translated into behaviours. Once this is done, behaviours will scale via social copying, not teaching and presentations (Viral Change™ Mobilizing Platform).

5. How to make change sustainable? (but not too much)

Sustainability in management needs to come with the 'but not too much' warning on the label.

The trick is to create a Company Operating System that allows for change and sustainability, but has reboot and mechanisms of renewal built in. (Many of my appliances at home will stop working when overheated. Why don't we have the same in our companies?).

The antifragile frame described by Nassim Taleb, which he never developed fully as far as the organization is concerned, is the best we have to at least force us to think in terms of change that changes itself, sustainable-to-a-point change.

These are fundamental questions, category 1! Don't spare effort.

MANY QUESTIONS OCCUPY AIRTIME. BUT SOME ARE SERIOUS SOURCES OF RESTLESSNESS,
OF THE HEALTHY TYPE. THESE ARE TOP RESTLESSNESS POTENTIAL.
IF YOU ARE VERY RELAXED ABOUT THEM, I AM SO SORRY.

THE 'CALL ME PETER' SCHOOL OF LEADERSHIP

I am reconstructing a fictitious reply from a senior middle manager to his CEO, in the way he expressed himself to me. He never wrote the memo, but this is what he would have said:

'Actually, no, Mr Johnson. I will not call you Peter. I appreciate the permission to break the social distance, but I quite like that distance, so I am not confused when I ask you for things.

I know that you have been given out permissions like this since you came in and this is appreciated. However, you hold a position of power and responsibility that is quite distant from me. If I call you Peter, I might just imagine that we have been mates since school or shop in the same supermarket on a Saturday, both so far from the truth'.

I saw on an American TV series that when somebody was elected as President of the United States, his main friend and campaign supporter stopped calling him by his name, even in private, and called him Mr President. I thought at first that he was nuts, but then I understood. As soon as Frank became POTUS, there was no business as usual anymore.

'You see, Mr Johnson, I want to relate to you as our leader. I won't have more or less respect for you by calling you Peter or Mr Johnson, but I want you to be where you are, in the Board, accessible of course, but not 'one of us' by forced design. Keep it like this and let's have lots of conversations, you from your high office, me from my low one. I truly believe that we will get much more understanding and things done by not pretending that by calling you as your friends do, we are already half way to our 'constructive dialogue'.

I hope you are not offended.

Warmest regards'

I have shared this with many clients, as a test, and I've got more or less 50/50 in terms of who thinks this is good, and who thinks it's just rubbish, and if Peter wanted to be called Peter, what was the fuss about. Yes, most of the latter are Americans.

Power distance is a well-known cultural measure. As such, it is not good or bad, it simply is. The high distance and the low distance people and cultures are very different. As for the stereotype that says, that 'Call me Peter' is American management, I can tell you that I have worked with white and blue-collar American managers, and Mr Johnson and Mrs James is the norm.

'Call me Peter' leadership is neither good nor bad until you have context. A universal desire for closeness and forced installing of a 'low distance' culture may be simply disastrous.

Leadership-power distance is something that cannot be constructed, most of the time it finds its own measures and doses, spontaneously, or by simple social copying within the tribes. In the UK, for example, medical doctors are 'doctors' (even if they don't have a doctorate) and surgeons are 'misters', which does not mean an inferior status at all, often the contrary. They are not Peter. This social code is strong and pervasive, used constantly even within the tribe itself.

In the UK parliament, when in session, members don't talk to each other as John or Mary, but as 'The Right Honourable Member for Basildon and Billericay'. In fact, they don't even talk to each other but to the Speaker. For example, 'Mr Speaker, The Right Honourable Member for Basildon and Billericay has just missed the point'. As opposed to 'For goodness sake, John, this is nuts'. All the distances are in place in this arcane system that, every Wednesday in Prime Minister Question time, produces the most unedifying and grotesque shouting that supposes to exemplify democracy.

I've seen an equal number of people embarrassed and delighted with a 'call me Peter' policy. Social proximity is a funny thing. I suspect we all have our own preferences. All is possible, all good or bad, but forcing it and imposing it as a pseudo-democratic shot, and social equaliser, is never, ever, a good idea.

AS A RULE OF THUMB, DON'T START WITH A 'CALL ME PETER', UNTIL THEY CALL YOU PETER, AT WHICH POINT YOU DON'T NEED TO SAY ANYTHING. UNLESS OF COURSE YOU PREFER A 'BOND, MY NAME IS BOND'.

THE LEADERSHIP TEAM TIPPING POINT: THE ARROW POINTS SOUTH

Some top management teams and leadership teams are created by the Internal Organizational Chart Robot Officer, that is, they are composed by whoever is below the boss and happens to be at that time in that place. I have called this 'The Accidental Management Team'. And, guess what, many stay like that. No evolution. But evolution is possible.

In my consulting work, I have a model of progression that starts as 'Accidental Management Team' and ends in 'Collective Leadership', with a few steps in between. I ask my clients to spot their GPS point in the evolution and then decide if they find it cosy or are restless, or how far they want to go.

I remember my early surprise, years ago, when I developed the model and many 'management teams' did not really want to progress that much and were happy to remain as 'accidental'.

But in the progression to higher levels of complexity and possibilities (I don't use the term 'high performance team' because the team is not an engine that can be described in terms of horse power), there is a tipping point, very often not reached. This is the point when the members of the team do not see themselves as representing their own functions or businesses (Finance, HR, Country A, R&D...) in the company, but they see themselves as representing the company in their functions, or business, or areas.

The arrow is inverted. I am not the Head of R&D representing 'the interests of R&D' (what I call an ambassadorial model) – arrow points North – but I am the Head of R&D representing the interests of the company in R&D - the arrow points South. It is a 180-degree shift in thinking and behaving.

I always have the expected 'well, it's both'.

But this is a trap. We always seem to need a compromise in thinking, the halfway, the 'it's both ways anyway'. Well, I have bad news, it isn't. It's one or the other.

That is the real tipping point in the complexity and possibilities of a leadership team. The arrow is inverted. It now goes South.

NOT MANY TEAMS REACH THAT TIPPING POINT, BUT, WHEN THEY DO, THE LEADERSHIP PRACTICE AND POTENTIAL HAS EXPONENTIALLY GROWN.

SO, THE QUESTION BEHIND THIS IS: WHO DO YOU (THINK YOU) REPRESENT IN THIS MANAGEMENT/LEADERSHIP TEAM? HOW YOU ANSWER DEFINES YOUR GPS POINT IN THE EVOLUTION TOWARDS HIGHER LEVELS OF SOPHISTICATION.

IT'S THE DIRECTION OF THE ARROW.

THE 'GREAT MAN' MODEL OF LEADERSHIP IS ALIVE AND WELL, DESPITE LARGELY EXAGGERATED ACCOUNTS OF ITS DEATH

THE GREAT MAN THEORY WAS BORN IN SCOTLAND, THE CHILD OF PHILOSOPHER AND HISTORIAN THOMAS CARLYLE (1795 –1881) – 'THE HISTORY OF THE WORLD IS BUT THE BIOGRAPHY OF GREAT MEN'. IT WAS COUNTER-ARGUED BY ENGLISH PHILOSOPHER, BIOLOGIST, ANTHROPOLOGIST, SOCIOLOGIST AND A FEW OTHER THINGS, HERBERT SPENCER (1820 – 1903) – 'GREAT MEN ARE THE PRODUCTS OF THEIR SOCIETIES AND THAT THEIR ACTIONS WOULD BE IMPOSSIBLE WITHOUT THE SOCIAL CONDITIONS BUILT BEFORE THEIR LIFETIMES'.

This dichotomy has lived ever since. Indeed, it is as old as humankind. But the anti-great-man theory has gained progressive ground in leadership. Not won the battle completely, but certainly more politically correct. It's not about him or her – the approach says – but about the team, the conditions, the collective.

Charismatic leadership, for example, has its adepts, but it's more politically correct to say that we don't really need these charismatic leaders, after all, there are plenty of examples of uncharismatic ones doing very well, thank you, and increasing earnings per share, what else do you want?

But on the same pages, where prominent and righteous management thinkers debunk the Great Man theory of leadership, we read about Jobs and Bezos and Gates and Page and... It seems

contradictory. And, indeed, if there is a Great Man or Women at the centre of success or failure, where do they come from? Do they land from the sky? Rise from the catacombs? Are they the sort of nomadic leaders that jump from corporate to corporate until the level of stock options is greater than the appetite to lead? Or, should we look at garages, at lofts, at rented hubs for people with laptops romanced by venture capitalists?

Pick a model, I'll give you the data to support it. The naked truth is that, as far as management affairs go, not much correlates with not much, and that those lists of 'research' with the '10 characteristics of outstanding leaders', have the solidity and strength of a cream cake.

Whether you like it or not, we are stuck with the Great Man/Woman approach no matter how much we adapt the concept to allow for a Spencer-like 'product of their societies', which, in today's context, it's only stating the obvious.

I don't have a big problem with this, on the contrary, I think that some anti-hero fighting is a waste, coming from management thinkers who have not much else to fight. That does not mean that we should depend on their magical appearance, or luck, or negate the need for some sort of leadership development. But, we would do a greater service to ourselves if we were to acknowledge that, when it comes to management and leadership, we are in massive Trial and Error territory. I prefer the uncomfortably humble view that we don't know much about it, coupled by a determined 'ok, let's try and make it happen', more than either the blind acceptance of the '7 habits', or 10, or 20, or the unconscious cloning of Saint Jobs.

THE WORLD IS FLAT, LEADERSHIP IS GLOBAL AND I WANT TO GO HOME

Where is home? Ask this question to an Irishman or woman. Even if they have been living abroad for 20 years, home is Ireland, not New York, not Liverpool, not Chicago, not Paris. If an Irishman tells you 'I am going home next week', he does not mean downtown Brooklyn or South Side Chicago. It means an airport heading for Shannon or Dublin.

Maybe it is the Celtic attachment to place and space. An attachment that is in the mind and the mind comes with you wherever you go. The Celtic imagination, humanity's greatest knew.

So, where is home in the global village? Other than for an Irishman. Globalisation, it seems, equalises humanity. Flat, very flat. (As a joke,

I think that *The World is Flat*, a book by Thomas Friedman of *The New York Times*, should have been written by the CEO of Ikea).

Global leadership? What is it? A set of universal principles, behaviours and styles that can work across the world? OK, it could be possible to map them and develop them. And indeed, there are very good people working in that direction.

But where is home? Is it on the Facebook pages? Wherever my smartphone is? Family! Oh! I forgot! Family. Wait 1 minute, they are also on Facebook, and now Snapchat, and Instagram.

Perhaps the question is where is the longing? The belonging? A place? A Space? A group? Where some people are? Biblical Ruth said it in moving

words: 'Don't urge me to leave you or to turn back from you. Where you go I will go, and where you stay I will stay. Your people will be my people and your God my God'. That was the Facebook-free, pre-globalisation, definition of love.

Maybe, actually, we have homes, in plural. That is, little homes that may be more or less connected with the Big Belonging Home. These are places of voluntary belonging, of engagement, perhaps of enhancement of the self. They are called organizations or companies, where we attach ourselves for an enormous amount of time of our lives. Physically, psychologically and to the server.

That 'attachment to people and place' does not make the company a family. I think this is a flawed concept. Companies have CEOs and CFOs; families have parents. But if we get this natural human attachment to place and people right, inside an organization, it is likely that the engagement, however you describe it (as long as it is not a score in a survey) will be high. Oh! my 'company of volunteers'!

For me it is a sign of good leadership, global or local, to provide these little homes, to create those 'home effects'. I have had the privilege of working, indirectly, with some deprived young kids in the US who have found 'home' in the school, or even in the safety and welcoming of a yellow school bus. Attachment to space, place and people, even on wheels, that is.

IMAGINE A WORKFORCE THAT SAYS 'I WANT TO GO HOME'. AND, IRISHMEN ASIDE, THEY MEAN MY PLACE OF WORK. IMAGINE THAT, IF YOU CAN. AND THEN YOU CAN THROW ALL THE MANUALS ON EMPLOYEE ENGAGEMENT IN THE BIN. AND WRITE YOUR OWN ONE.

THE LEADER WITH SEVEN FACES.
A MODEL OF LEADERSHIP
THAT REQUIRES A MIRROR.

As far back as 2006, it feels like a century ago, I developed a frame of Leadership that could help understand the topic from several angles, which I called faces. In fact, the model and the book, were called *The Leader with Seven Faces*. The primary goal was to avoid seeing leadership from the perspective of 'one face' only, for example, what leaders say. I pointed out, at that time, that some leaders are very visible by what they say, but less by what they actually do, or vice versa.

Today, the model has developed into a full Leadership Coaching one, individual and group level, and the Faces have been validated time after time.

THESE ARE:

1. What leaders say.

The issue of their language, what they say and what people hear, perhaps not the same. The meaning and intention of the language used. And I referred, for example, to the 'invitational' language of Jesus Christ versus the 'factual, bullet point' corporate language.

2. Where leaders go.

And take people with them. Here is the topic of destinations (or lack of), journeys and having a good map or not. The leader in this face appears a bit like a Cartographer.

3. What leaders build.

How leaders build spaces and protect time. How they build 'homes' to belong or to long for. And, of course, the key issue of legacy: what do leaders leave behind and whether that matters.

4. What leaders care about.

Here is the area of values and non-negotiables. And how deep we need to go, beyond words.

5. How leaders do it.

The 'how' is a question of style, but not in the sense of individual personalities, but more on the styles of bringing people along. For example, a race. A constant race. A pack. A marathon. I draw analogies from running (jogging) in solitary, or in a group.

6. What leaders are.

With an emphasis on the 'what', as in what kind of beast. There are three topics: awareness, responsibility and identity. This is the 'what' in the sense of the Jewish 'Book of the Fathers': 'If I am not for myself, who will be for me? And when I am for myself, what am 'I'? And if not now, when?' It's the what!

7. What leaders actually do.

The focus here is on role modelling, changeability and the overall practicing of the seven faces.

The Seven Faces allows us to project ourselves in different ways and to reflect on which of them are overgrown or underdeveloped. In fact, *The Leaders with Seven Faces* is cartography in itself, with a multitude of questions, not a list of answers.

Years later, my temptation has been to 'retire it'. But the lack of reflection, the epidemic that we suffer from and the abundance of ready-made beautiful answers to what sometimes feels like irrelevant questions, has convinced me that, in this area, we have just started.

MAY I INTRODUCE YOU TO OUR WORST ENEMY? THE WORD 'AVERAGE'.

RANDOM THOUGHTS:

People content with average achievements in the market, launch a party when the statistics show a few points above average.

Does the average company have average management?

Certainly an average management team can get things done.

What about average ideas, no different from anybody else?
Average positions and views?

Is it OK to accept average results on your kid's school progress report?

We refer to 'the average mortal', what is it? What does he or she look like?

What is an average employee? Would you hire one? Seriously, do you set out to hire the average in the short list?

Why the word average triggers so much comfort in some people and horrify others?

What is average performance? What does it mean if the overall company performance is low?

The maths definition: 'The term average may refer to the statistical mean, median or mode of a batch, sample, or distribution, or sometimes any other measure of central tendency'.

Guru Seth Godin says, 'Average stuff for average people is getting ever more difficult to sell. If that's all you've got, get something else'.

My analytics on Daily Thoughts readership says that I am miles above the average 'of the industry'. Should I launch a party?

Benchmarking got married to Best Practices and got an average family.

Enough average rambling.

I really believe that the word 'average' applied to our organizational world is simply lethal. The only question to deal with, is the type of prolonged agony. But the death certificate is ready.

Average services, average consulting, average corporate speech, average client, average effort, average progress, average ideas, they are all waiting to enter the Organizational Intensive Care Unit. There is a waiting list I am afraid, there are no beds available.

Years ago, I would have agreed that 'average' could be a reasonable place to be for some people, if they choose to; and that it would be harsh to push for the extraordinary. Today, having grown up a bit, I think that average is a terrible place to be. The harsh side today is to agree with the normalisation and the lower common denominator.

AVERAGE, WHOSE ORIGINS AND ETYMOLOGY COME FROM 'DAMAGED GOODS'
(EQUALISE LOSES AND GAINS), IS A WORD TO BE BANNED FROM THE ORGANIZATION,
FROM SCHOOLS, FROM SOCIAL CHANGE, FROM THE ASPIRATIONS OF MANKIND.
I KEEP QUOTING MY FAVOURITE MANAGEMENT CONSULTANT, MICHELANGELO, QUOTED,
I KNOW, A THOUSAND TIMES AND PERPETUATED ON MUGS AND POSTERS:
'THE GREATER DANGER FOR MOST OF US LIES NOT IN SETTING OUR AIM TOO HIGH
AND FALLING SHORT; BUT IN SETTING OUR AIM TOO LOW AND ACHIEVING OUR MARK'.

NOT AN AVERAGE SAYING.

STOP PRESS: THE C-SUITE PEOPLE, AND TOP LEADERSHIP, MAJOR PROBLEM REVEALED

For CEOs, CFOs, CHROs, and other Cs, and Divisional Ds, survey after survey try to identify their focus, their concerns, their attention, their worries, the 10 things they see as critical success factors. There is a whole industry of C-suite level surveys that run interviews and then package the answers under glorious headings such as 'Global Trends'. In those surveys (also called 'research'), leadership goes up and down, so does talent management, vision, culture and the rest of the management supermarket. These surveys are an interesting read.

Here is my Alternative Survey (sorry, Research). The major issue is fear, which is no more and no less than a legitimate human emotion, but one of imperialistic power. These are the top 20 fears that I see from my work with clients as an organizational consultant. Not exclusively of C and D suites by the way, also people below, but with focus on top leadership teams.

1. The unknown. Strategic Linear Planning does not do the trick anymore.

2. Fear of pronouncing the word 'unknown' as if it was a sin to accept that the unknown does exist and it's not their fault.

3. The untried. We want innovation, but you go first. (Can we have examples of where this has been done? Although when you give us the examples we will tell you that they come from the wrong industry and the wrong size of company).

4. The unconventional. We'd better bring in McKinsey, the Board will like that. Predictable, safe and expensive.

5. Fear of challenging, but not fear of saying that we should not have fear of challenging.

6. Fear of failure, although we say that mistakes are OK.

7. Fear of not knowing what could go wrong, because if we knew we may not have the skills, or guts, to address it.

8. Fear of disappointing others. The definition of others depends on your GPS position in the organizational chart.

9. Fear of losing control. That's it.

10. Fear of not being recognised.

11. Fear of being disrupted (also referred to as Uber-ised).

12. Fear of being redundant, which is not exactly the same as becoming redundant.

13. Fear of becoming irrelevant: C-people, D-people, the products, the company, the vision.

14. Fear of losing the plot, expressed in more circumvented ways.

15. Fear of being second.

16. Fear of being late (in the thinking, in the action).

17. Fear of being embarrassed by decisions not leading to total, unequivocal success.

18. Fear of spending too much money, although they know that the concept of 'much' is both relative and strategic.

19. Fear of being seen as too brave, in a culture where being seen as brave is good. (I suppose, this is fear of the borders).

20. Fear of being seen as having fear.

What differentiates leaders is the order, or the combinations, or the relative weight of these 20 fears.

When addressing challenges and when helping these executives, in whatever capacity you may act (boss, colleague, consultant, coach, service provider, friend), the trick and the wise move is to get into fear-hunting mode. The key question is: what fear(s) are behind the said and the unsaid?

This is always, always, the most productive way to understand what is going on.

THE FORMULA ABOUT WHAT TO DO WHEN 'LEADERSHIP DOES NOT GET IT', FINALLY REVEALED

THERE ARE ALWAYS PEOPLE WHO 'DON'T GET IT', ARE AGAINST CULTURAL CHANGE EFFORTS, DO NOT SUPPORT A PROGRAMME, TORPEDO IT, OR ARE SIMPLY TOXIC OF SOME KIND. SOME OF THEM MAY BE SENIOR PEOPLE WITH SENIOR BONUSES, OR AT THE VERY TOP, OR A BIT BELOW, OR COMBINATIONS.

The traditional thinking says: time out! There is nothing I can do, because if the top doesn't get it, nobody will. Let's spend the time trying to convince the top and the next level down, and the next, that this is good. Only then, we can change ... the company/the world/ anything. Which is a good explanation of why we are not that good at changing ... the company/the world/anything.

Rational PowerPoint presentations to the top, led by well-intentioned champions of the idea, internal and external consultants, trying to explain why 'this is what we need'. The tribunal (there is no other way to describe that Executive Committee) pushes back with things such as: give us examples, tell us something concrete, concrete, concrete, very concrete, and what exactly is going to happen on Wednesday 23rd in the afternoon.

Let's assume here that you have the extraordinary luck of a visionary leader who says: let's do it! When can we start?! So, you do. But you still have the problem of many others who 'don't get it'.

If revolutions were to start when everybody is convinced that the revolution is needed, including the ones who could, or should, start a revolution, or could torpedo it, no revolution would have ever taken place.

The aim of a large scale behavioural and cultural change (as we do in Viral Change™) is not to fight these people, disable them, argue with them, convince them, detoxify them or have a long and rational discussion to rehabilitate them. The goal is to reach a threshold of critical mass of engaged, committed, positive and forward looking people, who are actively making changes, that makes the other irrelevant.

It's a question of critical mass, not seniority or hierarchical power. When things are moving, changes are taking place, differences are noticed, the Opposition starts to fragment into different groups. One, the ones who continue to oppose and can't handle it. They either leave of have gastric ulcers. Two, the ones who can see and hear and become supporters. Three, the chronically neutral. By the way, a subgroup of Two are the ones who say, 'I have always believed that this was the right thing to do', even if they were the ones ready to kill you. This beautiful tribe deserves a big, big, big smile, followed by a 'thanks for your continuous support, sir'.

What if there is still a fierce opposition at the top? Many years of organizational consulting with companies across the world, many, many Viral Change™ programmes later, many years of living on both sides of the fence of leadership, have found me the perfect formula, which I am happy to share with you. Here it is.

IF YOU ARE IN A COMPANY, AS EMPLOYEE, MANAGER, EXTERNAL CONSULTANT OF ORGANIZATIONAL TYPE OF SOME SORT, WHERE THE TOP, OR QUASI TOP 'DON'T GET IT', ARE AGAINST CULTURAL CHANGE EFFORTS, DO NOT SUPPORT A PROGRAMME, TORPEDO IT, OR ARE SIMPLY TOXIC OF SOME SORT, WITH SOME OF THEM BEING SENIOR PEOPLE WITH SENIOR BONUSES, AT THE VERY TOP, OR A BIT BELOW, OR COMBINATIONS, THERE IS A CLEAR AND POWERFUL, ONE STRATEGY: LEAVE.

PS. IF YOU ARE A CONSULTANT, DON'T FORGET TO GIVE THEM THE TELEPHONE NUMBER OF YOUR COMPETITORS.

'YOU CAN HAVE ANY COLOUR OF LEADERSHIP AS LONG AS IT IS WHITE'. THIS IS OUR 'FORD TRANSLATION' IN ORGANIZATIONS.

HENRY FORD SAID THAT YOU COULD HAVE 'ANY COLOURS OF A CAR AS LONG AS IT'S BLACK'. THE COLOUR TO AVOID IN LEADERSHIP IS ACTUALLY WHITE. OUR CONSENSUS SYSTEMS (OF MANAGEMENT, OF LEADERSHIP, OF PROJECT MANAGEMENT, OF 'CULTURE OF') ARE WHITE. WHITE FROM THE START, SOMETIMES. THE ANCIENT COLOUR OF PURITY.

We need Newton. He brought in a prism and demonstrated that white light was actually a combination of the rest of the colours. You just did not see it. If we lead in white, we miss all the colours. White is the colour of total alignment and consensus, a clean, pristine colour with a lot of happiness around. This is what you see. Without a prism.

I have previously written about consensus as permanent state in the organization, as a 'collective coma'. Comments I receive on my Daily Thoughts on this subject tell me that the issue of leadership still bothers us. And, consensus, in particular, is a hot leadership issue: how to reach it and how to avoid it, at which times. Ah! The tension.

Consensus even reached the Paris talks on Climate Change a few years ago. Not widely publicised, this little note in *The Guardian*, gives us some insights into some of the 'mechanisms' used to reach that consensus.

'The French hosts have adopted a traditional South African negotiating format to speed up decision-making and bring opposing countries together in Paris.

Zulu and Xhosa communities use "indabas" to give everyone equal opportunity to voice their opinions in order to work toward consensus.

They were first used in UN climate talks in Durban in 2011 when, with the talks deadlocked and the summit just minutes from collapse, the South African presidency asked the main countries to form a standing circle in the middle of hundreds of delegates and to talk directly to each other.

Instead of repeating stated positions, diplomats were encouraged to talk personally and quietly about their 'red lines' and to propose solutions to each other.

By including everyone and allowing often hostile countries to speak in earshot of observers, it achieved a remarkable breakthrough within 30 minutes.

In Paris, the indaba format was used by France to narrow differences between countries behind closed doors. It is said to have rapidly slimmed down a ballooning text with hundreds of potential points of disagreements.

By Wednesday with agreement still far away, the indaba was refined, by splitting groups into two.

'It is a very effective way to streamline negotiations and bridge differences. It has the advantage of being participatory yet fair', said one West African diplomat. 'It should be used much more when no way through a problem can be found'.

To form a standing circle in the middle of hundreds of delegates and to talk directly to each other: I would call that a 'no-escape strategy'. The circle was the Newton prism. All the colours could be seen. Eventually there was a white. At least for now.

LEADERSHIP CAN'T AFFORD COLOUR BLINDNESS, AFTER ALL. THE ORGANIZATION IS A RAINBOW. KEEP IT LIKE THIS. MUCH BETTER THAN PURE WHITE.

A TSUNAMI OF NAVEL-GAZING, FORCE 11, IS IMPACTING BUSINESS, SOCIETY AND POLITICS. AND INDIVIDUAL IDENTITY.

I DON'T LIKE TO SOUND GLOOMY. BUT, IS THE CURRENT SELF-CENTRISM AN EPIDEMIC OF COLOSSAL PROPORTIONS? OR, ANOTHER WAY TO PUT IT, IS NAVEL-GAZING THE TSUNAMI COMING TO ALL OUR SHORES?

Individually, we are in a massive, toxic selfie epidemic. Millions of homo sapiens take pictures of themselves as if running out of time before any Second Coming of the Lord, or at least The Four Horsemen of the Apocalypse, drop by.

Companies look 90% at themselves and 10 at the market. And when they use the 10%, 90% of that 10%, it is looking at competitors, not the real buyers, not society.

Big Global Brands have such a high regard for themselves that they keep telling us about their attributes and their greatness, and their passions, which they have dissected into a million PowerPoints and multi million contract consultants, so that the rest of us, mortals, recognise a greatness that we don't care much about, and pay for that greatness that is not that great.

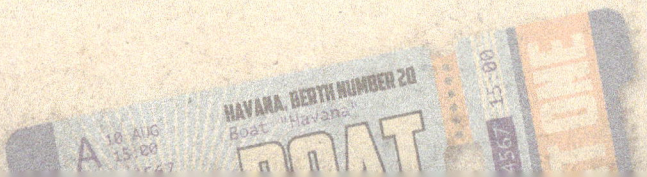

The Me Inc. is very strong and, dangerously, we believe that we are communal and resource-sharing loving people. Wow!

Across the world, self-centred-born organizations have become so sophisticated at navel-gazing that you wonder if they have inherited some sort of optical macular degeneration, aka blindness, in the process. Conservatives are hyper-conservatives because they want to conserve what they see in their navel-gazing exercises. Left-leaning organizations have lost the equilibrium, due to so much navel-gazing, that they are falling instead of just leaning and becoming irredeemably self-centred. Nationalist movements thrive because telling people to look after oneself and forget the rest, sells very well. Add in the salt and pepper of 'the others' are screwing you up, and, bingo, we all want independence in a Massive Interdependent World.

We need a counter-epidemic. It reads like this. People, can you open the windows? Actually you'll be amazed what you can see. You are not that important, we all are. Calm down. Your horse is getting a bit tired. Bosses, employees, politicians, journalists (that excludes the UK *Daily Mail*), decent men, we are here 'in transit'. Stop looking in. We are in this together. The answers are outside us, most of the time.

I know that my Unsexy Manifesto won't go too far but, come on, let's be serious. There is a thing called society, despite Mrs Thatcher's denial. Most of the things that look like 'I' or 'me' don't have a life within the 'us'.

P.S. I propose a Narcissus Tax. For every selfie,
10% of your phone battery is gone.
(Mr Crook? Mr Crooooook? Tim? Are you there?).

367

IS LEADERSHIP SO ELUSIVE?
OR ONLY IN THE HANDS OF ACADEMICS?

A publication I once received around the Mighty Davos meeting portrays the views of five expert academics on the topic of leadership for the future, probably all attending that-type-of-business-conclave. Here are their five vignettes:

1. 'The leaders who fare best at predicting the future are the ones who recognise that the future is unpredictable'.

2. 'Heightened uncertainty puts a premium on good judgement'.

3. 'Leaders must be able to build organizations that are agile and can routinely innovate'.

4. 'One key skill that all responsible leaders need to have today is a deep understanding of the key global trends driving change'.

5. 'The path to leadership is both an inner and outer journey'.

OK! Now, try to (a) disagree with any of these; (b) take the advice as an operational yardstick; (c) combinations…

Can we unpack it a bit please?

'The leaders who fare best at predicting the future are the ones who recognise that the future is unpredictable'. Please explain. So, what do they predict? That the future is unpredictable or a particularly unpredictable future?

'Premium on good judgement?' You bet. Bad judgement sounds like a bad idea, leaders or no leaders.

'Building organizations that are agile and can routinely innovate?' Yep. But, is there anything else? I heard that in the last decade.

'One key skill that all responsible leaders need to have today is a deep understanding of the key global trends driving change'. Sure. If you don't, you should not be paid, let alone be a 'responsible leader'. The irresponsible

ones presumably don't care.

'The path to leadership is both an inner and outer journey'. I could not agree more, but, what does it have to do with leadership that it does not for all of us as plain vanilla human beings?

Is leadership so elusive? Or only in the hands of academics?

It is frustrating that people who are portrayed as 'leaders and experts on leadership', generate platitudes of such a magnitude, which I would not tolerate from junior consultants applying for a job with us.

You could say that I have taken lines out of context. And I have. But I have also read the rest of that context and it does not add much to the position. It may well be that the journalist has edited them. That I could imagine. And I hope this is the case.

I PROMISE YOU, I DON'T WANT TO MAKE FUN OF THE ACADEMICS OR ANYBODY ELSE FOR THAT MATTER. NOT A GOOD USE OF MY TIME. JUST WANT TO FIND MEANINGFUL CONVERSATIONS ON LEADERSHIP STYLE, AND IT HAS BEEN A LONG, LONG TIME SINCE I HAD A GOOD AHA!

MAYBE IT'S JUST ME WHO DOES NOT GET IT. I DON'T GET THIS DAVOS STUFF.

CORPORATE GRAMMAR COULD LEARN FROM OBAMA'S SPELLING GUIDELINES

'THIS ISN'T A PERIOD, IT'S A COMMA, IN THE CONTINUING STORY THAT IS AMERICA', OBAMA SAID WHEN LEAVING OFFICE.

Well, very often we don't get our organizational punctuation right.

New CEOs come in and declare a full stop, period, new paragraph. But people may expect a comma, à la Obama. Other people are craving for a bit of a semicolon: please explain what so and so means.

We hire Big Consulting Groups whose grammatical expertise is the parenthesis, a big parenthesis in which all stops.

Corporate communications often provide the exclamation marks and HR the spell checker.

What about the question marks? Do we want them? Allow them? Seek them? In corporate life, the quote attributed to Neil Postman [1931-2003], applies: 'Children enter school as question marks and leave as full stops'. But we don't even have to leave the company to get quite domesticated with full stop production. People with lots of question marks could be enormously irritating.

I guess getting the corporate grammar right is a great leadership skill. Leaders who provide full stops when a comma is due or a comma when the full stop is, or exclamation marks in the form of corporate reports when it all should end as a question mark, etc., are walking misspellers. Confusion is then inevitable.

Just remember that a little piece of grammar (filioque) in the form of a single word caused the schism between the Eastern Orthodox and Western churches in Christianity! No kidding. Let's get our organizational punctuation right.

I promise you that these Daily Thoughts belong to the comma tribe.

MARTIN LUTHER KING'S 'I HAVE A DREAM' WAS NOT IN THE SCRIPT

Most of what is very good comes from discarding the standard or the good itself.

The best scripts I have ever had for my speaking engagements are the ones I have not used or the ones I have not followed. Writing a flow, a script, a story, gives your mind the comfort of a structure, of an outline. In doing so lots of collateral ideas come up. And those may take over.

This is the King's story as told by Adam Grant in *The Surprising Habits of Original Thinkers*:

'The night before the biggest speech of his life, the March on Washington, he was up past 3am rewriting it. He's sitting in the audience waiting for his turn to go onstage, and he is still scribbling notes and crossing out lines. When he gets onstage, 11 minutes in, he leaves his prepared remarks to utter four words that changed the course of history: "I have a dream." That was not in the script. By delaying the task of finalizing the speech until the very last minute, he left himself open to the widest range of possible ideas. And because the text wasn't set in stone, he had freedom to improvise'.

The more solid the preparation the better. For anything. Then, at 85-90% good, you stop and let it cook. The extra 10% coming later may change the course of the entire previous 80%.

'I HAVE A DREAM' CHANGED EVERYTHING HE SAID AFTERWARDS, BUT I BET IT WOULD NOT HAVE COME OUT HAD DR KING NOT SCRIBBLED AND STRUGGLED AND THEN DISCARDED. BECAUSE HE WAS WELL PREPARED, HE WENT OFF TANGENT. AND THE DREAM THING WAS HISTORY. OFF SCRIPT.

7 RULES TO NEGOTIATE AND LEAD (AND CONTROL YOUR DESTINY). NUMBER 5 IS THE TRICKY ONE.

1. **Control the conversation.** Control the dialogue. Don't accept a dialogue imposed on you. Common ground is OK, but only if it's really common. Reframe, before the (wrong) frame is given to you. A conversation on cost cutting may be reframed as investment and building. A vendor-buyer conversation can be reframed as forming partnership. An asymmetrical big corporation-small business consultancy can be reframed as those who need something and those who have the expertise.

2. **Control the emotions.** Start with the end. Ask, what emotion do I want to have in place at the end, to leave behind: awe, excitement, scare, mission impossible or the best thing ever, the 10 reasons why it would be foolish not to go that way.

3. **Control the time.** I call it 'the now and next': this is what we are discussing now (and what we are not) and this is what is next (including I don't know, but I will make sure you know ASAP). This is an hour's conversation or a three weeks decision. There is always a clock.

4. **Control the environment.** Where all that is taking place matters, the space, the psychology of the place, the branding if any. Don't hold innovation conversations in a call centre. Rent an incubator space if your counterparts are thinking of something new and risky. Get rid of tables and chairs and bring in sofas if you want to have a conversation instead of a 'meeting'. Don't use PowerPoints unless you show Gant charts or spreadsheets.

5. **Control your discomfort with the use of the word control. Get over it.**

6. **Surprise, always surprise.** Never be predictable.

7. **In doubt:** go back to number (1) and check you are doing a good job.

THE BEST QUESTION IS THE ONE WHICH HAS NO ANSWER

Recently, I keep finding myself going back all the time to 'the art of questioning', as something being at the core of good management and leadership. This is perhaps influenced by so many instances in which I have found myself under the tyranny of poor critical thinking. This has perhaps been absent in some client interactions. The rush for 'answers' and 'closure' has led to very bad decisions.

Questioning is powerful, potentially disruptive, and healthy. It's the behaviour behind curiosity, and curiosity is the state of mind behind innovation. Questions can be superficial or deep. The superficial ones come associated with a quick and comfortable answer. These are poor questions.

In the art of questioning, discomfort correlates with success. The perfect question has no good answer. The pursuit of perfect questions is not a masochistic affair but a discipline that leads to a better understanding of the world. Unrelenting curiosity will lead to the art of questioning leading itself to 'delivering the goods'.

In the past I have designed two large scale leadership and change programmes based entirely upon 'questions': 'the 10 questions people ask here', for example, has led to a much better and more agile culture. Its simplicity is very powerful. A 'Copernican Revolution', a client has called it, in contrast to super-complex models of leadership and change leading only to intellectual tourism.

QUESTIONS AND QUESTIONING ARE AT THE CORE OF LEADERSHIP. THIS ART OF QUESTIONING CAN BE MASTERED. IT'S PRAXIS, IT'S ABOUT EXERCISING IN THE MIND GYM.

NEVER UNDERESTIMATE THE POWER OF A GOOD SET OF QUESTIONS. THESE MAY BE ALL YOU NEED, FROM STRATEGY TO IMPLEMENTATION, TO PERFORM ON SOLID GROUND.

'OUR BEST DAYS ARE YET TO COME. OUR PROUDEST MOMENTS ARE YET TO BE. OUR MOST GLORIOUS ACHIEVEMENTS ARE JUST AHEAD'.

I AM BORROWING RONALD REAGAN'S LINES TO REMIND OURSELVES THAT, AS LEADERS IN AN ORGANIZATION, WE MUST VISUALISE A FUTURE. HE DID. AND WE MUST DO SO WITH TWO CAVEATS:

1. **We must be invitational.** We may visualise a future that is in our heads, a glorious and perhaps even enlightened one. But don't forget to invite. It is the 'come with me' that is often missing. Invitational language is often forgotten in leadership. The factual display of bullet points assumes that what needs to be done is obvious, and that the reader/recipient will read it as marching military orders. But it usually fails the invite test. The explicit one. 'I am going there, come with me, I need you, will you?' Then those bullet points suddenly look attractive.

2. **That future must not be closed.** Full picture, all done. I have all the answers. If there is no discovery on the journey, no room for the emergent, that future is unlikely to be as rich as it could be. Reagan did not say this is exactly what those best days look like, or what exactly you'll be proud of, or what achievements we are talking about. And he did not give it an ROI, by the way.

Reagan said what he said referring to America (that part of the world that most of us call The United States, not the entire continent, but hey) We could say, must say the same of our organizations, our companies, our plans.

In some parts of the Zen tradition, 'the beginner's mind' is a full, philosophical position, a world view. Hence the expression: 'In the beginner's mind there are many possibilities, in the expert's mind there are few'.

'Perpetual beginner' may be understood by zen-loving executives, but hard-wired MBA warriors may have a hard time with 'that stuff'. But all it means is that possibilities always emerge and that the key is how to work hard on a well-crafted journey that allows for that 'look out', that new 'aha!', a new discovery that may even question a bit of the path. Or even the whole.

Only on that 'best days are yet to come (...) proudest moments yet to be (...) most glorious achievements are just ahead' mentality, can one navigate a future that is truly rich and full of possibilities.

Invite, always invite.

And send an RSVP!

INVITATIONS ASSUME AN ANSWER: YES, NO, OF COURSE, MAYBE, OR MY GOD, OR WHATEVER. BUT YOU'LL KNOW WHERE PEOPLE ARE ON THAT JOURNEY, BECAUSE THEY ARE PART OF IT. SO YOU CAN DEAL WITH EXCITED FELLOW TRAVELLERS, PASSIVE BYSTANDERS, HIGH CYLINDER LEADERS, FILIBUSTERS, SLOW WALKERS, SPRINTERS AND PURE PASSENGERS OR VOYEURS. AS YOU DEAL WITH ALL OF THEM, 'ALWAYS REMEMBER, BEST DAYS YET TO COME, PROUDEST MOMENTS YET TO BE, AND MOST GLORIOUS ACHIEVEMENTS ARE JUST AHEAD'. THEN, WITH THAT IN MIND, THE FILIBUSTERS ARE JUST A SMALL LOCAL DIFFICULTY.

GOOD LEADERS ARE A BIT LIKE CORPORATE ANTHROPOLOGISTS, WITHOUT THE SIX MONTHS IN TANZANIA

Good leaders are a bit like corporate anthropologists. In fact, we are all exotics on the payroll. In my idiosyncratic view, social sciences, psychology and social psychology are busy with what is seen and said, whilst anthropology is annoyingly curious with what is unseen and unsaid. Leaders can't afford one without the other, but this is a conversation for another day.

In the Era of the Algorithm, we may just forget the social ones. And they are the fabric of the organizational culture.

Social algorithms are, indeed, the tapestry of the culture, the logic in its idea-logic (ideology), the nuts and bolts of its operating system. I call social algorithms the content of the organization's rule book that is mostly unwritten.

There are in fact, for me, two types of social algorithms: the underground ones and the ones that you as leader are installing, consciously or not. To do the latter well, and for good reasons, you need to understand what is going on in the former, in the 'organization's underworld'.

At first glance, social algorithms are shy and not completely obvious. Going a bit deeper, some of those rules start to emerge. I have a system to uncover them, but anybody can make the effort to find them. Once this is done, a whole new universe is discovered and a profound understanding of the organizational culture emerges.

Try to describe them first, imagining situations. It may take a little while to compile a full catalogue. Then, it may start looking like this. Just as an example, as a mixture of underworld and injected:

– If A, we always do B

– We never compromise on C

– In doubt, we do D

– E,F and G are non-negotiable

– H is always reason for dismissal

– When we reach X, we stop (decision, recruitment)

– If noise is up, we go to the source

– The lowest level makes the decision

– We always ask these 3 questions

– From 30 people in 30 days to 3 people in 3 days

– We escalate at Y, Z points

– We ignore N

– We don't execute straight away, we wait for M

My rule of thumb is that many organizations (as I can with my clients) work with about 20 of them.

THREE MAGIC QUESTIONS FOR LEADERS

1. **Will I regret not doing this?** Bezos, Amazon Chief. Here from an article published a few years ago: 'When faced with significant and tough decisions, Bezos is known for touting this framework as a way to help his decision making. When a big decision or idea presents itself to him, he thinks forward in time to when he is aged 80. He asks, 'Will I regret not doing this?' His goal in life is to minimise the number of regrets, so his decisions are guided by that principle. If 80-year-old Bezos will regret not doing it, then he will move forward with the idea. He would rather try something, even if he will fail, than not try it and regret it later.

2. **If not now, when?** Hillel the Elder, rabbi, died in 10 AD. Actually, you get three questions for the price of one here. Personally, I must confess they have influenced me more than perhaps I have cared to acknowledge (although featured in many of my books and writing).

   > 'If I am not for myself, who will be for me?
   > But if I am only for myself, who am I?
   > If not now, when?'
   > (*Ethics of the Fathers, 1:14*)

3. **What will I tell the children?** Me. If we can't answer this satisfactorily, I think we should be very restless. For me, it's not what I will tell my business partners, my clients, my bank manager, my friends, my social group, my political party (I don't have one) my tribe, my readers, my followers. #itsthechildrenstupid. My children. Their children. Your children. The next and next and next generations. It's legacy. But it does not have to be with a big L. It just needs to pass the test though: will I get a red face? Smiling face? What face?

3 QUESTIONS. THAT'S IT.

'WHAT IS IN IT FOR ME?' DON'T ANSWER THAT FOR ANYBODY.

This is a question always tempting leaders to give an answer. Eager to show that people will benefit, we spend time explaining: good for your development, good for your knowledge, good for you as a professional etc. If people could not figure this out for themselves it may be not worth asking them to do anything!

Employees are not your kids. If people in your teams, your groups, the organization, don't see it, you are running a sad place in a poor state of affairs.

This is the script: If you can't figure it out for yourself

'I can't speak for you'.

'The company is not going to tell you'.

'Consider being somewhere else where you can find the answer'.

In my experience, 'the question' often exists more in the mind of the manager, worried about answering, having a ready-made answer just in case, than anything

else. We even have an acronym, could you believe it? WIIFM. As in many other situations, we tend to extrapolate and elevate issues to the category of universal problems. Yes, perhaps we have had a few of these asking those questions. Perhaps we did struggle with an answer. But, perhaps, we were not strong enough to say: I don't know, you tell me, I am not you.

Giving a pair of glasses to people who are blind, can't see, is not going to solve the problem. The most you can say, if you insist on a path of dialogue and answers may be:

'I don't know about you, but for me it is, etc.'

'Other people like you have found that doing X works'.

BUT NEVER GIVE AN ANSWER THAT EXPLAINS WHAT YOU THINK THE OTHER PERSON SHOULD SEE BUT DOESN'T. REFLECTION AND SEEING CAN'T BE OUTSOURCED.

THE TRAGEDY OF CORPORATE SHALLOWNESS.
A CALL TO WAKE UP.

These are the symptoms. Indicators, red flags, culture makers. If you have more than 5, you are in trouble. 6 to 10, it's serious. 11 to 15 life threatening. More than 15, you need a big shake up, earthquake, shock, a battalion of emperor-with-no-clothes hunters, bubble punching at a scale. A revolution.

Resist shallowness. Life in the shallows is not worth living. We can do better than this. Resist. Work could be remarkable. Seriously. Get out of your Plato's cave. Life is short.

CRITICAL TEST:

1. Innovation is catching up with everybody else in the world.

2. Group presentations are permanent after dinner speeches but served any time.

3. Panel discussions are a parade of platitudes in 10 min slots praised as profound contributions.

4. External speakers are entertainment.

5. Discussions are monologues occasionally crossing each other.

6. Management talk is clichés + jargon + airport bookstore book.

7. Lives are calendars.

8. Continuous learning is watching a TED Talk.

9. People develop severe back and neck pain of pandemic proportions by constantly looking up to the top leaders for approval, nodding, Oracle revelations or marching orders.

10. Teams are meetings.

11. Diversity is the number of women on the Board.

12. People refer to management as 'they'.

13. Presidents drop the P.

14. Workshops are word-shops (and occasionally war-shops).

15. Mission statements are created by word permutation software.

16. PowerPoints have neither power nor points.

17. Critical thinking is asking for more information.

18. New Idea is one book.

19. Mediocrity is rewarded.

20. Not even members of the Leadership team can remember the list of values on the wall.

THE ARITHMETIC OF SUFFERING IS FLAWED. LEAVE THE TAPE MEASURE AT THE DOOR.

I don't know about you, but I have used the expression 'in the grand scheme of things' many times in my life as a way of putting my own discomfort into perspective. 'In the grand scheme of things', our daily inconveniences seem nothing compared with the populations with no food or great poverty. 'In the grand scheme of things', the extra burden of today is small compared with the daily burden of others. 'In the grand scheme of things', having to stay at home is nothing compared with those health care workers on the front line.

'In the grand scheme of things' works as a mechanism of consolation. Self-generated and free, at the expense of somebody else's problem. It works.

But, as useful as it is for our self-conviction that our problems are minor, it opens the door to the arithmetic of suffering. And this is dangerous territory.

I learnt this in the trade. In my early years as a clinical psychiatrist, I soon understood that the official classification of mental suffering was flawed. We catalogued some anxiety disorders as minor compared ('in the grand scheme of things') with, say, schizophrenia. My clinical reality told me otherwise. Some schizophrenics were out of touch with reality, undoubtedly a terrible situation, but they may not have been able to even feel their own trouble and disconnect. However, that young woman who could not leave the house because of extreme paralysing anxiety, was officially classified as a minor trouble. The metrics seemed to be flawed and unfair.

Maybe that is why today I have a natural dislike for the advocates of moral equivalence or comparative suffering.

We seem to possess some strange power of measuring other people's lives. Our language has also created similar tricks. For example, when we talk to somebody who has suffered a loss, we say: 'I know how terrible this may be' or (even more assertively) 'I know how you feel'. No, you don't. Even if you went through a similar tragedy before, you can't compare suffering A with suffering B.

Suffering is at least as subjective as physical pain. Professionals like doctors or physiotherapists will ask you: 'on a scale of 1 to 10, what is your pain today?' The professionals can only trust you. That is the only thing they can do. Your answer, by the way, only starts to have some value when asked again another day, and another day. You going from 9 to 6 is good, and going from 3 to 7 is bad. That's it. That is the science.

Suffering does not have a thermometer. It does not come in half a litre or 1 litre. It's neither pink, nor black. It's not 8, or 7, or 1.

Since we are natural incubators of feelings, not content with suffering just a bit ('in the grand scheme of things'), we add a bit of salt and pepper in the form of guilt. The worker that now has to work from home feels guilty that others have to expose themselves to the vagaries of the Covid-19 pandemic.

Feelings don't have thermometers either. Could you imagine, 'I love you about a 4.5'.

FEELING COMPASSION OR EMPATHY IS ONE THING, ADDING THE COMPARATIVE ARITHMETIC IS NOT GOOD. IN THE COVID-19 CRISIS, THE BEST WE CAN DO IS TO RESPECT EACH OTHER'S FEELINGS, FEEL UNRESTRICTED SYMPATHY, EMPATHY, AND LEAVE THE TAPE MEASURE IN THE DRAWER.

GOING BACK TO NORMAL POST COVID-19, WHEN NORMAL IS NOT WAITING FOR US

[1] When on the road going back to normal, with catching up in mind, as if trying to find the old furniture, the old clothes, the old shoes waiting in the cupboard, we may find that the place is not there anymore. What happened to normal? We will feel cheated. Normal was not waiting for us.

Maybe that normal was not really normal, we will say, scratching our heads in consolation. We had smelled one or two abnormalities, after all. Maybe that is why.

Much better to put the energy into shaping what people often call 'a new normal' (a linguistic irritation that wants to be smart). A new house, the new reality, the new game, new space in the world. Better to shape a future, now that we can, than being given one later, one that we didn't want.

This would be terrible: that we were distracted finding our way back to normal and we missed the fork in the road to that future. How did that happen? We did not notice, busy as we were travelling the old road back and imagining what normal had kept safe for us.

But normal was not waiting for us. How inconsiderate.

[2] Back to normal is for true survivors. These are the only ones for whom normal is waiting. Normal will be kind to them. Because they need a space to breathe to keep going. We must respect them big time.

But, if you are anything like me, we are in part pseudo-survivors, maybe with a bit of impostor syndrome. We feel a bit guilty for occupying the same surviving space as the real ones.

It's a crowded place around here.

Those who were never under any threat other than in their minds.

Those who were under some threat, but they could control it.

Those who won a battle that they never fought.

Those who usually defend themselves against no attackers.

Those who suffered unsettlement, disruption, discomfort, even loss, but are still standing.

Those who were a bit scared, a bit worried, a bit shocked.

People like me.

A mixed bag. Who am I to catalogue?

[3] We need to feed-forward. Not feed-back. We don't need a thermostat. We need a compass. Move North or East or West or South, but never back to normal. Because normal is not waiting for us.

The so called 'new normal' (this thing is sticky) is for creators, makers, builders. Not for decorators of the same old room. Not going back to the pot of paint to finish the ceiling, that was left behind. And, when thinking about it, that dark blue was really horrible anyway.

[4] For some of us, we can say that we are not on a Sabbatical.

We are not working from home. We are working at home.

We are not on pause.

We are not waiting for a reality that sits in the past.

We are not in suspension mode.

We are not in rehearsal for when we are back to the streets, kids back to school, when we meet again in the office, when flights take off once more.

There is no if, there is no green room, there is no intermission, there is no when. It's now and next. And, you know what? I am beginning to see all sorts of possibilities!

Once in a generation we have a lot of blank space on the canvas. (And your chance to drop that dark blue, for goodness sake).

Granted, we don't know what this *terra incognita* truly looks like, but one thing is for sure, it's Hernán Cortés all over, the ships are burning in the harbour and there is only one way, up the hills to explore and build.

Because normal is not waiting for us.

LIKE THE BARBARIANS OF CAVAFY, (WAITING FOR THEM, DRESSED IN THEIR BEST ROBES, PREPARING TO IMPRESS THEM, BUT THEY NEVER CAME, 'WHAT ARE WE GOING TO DO NOW'? – HE SAYS – THOSE BARBARIANS WERE A KIND OF SOLUTION), LOCKDOWN WAS 'THE SOLUTION' TO OUR EXTREME ABILITY TO POSTPONE.

BUT NORMAL NEVER WAITS. WE ONLY HAVE ITS PHOTOGRAPH.

SOLIDARITY AS A FORM OF ORGANIZATIONAL CULTURE IS BOTH A SOFT LABEL AND A SECRET WEAPON

SOLIDARITY IS ONE OF THOSE TERMS THAT CAN BE USED IN MANY WAYS. IT OFTEN BRINGS A CONNOTATION OF SYMPATHY OR AN ASPECT OF UNITY UNDER THREAT, SUCH AS THE 80'S SOLIDARITY MOVEMENT IN POLAND.

In traditional Catholic Social Teaching (a powerful set of loosely connected positions on social matters, solid, I insist, regardless of your religious beliefs), solidarity is about 'valuing our fellow human beings and respecting who they are as individuals', so the website says. The same website, that is, in which some 'missing-the-point-completely' webmaster has attached a picture of two high level bishops, a Catholic and an Anglican in forced 'high five', to the box of the definition of solidarity. I confess my embarrassment as a Catholic. A Catholic and an Anglican bishop in 'high five' mode is the last thing that comes to my mind on this topic. I bring in the Catholic connotation because my original post was triggered by an invitation to speak at a Catholic forum and that forced me to imagine that 'solidarity in action'.

Years later, it seems to me more pertinent than ever to go back to imagine a workplace where all those elements of unity, empathy, collaboration, cohesion and everything else in the thesaurus dictionary, could be at the core of culture. Yet, I don't find many places (business organizations), where the term sits prominently in a value system, let's say, compared with empowerment, ownership or accountability.

My hypothesis is that this is because empowerment, ownership and accountability are 'things given to you' (and taken or not), that is top-down created, whilst solidarity is something that is not given to you, it is created by you and others, collectively, bottom up. And most value systems are dictated from the top and cascaded.

In any case, I am convinced that solidarity has more glue power than anything else.

HERE IS WHAT I IMAGINE A 'CULTURE OF SOLIDARITY' MAY LOOK LIKE:

1. There will be a strong **sense of interdependence** in the place. This is contrary to a culture of Social Darwinism, with excessive internal competition. 'My safety is your safety' or 'my success is your success', for example, would be wonderful examples of this achievement.

2. It will require a great deal of **Social Intelligence:** listening, putting oneself in other people's shoes. Something organizations desperately need and that has become a topic of much conversation in recent years.

3. It will engender a **sense of 'the collective'**. Suddenly, questions such as 'who needs to know?' and the subsequent action and sharing, will make real sense.

4. It will spread a sense of **accountability and responsibility**. You need to know what you and others are responsible for, to be able to contribute. Vagueness will not be supported.

5. It will also create **awareness of the impact of my actions** (of my work with others) on individual and collective commitments.

6. It will foster genuine **co-operation, beyond connectedness**. Connectivity per se is not collaboration.

7. It will go far beyond a defensive attitude (I can be hurt, I am likely to be a victim), to reach the proactive **'we are all agents (of our destiny) here'**.

8. It won't feel like 'theory' or just good works. **It will be action** (the word activism contains the word act).

9. It will require **authentic leadership** that supports all of the above.

10. It will **generate trust**. Vulnerability is OK, 'I won't be punished, we are all in this together'.

So, there you are. Solidarity may be the above package; far more than people with placards. 'We are all Charlie' is a show of sympathy. 'We are all in this together, we depend on each other, and we act collectively, without organizational chart barriers', may be the expression window of a 'solidarity culture'.

If you have one of these, you have a community, not a company. And this, believe me, is not bad at all.

Or should I say, tremendous, it is tremendous. #tremendous.

THE 6 STAGES OF MANAGEMENT TEAMS.
THE ORIGIN AND EVOLUTION OF THESE SPECIES ON ONE PAGE.

STAGE 1: **The Accidental Management team.** The team is composed of whoever reports to the top. You are in that place, at that time. You are part of the management team. Period. Well, not quite a team but a juxtaposition of direct reports to the boss. The team members don't talk to each other much (other than in meetings) because they don't have to. The team is managed via one-one-ones, which the boss sort of likes. The team is a collection of binary relationships with the boss.

STAGE 2: **The Utilitarian Management Team:** As above, but some alliances are formed and two or three members work together when needed, if needed, if they feel like it. That excludes the more useless members who are still consoled by the monthly one-to-one. Collaboration does exist, don't get me wrong, but as long as I can benefit from somebody else.

STAGE 3: **The Maturing Management Team, SPAMETO model.** The dynamics between the members are in all directions; cross collaboration takes place; all starts looking like a proper team. Small detail, everybody is equal but Some People Are More Equal Than Others (SPAMETO). Yes, Finance, Sales and Marketing dominate the airtime in meetings, whilst HR, IT and R&D look at emails in monastic silence. And I am committing here the sin I hate most. I am equating team and meeting. But, frankly, in Stage 3, most activity is 'in meetings'.

STAGE 4: The Balanced Management Team. Cross collaboration and fertilisation take place. Performance is the focus. Everybody is contributing. Everybody counts and everybody accounts. They may be 'high performance' or not depending on what you call performance. Well-balanced and high-performance, is not a bad place to be.

STAGE 5: The Leadership Team. There is a bit of jump here. Maybe more than a bit. The team leads the organization. The functional, operational and business representation is clear: as in Stage 4, there may be a CEO, CFO, COO, Head of R&D etc. But they have switched the 'direction of the representational arrow'. They don't represent anymore their areas into the company, they represent the company into the areas, the functions, business units, operations. No switch of 'the direction of the arrow' (in mind and heart), no Leadership Team, no Stage 5.

STAGE 6: Collective Leadership. As above but members share the collective drive. They are interchangeable, with the only limitation of their skill base, not the area of 'expertise'. The Head of HR may not be able to run Finance but must be able to present to the entire company, if needed, the financial results or the budget. The Head of Finance may not be able to run HR, but must be able to stand up and articulate the Human Capital Plan for the company in full detail, etc. One of the tests for this stage is The Empty Chair Test. Mr or Mrs X, member of the team, has disappeared for 3 months to run an acquisition, or to look deep into a project, but nobody has noticed. The empty chair (functional, operational, or otherwise) is largely invisible outside the team itself. Mr or Mrs X's job has been naturally absorbed by others, temporarily, and the sky is not falling at all. If this has happened, it is not because the CEO said so, but because the reallocation was spontaneous, natural, and with no fuss.

NOT ALL MANAGEMENT TEAMS REACH HIGH LEVELS. NOT REACHING HIGH LEVELS DOES NOT MEAN POOR PERFORMANCE. HOW FAR TO PROGRESS, WHAT SPEED, WHERE TO TARGET, ARE CHOICES. BUT THE CONVERSATION MUST TAKE PLACE.

NO MILK, NO HONEY, ENJOY THE JOURNEY

MOSES' LEADERSHIP WAS BAD. HE PROMISED HIS PEOPLE A LAND OF MILK AND HONEY. INSTEAD, THEY GOT A TERRIBLE HIKE FOR FORTY YEARS WITH NO MILK AND NO HONEY AT THE END. HE WOULD NOT BE RE-ELECTED TODAY AS CEO (ALTHOUGH, MAYBE, HE COULD STILL GET A FEW MILLION WHEN QUITTING).

The 'journey' and the 'travelling' are universal analogies. The hero's journey is an archetype for mankind. Perhaps nobody has put it better than Joseph Campbell (1904 – 1987) in his seminal *The Hero with a Thousand Faces* (first published in 1949, then 1968 and 2008).

As mentioned before, there is 'journey leadership' and 'destination leadership'. 'Destination leadership' is OK if real and honest. But, promise too much honey and you may be in trouble. The problem with many 'destinations', is that they are like those holiday brochures that show a swimming pool in the compound, but not the building work next door and the mosquitos in the bathroom with no hot water.

The ancient Greeks knew a thing or two about journeys. Odysseus lived on the Greek island of Ithaca and Homer wrote a whole epic about reaching this 'promised land', incidentally describing the island's features in a way that don't match the real island of Ithaca. But, who cares? The principle is the journey.

Constantine P. Cavafy's poem 'Ithaca' is required reading in my Leadership Programme. It describes the exciting prospect of reaching Ithaca, but soon warns that you should pay attention to every bit of the journey: 'A long one, full of adventure, (and) full of discovery'. And he recommends not to hurry the journey at all. 'Better if it lasts for years, so you are old by the time you reach the island, wealthy with all you have gained on the way, not expecting Ithaca to make you rich'.

We have a boring term for this in management: 'managing expectations'.

It warns you that Ithaca may even disappoint you, because after your 'marvellous journey', Ithaca may have 'nothing left to give you'. 'And if you find her poor, Ithaca won't have fooled you. Wise as you will have become, so full of experience, you will have understood by then what these Ithacas mean'.

LEADERSHIP MAY BE, AFTER ALL, THE ART OF TAKING PEOPLE ON A JOURNEY TO ITHACA, NOT THE PRESCRIPTION OF HOW TO REACH IT.

IT'S THE JOURNEY, NOT THE MILK AND HONEY.

WHAT I LEARNT FROM THE MONKS: A LITTLE ANTHROPOLOGY OF LEADERSHIP AND SPACE ON ONE PAGE

I return to my friends, the monks of a Benedictine monastery in the Highlands of Scotland, who spend most of the time in silence. I mean, when not chanting to each other in the church seven times a day.

Yet, that silence needs the space in order to be heard. A while ago, they designed a garden, a sort of a maze, so that they could walk in a direction without bumping into each other. One of them, a friend for many years, leaves from time to time to live completely on his own, for a week, in one of the nearby cottages, as if in a detox regime. When I asked him moons ago about 'that need' he looked at me puzzled: wasn't it obvious? When he is away, he walks down the valley every day for the communal Mass and back. When coming in, the other monks avoid him (during that week) so to respect the space he has created for himself.

There is something special about creating space. For me, leadership is mainly architectural: create the conditions, find the spaces, protect them, make them liveable. Architects also have maps, and compasses. The leader needs to provide maps (frameworks, such as the non-negotiable behaviours) and navigation tools (a value system). But, above all, it's about space.

Providing spaces for people to breath, to grow, to deliver something, to get better, to think critically, to interact, to collaborate, to travel together. This is all about space. Space is the psychological sister of place. Space may be only, or mainly, mental. As such, it is a precious asset. No wonder the word space has been often associated to the word sacred. As in sacred spaces. To provide space, to create and protect spaces for others, is something a good leader does. It's a great deal of his servant-ship.

But we, sometimes, are not very good at this. We take over other people's spaces by insisting on discussing, wanting to 'go deeper', being intolerant with leaving things open, dictating our own terms and providing unreasonable borders to their spaces.

At a threshold point of two people living together in one place, they may come to inhabit one single space. It requires a lot of maturity to live in one single space with others. Occupying one single place, is the easier part, space is not. Indeed, that single space may end up being too much to ask.

It may be better to have separate spaces to respect, often overlap. Psychotherapists have known for many years that a temporary split, or making tangential connections for a while, may be the solution to some problems. Unbundle the spaces that have become blurred, that is.

Spaces could be rich and beautiful or could also be toxic. In a relationship of spaces, if one is toxic, the whole may become contaminated. Also, the more personal, protected space one has, the more one can give. This is 'the border diet' of my old TEDx talk.

SPACE IS A GOOD WAY TO START A LEADERSHIP DEVELOPMENT CONVERSATION. MUCH BETTER THAN VISION, CHARISMA, DETERMINATION OR ROLE MODELLING. THE LEADER AS AN ARCHITECT IS A MUCH RICHER MODEL. ARCHITECTS OF OUR OWN SPACES, AND PROVIDERS AND KEEPERS OF SPACES FOR OTHERS.

WATCH THIS SPACE.

PLACES

The concept of place has always intrigued me, together with its rocky relationship with its sister, space. Sometimes you can have a lot of space in a small and creepy place, or be in a magnificent place, high tech and high everything, with no space at all. Places always trick us. The modern trend of open spaces in offices came with the assurance that they would be liberating and that they would be fostering collaboration, communication, even joy. After many years, some of these places had produced a lot of that, indeed, but many had become another form of prison where privacy doesn't exist and where your computer screen is the new silo.

Places have always had a profound impact on me beyond the bits and pieces of memory. Some places are mini worlds where the concept of space and time gets completely disrupted, even mixed up, as soon as you arrive. Arriving in one of these places is more than crossing their borders.

Some of these places, at least for me, have truly magnetic properties. Why them and no others, who knows? I have always been intrigued by what the Celts called 'thin places'. Those where the border between the divine and the human was imperceptible. It's a beautiful concept. I know some of those. But I think that many others, although they may not be that thin, still have a fluid border and occupy some special place in my mind, beyond the anecdotal. There is a piece of the soul that gets stuck.

The six places in this book have these properties. I could not tell you why. They have all agreed to host the content of the book. How kind of them.

Kinvara, The Harbour

Kinvara is a tiny place in County Galway, Ireland. You can't miss the harbour. All streets seem to land you there. In summer, you may be there for a festival of their distinctive cargo boats called *Hookers*. Big red sails, ready to fight the Atlantic, displayed in a way that, to the foreigner, look more Viking than local. Indeed, it may have been a Viking boat design in the first place. They used to be the main way of transport between Galway and Connemara, grain in one direction, turf in the other.

Ireland is a very special place for me. It's full of memories of escapades, joy and freedom. In the last 3 years, my business life has taken me to Dublin and Shannon airports several times a month. Arriving in Ireland is always different for me. An irrational sense of belonging gets through the skin. I am incredibly antisocial in taxis. No small talk, big talk, any talk. Not in Ireland. Well, after all, you can't be in Ireland and not talk.

I understand why the Irish call it home. That may not sound particularly special, but I'm talking about Irish people maybe having a chat on 5th Ave in New York and asking each other 'when are you going home?' They are not referring to taking the bus, or a cab, back to their suburban house in the State. There is no home other than Ireland, the rest is another kind of place. Going home is going back to Ireland, or it isn't. I remember well the first time my Irish wife, and best friend, said in the middle of London, 'we need to think about going home', and I said 'so early, we have just arrived here? Are you OK?'. 'I mean home', she said, then smiled as if suddenly she understood. And forgave me for not getting it. It has never happened again since that day.

I thought that I had adopted Ireland, at least as a piece of home, but Ireland has adopted me. Symbolically, the name of my house in the UK is Kinvara. Although, it's mainly the postman who knows that, and he never seems to be particularly excited, busy as he is with the deliveries. I may get a 10 second conversation about the weather. He is Australian and always wears shorts. Any month.

A cottage by the sea near Kinvara, and near Ballinderreen, has a special place in my mind. But that's a story for another day. A story of turf, fire and the magnificent Atlantic in front.

OXFORD, BLACKWELL'S

The basement in Blackwell's, the historical bookshop in Oxford, is not a basement, it's a catacomb full of discoveries that always invites me to look at books that my routine business life would not consider 'useful'.

So, I keep my travels secret.

In the old days, possessing a physical copy of the Blackwell's catalogue (well, in plural really) was a kind of quarterly trophy. They always deserved a place in libraries, on their own merits. Having the Blackwell's catalogue was the closest thing to nobility for commoners like me. Today, it's all a click away. But not that basement. I live less than one hour away from it.

You get to the catacombs through tiny doors and narrow steps, leaving behind, outside in the streets, hordes of Japanese tourists following an umbrella. If heaven was a bookshop, the Blackwell's basement would be the Gold Card lounge. There are other floors as well, but ascending to the top to the second hand section is less exhilarating than going down to the huge cavern.

My favourite day was always a Saturday morning. If you go really early, you can park in the street and wait for the bookshop to open whilst having a coffee in one of the many coffee shops around, served by a first year anthropology student or somebody writing a dissertation about some obscure Elizabethan author. Then, you go in when many people are still not in the street, and you come out hours later to be greeted by full occupation of the streets by the entire world. Tourists, lots of them, catapulted in high tech buses from London, taking pictures of themselves at the door of a College, mix with the tolerant locals and peripatetic modern prophets with placards announcing the end of the world and asking you to repent.

And if you go at the end of term, when the kids have gone home for good, you'll find places with mountains of abandoned black bikes, not worth the price of their disposal. A cemetery of memories.

I have always been fascinated by how countries and cultures classify books. In Britain, you will not find the equivalent of the French 'Sciences de l'Homme' (human sciences), a big basket of fraternal topics. It's more of a detailed supermarket with well labelled shelves. But still there are topics that defy traditional classifications. So, you never know how the topic was baptised. Down, left and down again in the Blackwell's basement, there is always a gem wanting to be discovered. The question is which label. As for repenting, I am an incorrigible book buyer.

CADAQUÉS, EL MARITIM

The tramontana wind from the North can be so strong that, on winter days, you don't just walk, you fight your way in the street. On those days, boats have a hard time coming back to bay. I can testify. People from Cadaqués, a tiny Catalan place by the sea, close to the border with France, salute each other with a 'fa tramuntana' or 'no fa tramuntana'. In Catalan, there is tramontana wind or there isn't. That is the local 'hey, good morning, how are you?' The baseline for the day.

Cadaqués is an island that has been forced to be inland. They even have their own dialect from Catalan. Until modern times, the only way in and out was by sea. Today, a single windy road from Rosas is the way. Too windy for tourist buses, God bless. There are stories, lots of stories, about pirates coming down from France, being kept at bay by the locals by leaving fresh water on the prominent rocks in the middle of the sea. Given the number of French people who cross the border today to come to town to flood their restaurants, it's tempting to think that they are their descendants finally succeeding to get in.

El Maritim is a bar in Cadaqués, by the sea. It opened when the Civil War started and has survived to this day, same size, same look, occasionally redecorated. In the '70s, I used to go there very often with friends, as a student and as a young doctor. Sometimes we just went 'for a coffee' after finishing our shifts in the hospital. Small detail, the coffee was two and a half hours away from the Barcelona hospital. 'Let's go to Cadaqués' was the liberating call to action.

It took us from members of the establishment wearing white coats to imaginary adventurers and armchair revolutionaries just trying to break with the standard reality a little bit, but not too much. After all, the Gauche Divine, the Catalan version of 'Champagne socialists', gathered there over the weekend. My political awareness at the time was minus five on a scale of zero to ten. Ditto for my friends. But we all knew that lots of things were cooking there. In that bar terrace, there were a million conversations about saving the world, which have proved incredibly successful over time, as anybody can see. We were radicals by proxy.

I did not go back for many years, but now, a few minutes from El Maritim we have a family place, a second home, where I can open the windows and see the sea. Even in tramontana. I have to see the Mediterranean Sea to be half normal. And my grown-up kids still have their toddler toys in the basement. Most of the year the house is empty, I would not let any pirate in, not even if they paid.

SALAMANCA, LA PLAZA MAYOR

Salamanca ('Small Rome' we used to call it, with a few drops of Spanish imagination) is a provincial town in Castilla, Spain. I was born in a town about one hour away. On current Google terms. For us it was one day away, or perhaps something you did twice a year.

I remember the bus. I remember the seats. I remember the cold. I remember the 8 o'clock in the morning at the bus stop by the park. I left the area when I was 12. My family moved. When I think about it, such a tiny part of my life, it feels almost odd that I have such vivid memories, both of realities and myths. In the very few times I have been back over the years, I have reconstructed my history, as any history always is.

Children engrave in their brains patterns of space, time, dimensions, colours or smells. This is why when, after a long period, we go back as adults to a childhood place, we often find those places tiny. The first time I went back to what was my childhood house, I found the street door so tiny. But it used to be gigantic! And the shoe shop next door, still there, still with boxes piled high, maybe the same ones, so small. But it used to be massive!

However, the main square in Salamanca, la Plaza Mayor, has defied any cognitive engrave. It was monumental, it's monumental and gets bigger and bigger each time. Salamanca has the third oldest university in Europe, after Bologna and Oxford. It's still a pure university town, winter and summer. The Plaza Mayor is a gigantic (of course) square with big (gigantic) arcades all the way around. You can walk for hours under the arcades and stop in any of what seems a myriad of cafeterias to practice the Spanish, provincial, all weather sport, of watching people pass by. That is why on those terraces you don't sit in front of each other but next to each other, so both of you can watch people and still hold a conversation.

And if you were a student, and with not much money to spare on chocolate con churros, you just walked. In the old days, you walked in groups of young comrades. Divided by gender. Boys groups walked clockwise and girls anti-clockwise. Under the protection of the huge arcades. That ensured that, every ten or so minutes, you would always re-encounter the same group of the opposite gender. At a normal pace, you then had anything from five to seven seconds to look at her, or him, or them, and smile, laugh, whisper, blush, feel shy or feel suddenly like you had a world full of possibilities in front of you. Then repeat. Until you had to go home.

The romantic in me wants to believe that the tradition is still there and that the young men still look straight at the eyes of the young women, and vice versa, and not at their phones. And if you know that this is gone, I beg you not to tell me. It counts as charity.

Santiago de Compostela, Praza Do Obradoiro

My first memory of Santiago de Compostela is not very uplifting or inspirational. My friends and I were about to finish medical school and went to attend a Psychiatry conference. We booked ourselves into the 5 star Hostal de los Reyes Católicos, a splendid Parador, the estate owned chain of hotels. I imagine we must have got a good conference rate because we could not afford even a 3 star. The place was called 'the most beautiful hotel in Europe' for a reason.

Hotel, hostal, hospital, they all have the same root: hospes in Latin, or guest. Whether people on a pilgrimage, from centuries ago to today, reaching the point of destination of the *Camino de Santiago*, or exhausted medical students with sleep deprivation coming to a congress and landing in the most exotic place, everybody is a guest in Santiago de Compostela, in Galicia, Spain.

Exhausted we were. We arrived late in the evening, we went to the venue to pick up our IDs and bags (the congress ritual), ate a bite and went to bed. When I woke up, I found it very strange that it was still dark outside. Such a short night, but relaxing. I felt new and ready for the first day of the congress. Soon I realised it would be the second day. I had slept for 24 hours. The 'do not disturb' card was still hanging outside.

At that time, there was no such thing as a mobile phone, so it took me a while to find out about my friends. Eventually I did. Another one was in exactly the same resurrected condition as me. Of the other three, only one had survived the first day of the congress, the other two went, fell asleep and having been woken up by irritated seniors, came back to the hotel as well. For a nap. Extended that is.

Around the Praza do Obradoiro, the big square where the Cathedral and its Hostal are (Galician for 'Square of the Workshop') are shops selling jewellery, leather goods and of course souvenirs. And scallop shells. Lots of them. The scallop shell is the sign of the *Camino de Santiago*. There are many theories about it, but a sensible one is that pilgrims carried it as a substitute for a bowl to drink water. Santiago is the Spanish word that translates into other languages as James (English) or Jacques (French). If you like French food, you will know that the 'Coquille de Saint Jacques' is precisely that shell.

All roads may lead you to Rome, but all pilgrimages lead you to Santiago de Compostela. It is the point of all destinations. And then, there is Albariño.

LA HABANA, PARQUE CENTRAL

La Habana is shock treatment of the senses. Once there, your sensory system has changed for ever. I can't get rid of my romantic view of Cuba. Even if there is nothing romantic about the poor conditions in which this resilient population lives. Of all American places, Spaniards have a particular affection for Cuba. That was the place where our grandparents or great, great grandparents used to go 'to make money'. When somebody turned up in Spain with a small fortune or had suddenly adopted a bit of a luxury life, we used to say, 'he must have an uncle in La Habana'. There are no more uncles in La Habana anymore.

I immersed myself in La Habana's life like any other tourist does, but with the advantage of knowing the language. And it helps. During the trip, all the emotions were mixed in one single afternoon. Music and food, and decrepit walls, were a constant bombardment to the senses. It was difficult not to romanticise the place.

The best description of the place, as always, was made by my wife Caroline. She said to me 'these people wear a veil'. It took me a minute to understand, and then I did. There was always a veil through which they spoke, smiled, served you food, or offered you a ride in their 50's Cadillacs. You desperately wanted to take their veil off. But you couldn't.

You very soon got used to the absurdities and inefficiencies of the place, and you were willing to include them into the exotic, seduced by the narrative of suffering or resilience or the blockade. The most stupid blockade in history. Basically, nothing works. But somehow it works. In Cuba, the non-working works. Cuba has invented the non-working work. Internet is a concept (and a scrap card). Jobs are a concept (and a veil).

In my inevitable escapade to the beach, to the inevitable resort, beautifully built, with a beautiful bar, with a beautiful one single coffee espresso machine for the entire huge terrace, I made my first, very important enquiry in the beautiful reception. 'Where can I buy cigars?'. 'Oh, umm, oh, in town, you need to take the bus, we don't have them here'. I believed it for about five long seconds. On my way just around the corner to find the toilets, behind the reception, within the resort of course, I found a huge purpose built shop, government owned, with tons of cigars, any type and size. I asked the one lady-cum-veil vendor why she thought the receptionist said that. 'We've been here since the opening of the hotel; maybe he never comes this way'. This is the Cuban logic. What a place.

The same day, by the beach, we had the most exhilarating, unforgettable, hours of Cuban dancing and singing, still engraved in my mind.

Something that was sleeping in me awoke there. I still today don't know what that was.

ABOUT THE AUTHOR:
LEANDRO HERRERO

I am the CEO of The Chalfont Project, an international firm of organizational architects, and the designer of its products and services in the areas of large scale, behavioural change (Viral Change™), collective leadership and smart organizational designs. I have written several books in these areas and I am also, if lured into it, an international speaker on organizational culture and leadership topics.

Today, I am proud to say that Viral Change™, the flagship of The Chalfont Project, had an impact on more than a quarter of a million employees so far, in both the private and public sectors, across geographies.

Before this wonderful 20 year adventure, with a fantastic team, I spent many years as a hands-on leader in several world class companies, in areas such as pharma R&D, commercial health care roles and health economics. That means, I have been on the other side of the fence. And, before that, I was a practicing clinical psychiatrist, treating patients and teaching at university at the same time. I wasn't one of those couch types of psychiatrists. I wore lots of white coats. And I wrote 3 books as well.

I also have an MBA, which I completed at the same time as working in the pharmaceutical industry and it helped me to transition from medical doctor (basically an alien) to manager (basically an indigenous species). It also allows me to make bad jokes about MBAs, probably its most useful outcome...

I am a Fellow member of several management bodies keeping alive some appearance of faithful tribalism.

I have lived in the United Kingdom for more than 30 years now and escape to my home country, Spain, with my family as much as I can in search of the Mediterranean light.

I am above all a European citizen, therefore an immigrant in Britain, a wonderful place where I have always felt at home.

Drawing on his behavioural sciences background and acute observations from his extensive body of work as an Organizational Architect, Leandro Herrero, consultant, author and international speaker, seeds this thinking in his Daily Thoughts blog and in his other books.

OTHER BOOKS BY LEANDRO HERRERO:

The Flipping Point – Deprogramming Management

A flipping point in the trend for adopting absurd management ideas needs to be reached. Management needs deprogramming. This book of 200, tweet-sized, vignettes, looks at the other side of things - flipping the coin. It asks us to use more rigour and critical thinking in how we use assumptions and management practices that were created many years ago.

Our real and present danger is not a future of robots and AI, but of current established BS. In this book, you are invited to the Mother of All Call Outs!

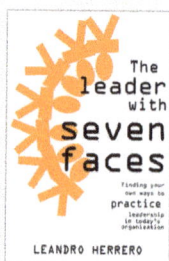

The Leader with Seven Faces:
Finding your own ways of practicing leadership in today's organization

After all the books written about leadership, you'd think we know a thing or two about leadership. However, nothing seems to be further from the truth.

The Leader with Seven Faces provides a novel approach to leadership where the questions to ask (about what leaders say, where they go, what they build, care about, do, how they do it and 'what' they are) take priority over producing 'universal answers'.

For anybody interested in leadership of organisations… and in seeing things through a new pair of glasses.

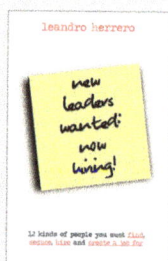

New Leaders Wanted: Now Hiring!
12 kinds of people you must find, seduce, hire and create a job for

A small percentage of the workforce has the key to success. A selected group of managers make all the difference. But what are the skills these people have that enable them to create business success?

The job advertising pages don't often describe those new skills. There is a tendency to play safe and look for people with a conventional set of skills and a proven track record. However, to get spectacular success, you need an 'internal engine' of people who think and behave differently. Who are these people? Where could they be? Do I have them already or do I need to find them? You cannot ignore these questions and your number one priority should be to find these people.

New Leaders Wanted explores those new skills and new approaches to reality and will guide you in your search to find those people.

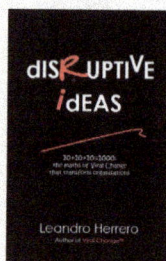

Disruptive Ideas
10+10+10=1000: the maths of Viral Change™ that transform organizations

In a time when organisations simultaneously run multiple corporate initiatives and large change programmes, *Disruptive Ideas* tells us that - contrary to the collective mindset that says that big problems need big solutions - all you need is a small set of powerful rules to create big impact.

In his previous book, *Viral Change™*, Leandro Herrero described how a small set of behaviours, spread by a small number of people could create sustainable change. In this follow-up book, the author suggests a menu of 10 'structures', 10 'processes' and 10 'behaviours' that have the power to transform an organisation.

These 30 'ideas' can be implemented at any time and at almost no cost; and what's more… you don't even need them all. But their compound effect will be more powerful than vast corporate programmes with dozens of objectives and efficiency targets…

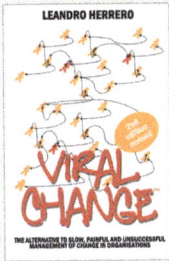

Viral Change™
The Alternative To Slow, Painful and Unsuccessful Management of Change in Organizations

Lasting change in modern organizations has less to do with massive 'communication to all' programmes and more with the creation of an internal epidemic of success led by a small number of people focused on a small set of non-negotiable behaviours.

This is the basis for *Viral Change™*, an unconventional approach to the management of change for any company.

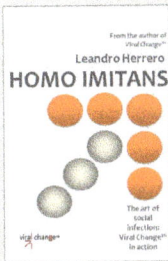

Homo Imitans
The art of social infection: Viral Change™ in action

Managing sustainable change is mastering the art of social infection, both in the micro- and macro-social world. In *Homo Imitans*, Leandro Herrero shows us how to achieve this through his successful *Viral Change™* approach.

Homo Imitans explores the power of social copying and social imitation and explains how to orchestrate change by using that largely untapped power.

It shows you how to create social epidemics of success based on the five pillars of change: behaviours, influence, networks, stories and distributed leadership.

Cultural change in organizations and the macro-social world is *Viral Change™*. Cultures are not created by training or information cascades. Behaviours create culture, not the other way around. Homo Imitans explains why and how.

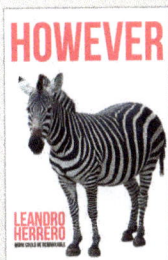

However: Work Could Be Remarkable

There are two types of people in organizations: 'Therefore People' and 'However People'. The 'Therefore People' have all the pieces of reality in front of them and conclude, "We must do X". The 'However People' have the same pieces, but conclude, "It looks like we should do X, however, we could also explore Y or Z. We always have options". This is a book about ideas, about people, about work in organizations. It is born out of the belief that work can be remarkable. 'However' thinking is Leandro Herrero's path to uncovering possibilities.

In each of the short chapters of the book, he encourages us to look at contrarian or unconventional views, to reframe obvious questions, to be brave and to challenge the many default positions that are usually well-entrenched. Organizations are in desperate need of an epidemic of 'However'. This is a 'However' book. It is an invitation to think critically and to engage in work with the be-lief that it can be remarkable.

Contact us at: meetingminds@thechalfontproject.com to:

Order extra copies or make a bulk order of *Camino* or other books.

Order customised editions: we'll create special editions for a specific audience, such as a company or organization. Relevant company resources can be added to the core content, e.g. in-house case studies or toolkits, as well as a special foreword or tailored introduction. The book cover can also be adapted.

Continue the conversation: Engage Dr Leandro Herrero, from speaking opportunities to consulting services. Details can be found at www.thechalfontproject.com or his personal website www.leandroherrero.com

All books are available from major online bookshops such as amazon.com, amazon.co.uk and barnesandnoble.com

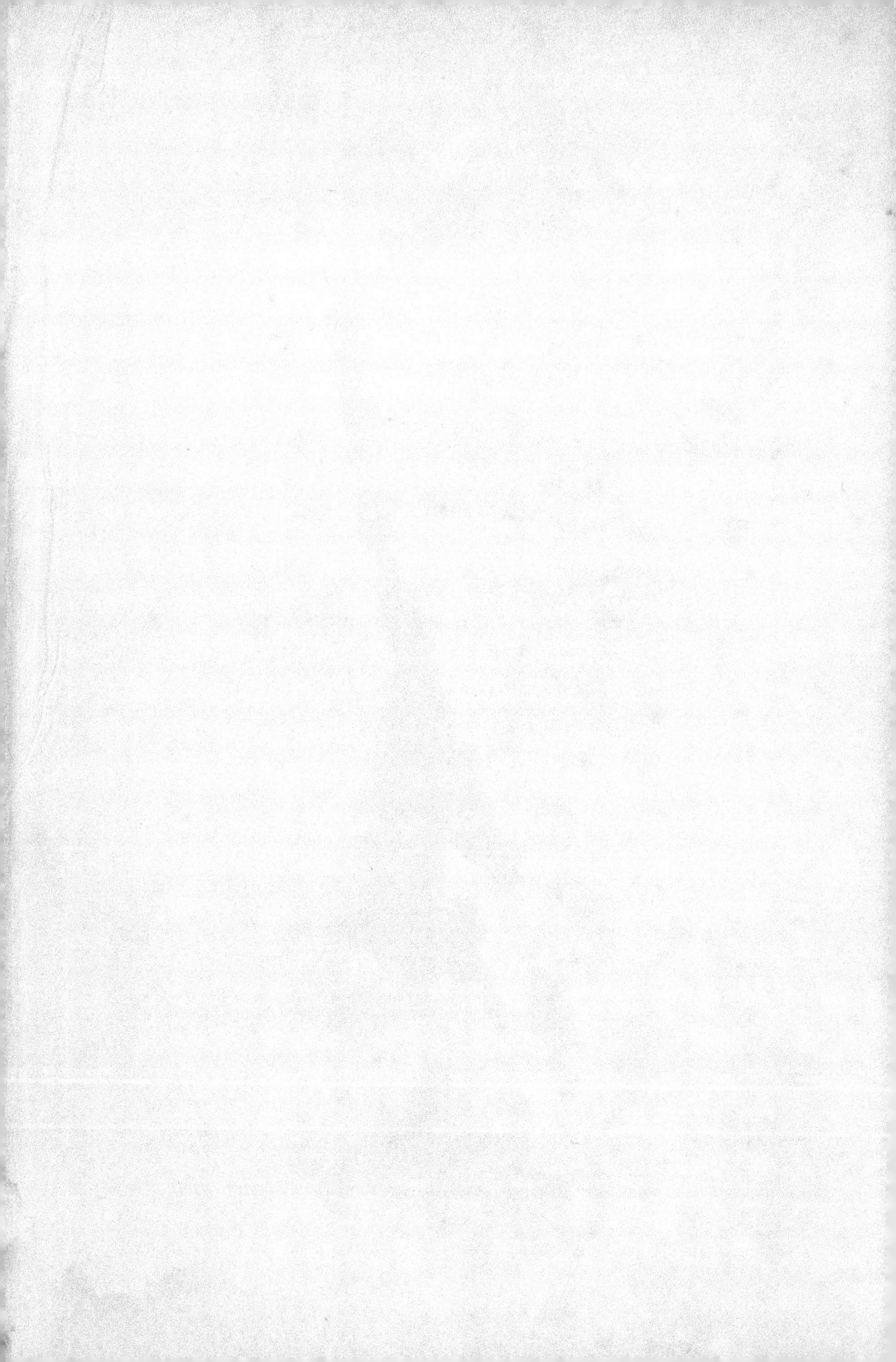

,,DAILY
THOUGHTS
BY LEANDRO HERRERO
24/7, 08:00 a.m GMT @leandroherrero.com

Leandro Herrero writes a daily blog 'Daily Thoughts' at
leandroherrero.com/subscribe-to-the-blog

To be part of this community subscribe now.

Follow us on:

Linked **in**

@LeandroEHerrero, @chalfontproject, @viralchange

THE CHALFONT PROJECT
ORGANIZATION ARCHITECTS
BUILDING REMARKABLE ORGANIZATIONS

WE ARE YOUR ORGANIZATIONAL ARCHITECTS

If you want to build a remarkable organization or challenge your status quo, we are your organizational architects. If you need the best leadership, if you want a collaborative environment, if you want to master change or instil radical management innovation: we promise you will have them. Work with us. We won't tell you things just because you want to hear them.

We will advise you, work with you and we will make a difference. We don't do 'small difference' – if this is what you have in mind, don't hire us. We work with people with ambition, who see possibilities, who have a sense of urgency and who want to make a difference in their worlds – teams, leaders, companies, society. Also, we don't do misery. Pain is sometimes inevitable, but misery is always a choice. (Not ours though, life is short).

Warning: we have a bias for behaviours in everything we do. Others may ignore them in favour of processes or structures, but for us there is no change of any kind unless there is behavioural change. So, talk to us.

www.thechalfontproject.com
uk-office@thechalfontproject.com
+44 1895 549158

www.ingramcontent.com/pod-product-compliance
Lightning Source LLC
Chambersburg PA
CBHW050038220326
41599CB00041B/7200